EARLY AND LATE PAPERS.

EARLY AND LATE PAPERS

HITHERTO UNCOLLECTED.

BY

WILLIAM MAKEPEACE THACKERAY.

BOSTON:
TICKNOR AND FIELDS.
1867.

UNIVERSITY PRESS: WELCH, BIGELOW, & CO.,
CAMBRIDGE.

NOTE.

Several years ago, when the author of these papers visited America, he had the pleasant habit of quoting to his friends phrases, and sometimes long paragraphs, from his earlier contributions to the English periodicals; and when asked why he had not included these magazine articles among his other miscellanies, he replied, "They are small potatoes," adding, at the same time, "but pretty *good* small potatoes, I believe." The collector of these Thackeray-valuables remembers also when he begged the author to bring together his scattered contributions to "Fraser" and "Punch," he replied: "Do it yourself, *mon ami;* write the preface, and I 'll stand by you."

It seems a real loss to the admirers of that fine genius to allow so much that he has written to remain longer shut up in the somewhat inaccessible pages of foreign periodicals, and this volume is published for those who treasure everything that came sparkling from Thackeray's pen. Much yet remains uncollected of this great master's contributions to the current magazine literature of his day, and at some future time other volumes, similar in character to this one, may appear from the same press.

J. T. F.

BOSTON, May, 1867.

CONTENTS.

MEMORIALS OF GORMANDIZING.

IN A LETTER TO OLIVER YORKE, ESQ., BY M. A. TITMARSH.

PARIS, May, 1841.

IR, — The man who makes the best salads in London, and whom, therefore, we have facetiously called Sultan Saladin, — a man who is conspicuous for his love and practice of all the polite arts, — music, to wit, architecture, painting, and cookery, — once took the humble personage who writes this into his library, and laid before me two or three volumes of manuscript year-books, such as, since he began to travel and to observe, he has been in the habit of keeping.

Every night, in the course of his rambles, his highness the Sultan (indeed, his port is sublime, as, for the matter of that, are all the wines in his cellar) sets down with an iron pen, and in the neatest handwriting in the world, the events and observations of the day; with the same iron pen he illuminates the leaf of his journal by the most faithful and delightful sketches of the scenery which he has witnessed in the course of the four-and-twenty hours; and if he has dined at an inn or restaurant, gasthaus, posada, albergo, or what not, invariably inserts into his log-book the bill of fare. The Sultan leads a jolly life, — a tall, stalwart man, who every day about six o'clock in London and Paris, at two in Italy, in Germany and Belgium at an hour after noon, feels the noble calls of hunger agitating his lordly bosom (or its neighborhood, that is), and replies to the call by a good dinner. Ah! it is wonderful to think how the healthy and philosophic mind can accommodate itself in all cases to the varying circumstances of the time, — how, in its travels through the world, the liberal and cosmopolite stomach recognizes the national dinner-hour! Depend upon it that, in all countries, nature has wisely ordained and suited to their exigencies THE DISHES OF A PEOPLE. I mean to say that olla podrida is good in Spain (though a plateful of it, eaten in Paris, once made me so dreadfully ill that it is a mercy I was spared ever to eat another dinner), — I mean to say, and have proved it, that sauer-kraut is good in Germany; and I make no doubt that whale's blubber is a very tolerable dish in Kamschatka, though I have never visited the country. Cannibalism in the South Seas, and sheepsheadism in Scotland, are the only practices that one cannot, perhaps, reconcile with this rule, — at least, whatever a man's private opinions may be, the decencies of society oblige him to eschew the expression of them, upon subjects which the national prejudice has precluded from free discussion.

Well, after looking through three or four of Saladin's volumes, I grew so charmed with them that I used to come back every day and study them. I declare there are bills of fare in those books over which I have cried; and the reading of them, especially about an hour before dinner, has made me so ferociously hungry, that, in the first place, the Sultan (a kind-hearted, generous man, as every man is who loves his meals) could not help inviting me to take potluck with him; and, secondly, I could eat twice as much as upon common occasions, though my appetite is always good.

Lying awake, then, of nights, or wandering solitary abroad on wide commons, or by the side of silent rivers, or at church when Dr. Snufflem was preaching his favorite sermon, or stretched on the flat of my back smoking a cigar at the club when X was talking of the corn-laws, or Y was describing that famous run they had with the Z hounds, — at all periods, I say, favorable to self-examination, those bills of fare have come into my mind, and often and often I have thought them over. "Titmarsh," I have said to myself, "if ever you travel again, do as the Sultan has done, and *keep your dinner-bills.* They are always pleasant to look over; they always will recall happy hours and actions, be you ever so hard pushed for a dinner, and fain to put up with an onion and a crust: of the past fate cannot deprive you. Yesterday is the philosopher's property; and by thinking of it, and using it to advantage, he may gayly go through to-morrow, doubtful and dismal though it be. Try this lamb stuffed with pistachio-nuts; another handful of this pillau. Ho, you rascals! bring round the sherbet there, and never spare the jars of wine, —'t is true Persian, on the honor of a Barmecide!" Is not that dinner in the "Arabian Nights" a right good dinner? Would you have had Bedreddin to refuse and turn sulky at the windy repast, or to sit down grinning in the face of his grave entertainer, and gayly take what came? Remember what came of the honest fellow's philosophy. He slapped the grim old prince in the face; and the grim old prince, who had invited him but to laugh at him, did presently order a real and substantial repast to be set before him, — great pyramids of smoking rice and pillau (a good pillau is one of the best dishes in the world), savory kids, snow-cooled sherbets, luscious wine of Schiraz; with an accompaniment of moon-faced beauties from the harem, no doubt, dancing, singing, and smiling in the most ravishing manner. Thus should we, my dear friends, laugh at Fate's beard, as we confront him, — thus should we, if the old monster be insolent, fall to and box his ears. He has a spice of humor in his composition; and be sure he will be tickled by such conduct.

Some months ago, when the expectation of war between England and France grew to be so strong, and there was such a talk of mobilizing national guards, and arming three or four hundred thousand more French soldiers, — when such ferocious yells of hatred against perfidious Albion were uttered by the liberal French press, that I did really believe the rupture between the two countries was about immediately to take place; being seriously alarmed, I set off for Paris at once. My good sir, what could we do without our Paris? I came here first in 1815 (when the Duke and I were a good deal remarked by the inhabitants); I proposed but to stay a week; stopped three months, and have returned every year since. There is something fatal in the place, — a charm about it, — a wicked one very likely, — but it acts on us all; and perpetually the old Paris man comes hieing back to his quarters again, and is to be found, as usual, sunning himself in the Rue de la Paix. Painters, princes, gormands, officers on half-pay, — serious old ladies even acknowledge the attraction of the place, — are more at ease here than in any other place in Europe; and back they come, and are to be found sooner or later occupying their old haunts.

My darling city improves, too, with each visit, and has some new palace, or church, or statue, or other gimcrack, to greet your eyes withal. A few years since, and lo!

on the column of the Place Vendôme, instead of the shabby tri-colored rag, shone the bronze statue of Napoleon. Then came the famous triumphal arch; a noble building indeed! — how stately and white and beautiful and strong it seems to dominate over the whole city. Next was the obelisk; a huge bustle and festival being made to welcome it to the city. Then came the fair asphaltum terraces round about the obelisk; then the fountains to decorate the terraces. I have scarcely been twelve months absent, and behold they have gilded all the Naiads and Tritons; they have clapped a huge fountain in the very midst of the Champs Elysées, — a great, glittering, frothing fountain, that to the poetic eye looks like an enormous shaving-brush; and all down the avenue they have placed hundreds of gilded, flaring gas-lamps, that make this gayest walk in the world look gayer still than ever. But a truce to such descriptions, which might carry one far, very far, from the object proposed in this paper.

I simply wish to introduce to public notice a brief dinner-journal. It has been written with the utmost honesty and simplicity of purpose; and exhibits a picture or table of the development of the human mind under a series of gastronomic experiments, diversified in their nature, and diversified, consequently, in their effects. A man in London has not, for the most part, the opportunity to make these experiments. You are a family man, let us presume, and you live in that metropolis for half a century. You have on Sunday say, a leg of mutton and potatoes for dinner. On Monday you have cold mutton and potatoes. On Tuesday, hashed mutton and potatoes; the hashed mutton being flavored with little damp, triangular pieces of toast, which always surround that charming dish. Well, on Wednesday, the mutton ended, you have beef; the beef undergoes the same alternations of cookery, and disappears. Your life presents a succession of joints, varied every now and then by a bit of fish and some poultry. You drink three glasses of a brandyfied liquor called sherry at dinner; your excellent lady imbibes one. When she has had her glass of port after dinner, she goes up stairs with the children, and you fall asleep in your arm-chair. Some of the most pure and precious enjoyments of life are unknown to you. You eat and drink, but you do not know the *art* of eating and drinking; nay, most probably you despise those who do. "Give me a slice of meat," say you, very likely, "and a fig for your gourmands." You fancy it is very virtuous and manly all this. Nonsense, my good sir; you are indifferent because you are ignorant, because your life is passed in a narrow circle of ideas, and because you are bigotedly blind and pompously callous to the beauties and excellences beyond you.

Sir, RESPECT YOUR DINNER; idolize it, enjoy it properly. You will be by many hours in the week, many weeks in the year, and many years in your life, the happier if you do.

Don't tell us that it is not worthy of a man. All a man's senses are worthy of employment, and should be cultivated as a duty. The senses are the arts. What glorious feasts does Nature prepare for your eye in animal form in landscape and painting! Are you to put out your eyes and not see? What royal dishes of melody does her bounty provide for you in the shape of poetry, music, whether windy or wiry, notes of the human voice, or ravishing song of birds! Are you to stuff your ears with cotton, and vow that the sense of hearing is unmanly? — you obstinate dolt you! No, surely; nor must you be so absurd as to fancy that the art of eating is in any way less worthy than the other two. You like your dinner, man; never be ashamed to say so. If you don't like your victuals, pass on to the next article; but remember that every man who has been worth a fig in this world, as poet, painter, or musician, has had a good appetite and a good taste. Ah, what a poet Byron would have been had he taken his meals properly, and allowed himself to grow fat, — if nature intended him to grow fat, — and not have physicked his intellect with wretched opium pills and acrid vinegar, that sent his principle to sleep, and turned his feelings sour! If that man had respected his dinner, he never would have written "Don Juan."

Allons donc! enough sermonizing; let us sit down and fall to at once.

I dined soon after my arrival at a very pleasant Paris club, where daily is provided a dinner for ten persons, that is universally reported to be excellent. Five men in England would have consumed the same amount of victuals, as you will see by the bills of fare: —

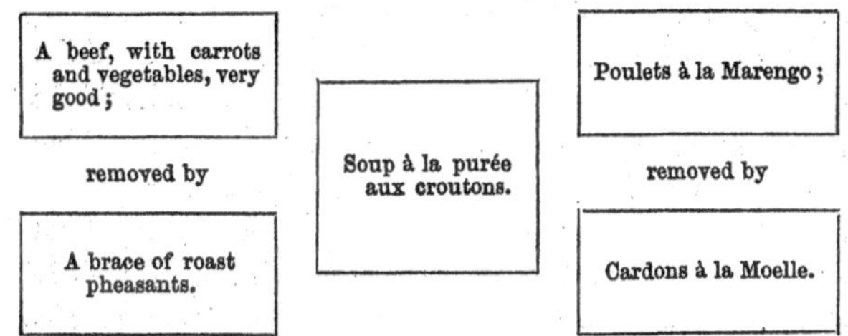

Desserts of cheese. Pears and Fontainebleau grapes.
Bordeaux red, and excellent chablis at discretion.

This dinner was very nicely served. A venerable *maître d'hôtel* in black, cutting up neatly the dishes on a trencher at the side-table, and several waiters attending in green coats, red plush tights, and their hair curled. There was a great quantity of light in the room; some handsome pieces of plated ware; the pheasants came in with their tails to their backs; and the smart waiters, with their hair dressed and parted down the middle, gave a pleasant, lively, stylish appearance to the whole affair.

Now I certainly dined (by the way, I must not forget to mention that we had with the beef some boiled kidney potatoes, very neatly dished up in a napkin), — I certainly dined, I say; and half an hour afterwards felt, perhaps, more at my ease than I should have done had I consulted my own inclinations, and devoured twice the quantity that on this occasion came to my share. But I would rather, as a man not caring for appearances, dine, as a general rule, off a beefsteak for two at the Café Foy, than sit down to take a tenth part of such a meal every day. There was only one man at the table besides your humble servant who did not put water into his wine; and he — I mean the other — was observed by his friends, who exclaimed, "Comment vous buvez sec," as if to do so was a wonder. The consequence was, that half a dozen bottles of wine served for the whole ten of us; and the guests, having despatched their dinner in an hour, skipped lightly away from it, did not stay to ruminate and to feel uneasy, and to fiddle about the last and penultimate waist-coat button, as we do after a house-dinner at an English club. What was it that made the charm of this dinner? — for pleasant it was. It was the neat and comfortable manner in which it was served; the pheasant-tails had a considerable effect; that snowy napkin coquettishly arranged round the kidneys gave them a *distingué* air; the light and the glittering service gave an appearance of plenty and hospitality that sent everybody away contented.

I put down this dinner just to show English and Scotch housekeepers what may be done, and for what price. Say, —

		s.	d.
Soup and fresh bread Beef and carrots .	prime cost .	2	6
Fowls and sauce		3	6
Pheasants (hens)		5	0
Grapes, pears, cheese, vegetables .		3	0
		14	0

For fifteen pence *par tête*, a company of ten persons may have a dinner set before them, — nay, and be made to fancy that they dine well, provided the service is handsomely arranged, that you have a good stock of side-dishes, &c., in your plate-chest, and don't spare the spermaceti.

As for the wine, that depends on yourself. Always be crying out to your friends, "Mr. So-and-so, I don't drink myself, but pray pass the bottle. Tomkins, my boy, help your neighbor, and never mind me. What! Hopkins, are there two of us on the Doctor's list? Pass the wine; *Smith* I'm sure won't refuse it"; and so on. A very good plan is to have the butler (or the fellow in the white waistcoat, who "behaves as sich") pour out the wine when wanted (in half-glasses, of course), and to make a deuced great noise and shouting, "John, John, why the devil, sir, don't you help Mr. Simkins to another glass of wine?" If you point out Simkins once or twice in this way, depend upon it, *he* won't drink a great quantity of your liquor. You may thus keep your friends from being dangerous by a thousand innocent manœuvres; and, as I have said before, you may very probably make them believe that they have had a famous dinner. There was only one man in our company of ten the other day who ever thought that he had not dined; and what was he? A foreigner, — a man of a discontented, inquiring spirit, always carping at things, and never satisfied.

Well, next day I dined *au cinquième* with a family (of Irish extraction, by the way), and what do you think was our dinner for six persons? Why, simply, —

Nine dozen Ostend oysters;
Soup à la mulligatawny;
Boiled turkey, with celery sauce;
Saddle of mutton rôti.
Removes. Plompouding; croute de macaroni.
Vin Beaune ordinaire, volnay, bordeaux, champagne, eau chaude, cognac.

I forget the dessert. Alas! in moments of prosperity and plenty, one is often so forgetful: I remembered the dessert at the Cercle well enough.

A person whom they call in this country an *illustration littéraire*, — the editor of a newspaper, in fact, — with a very pretty wife, were of the party, and looked at the dinner with a great deal of good-humored superiority. I declare, upon my honor, that I helped both the illustration and his lady twice to saddle of mutton; and as for the turkey and celery sauce, you should have seen how our host dispensed it to them! They ate the oysters, they ate the soup ("*Diable! mais il est poivré!*" said the illustration, with tears in his eyes), they ate the turkey, they ate the mutton, they ate the pudding; and what did our hostess say? Why, casting down her eyes gently, and with the modestest air in the world, she said, "There is such a beautiful piece of cold beef in the larder; do somebody ask for a little slice of it."

Heaven bless her for that speech! I loved and respected her for it; it brought the tears to my eyes. A man who could sneer at such a sentiment could have neither heart nor good-breeding. Don't you see that it shows

Simplicity,
Modesty,
Hospitality.

Put these against

Waiters with their hair curled,
Pheasants roasted with their tails on,
A dozen spermaceti candles.

Add them up, I say, O candid reader, and answer, in the sum of human happiness, which of the two accounts makes the better figure?

I declare, I know few things more affecting than that little question about the cold beef; and considering calmly our national characteristics, balancing in the scale of quiet thought our defects and our merits, am daily more inclined to believe that there is something in the race of Britons which renders them usually superior to the French family. This is but one of the traits of English character that has been occasioned by the use of roast beef.

It is an immense question, that of diet. Look at the two bills of fare just set down,—the relative consumption of ten animals and of six. What a profound physical and moral difference may we trace here. How distinct, from the cradle upwards, must have been the thoughts, feelings, education of the parties who ordered those two dinners. It is a fact which does not admit of a question, that the French are beginning, since so many English have come among them, to use beef much more profusely. Everybody at the restaurateur's orders beefsteak and pommes. Will the national character slowly undergo a change under the influence of this dish? Will the

French be more simple? broader in the shoulders? less inclined to brag about military glory and such humbug? All this in the dark vista of futurity the spectator may fancy is visible to him, and the philanthropist cannot but applaud the change. This brings me naturally to the consideration of the manner of dressing beefsteaks in this country, and of the merit of that manner.

I dined on a Saturday at the Café Foy, on the Boule vard, in a private room, with a friend. We had

> Potage julienne, with a little purée in it;
> Two entrecotes aux épinards;
> One perdreau truffé;
> One fromage roquefort;
> A bottle of nuits with the beef;
> A bottle of sauterne with the partridge.

And perhaps a glass of punch, with a cigar, afterwards: but that is neither here nor there. The insertion of the purée into the julienne was not of my recommending; and if this junction is effected at all, the operation should be performed with the greatest care. If you put too much purée, both soups are infallibly spoiled. A much better plan it is to have your julienne by itself, though I will not enlarge on this point, as the excellent friend with whom I dined may chance to see this notice, and may be hurt at the renewal in print of a dispute which caused a good deal of pain to both of us. By the way, we had half a dozen sardines while the dinner was getting ready, eating them with delicious bread and butter, for which this place is famous. Then followed the soup. Why the deuce *would* he have the pu—; but never mind. After the soup, we had what I do not hesitate to call the very best beefsteak I ever ate in my life. By the shade of Helio gabalus! as I write about it now, a week after I have eaten it, the old, rich, sweet, piquant, juicy taste comes smacking on my lips again; and I feel something of that exquisite sensation I then had. I am ashamed of the delight which the eating of that piece of meat caused me. G. and I had quarrelled about the soup (I said so, and don't wish to return to the subject); but when we began on the steak, we looked at each other, and loved each other. We did not speak,—our hearts were too full for that; but we took a bit, and laid down our forks, and looked at one another and understood each other. There were no two individuals on this wide earth,—no two lovers billing in the shade,—no mother clasping baby to her heart, more supremely happy than we. Every now and then we had a glass of honest, firm, generous Burgundy, that nobly supported the meat. As you may fancy, we did not leave a single morsel of the steak; but when it was done, we put bits of bread into the silver dish, and wistfully sopped up the gravy. I suppose I shall never in this world taste anything so good again. But what then? What if I *did* like it excessively? Was my liking unjust or unmanly? Is my regret now puling or unworthy? No. "*Laudo manentem!*" as Titmouse says. When it is eaten, I resign myself, and can eat a two-franc dinner at Richard's without ill humor and without a pang.

Any dispute about the relative excellence of the beefsteak cut from the filet, as is usual in France, and of the *entrecote*, must henceforth be idle and absurd. Whenever, my dear young friend, you go to Paris, call at once for the *entrecote;* the filet in comparison to it is a poor *fade* lady's meat. What folly, by the way, is that in England which induces us to attach an estimation to the part of the sirloin that is called the Sunday side,—poor, tender, stringy stuff, not comparable to the manly meat on the other side, handsomely garnished with crisp fat, and with a layer of horn! Give the Sunday side to misses and ladies' maids, for men be the Monday's side, or, better still, a thousand-fold more succulent and full of flavor, — the *ribs of beef*. This is the meat I would eat were I going to do battle with any mortal foe. Fancy a hundred thousand Englishmen, after a meal of stalwart beef ribs, encountering a hundred thousand Frenchmen, who had partaken of a trifling collation of soup, turnips, carrots, onions, and Gruyère cheese. Would it be manly to engage at such odds? I say no.

Passing by Vérey's one day, I saw a cadaverous cook with a spatula, thumping a poor beefsteak with all his might. This is not only a horrible cruelty, but an error. They not only beat the beef, moreover, but they soak it in oil. Absurd, disgusting barbarity! Beef so beaten loses its natural spirit; it is too noble for corporal punishment. You may by these tortures and artifices make it soft and greasy, but tender and juicy never.

The landlord of the Café de Foy (I have received no sort of consideration from him) knows this truth full well, and follows the simple, honest plan; first, to have good meat, and next to hang it a long time. I have instructed him how to do the steaks to a turn; not raw, horribly livid and blue in the midst, as I have seen great flaps of meat (what a shame to think of our fine meat being so treated!), but *cooked* all the way through. Go to the Café Foy then, ask for a BEEFSTEAK À LA TITMARSH, and you will see what a dish will be set before you. I have dwelt upon this point at too much length, perhaps, for some of my readers; but it can't be helped. The truth is, beef is my weakness; and I do declare, that I derive more positive enjoyment from the simple viand than from any concoction whatever in the whole cook's cyclopædia.

Always drink red wine with beefsteaks; port, if possible; if not, Burgundy, of not too high a flavor, — good beaune say. This fact, which is very likely not known to many persons who, forsooth, are too magnificent to care about their meat and drink, — this simple fact I take to be worth the whole price I shall get for this article.

But to return to dinner. We were left, I think, G. and I, sopping up the gravy with bits of bread, and declaring that no power on earth could induce us to eat a morsel more that day. At one time we thought of countermanding the perdreau aux truffes, that to my certain knowledge had been betruffed five days before.

Poor blind mortals that we were! ungrateful to our appetites, needlessly mistrustful and cowardly. A man may do what he dares; nor does he know, until he tries, what the honest appetite will bear. We were kept waiting between the steak and the partridge some ten minutes or so. For the first two or three minutes, we lay back in our chairs quiet, exhausted indeed. Then we began to fiddle with a dish of toothpicks, for want of anything more savory; then we looked out of the window; then G. got in a rage, rung the bell violently, and asked, "Pourquoi diable nous fait on attendre si long temps?" The waiter grinned. He is a nice, good-humored fellow, Auguste; and I heartily trust that some reader of this may give him a five-franc piece for my sake. Auguste grinned and disappeared.

Presently, we were aware of an odor gradually coming towards us, something musky, fiery, savory, mysterious, — a hot, drowsy smell, that lulls the senses, and yet inflames them, — the *troufles* were coming! Yonder they lie, caverned under the full bosom of the red-legged bird. My hand trembled as, after a little pause, I cut the animal in two. G. said I did not give him his share of the troufles; I don't believe I did. I spilled some salt into my plate, and a little cayenne pepper, — very little: we began, as far as I can remember, the following conversation: —

Gustavus. "Chop, chop, chop."

Michael Angelo. "Globlobloblob."

G. "Gobble."

M. A. "Obble."

G. "Here 's a big one."

M. A. "Hobgob. What wine shall we have? I should like some champagne."

G. "It 's bad here. Have some sauterne."

M. A. "Very well. Hobgobglobglob," &c.

Auguste (opening the sauterne). "Cloo-oo-oo-oop!" The cork is out; he pours it into the glass, glock, glock, glock.

Nothing more took place in the way of talk. The poor little partridge was soon a heap of bones, — a very little heap. A trufflesque odor was left in the room, but only an odor. Presently the cheese was brought: the amber sauterne flask had turned of a sickly green hue; nothing save half a glass of sediment at the bottom, remained to tell of the light and social spirit that had but one half-hour before inhabited the flask. Darkness fell upon our little chamber; the men in the street began crying, "*Messager! Journal du Soir!*" The bright moon rose glittering over the tiles of the Rue Louis de Grand, opposite, illuminating two glasses of punch that two gentlemen in a small room of the Café de Foy did ever and anon raise to their lips. Both were silent; both happy; both were smoking cigars,—for both knew that the soothing plant of Cuba is sweeter to the philosopher after dinner than the prattle of all the women in the world. Women,—pshaw! The man, who, after dinner,—after a good dinner,—can think about driving home, and shaving himself by candle-light, and enduing a damp shirt, and a pair of tight glazed pumps to show his cobweb stockings, and set his feet in a flame; and, having undergone all this, can get into a cold cab and drive off to No. 222 Harley Street, where Mrs. Mortimer Smith is at home; where you take off your cloak in a damp, dark back parlor, called Mr. Smith's study, and containing, when you arrive, twenty-four ladies' cloaks and tippets, fourteen hats, two pair of clogs (belonging to two gentlemen of the Middle Temple, who walk for economy, and think dancing at Mrs. Mortimer Smith's the height of enjoyment);—the man who can do all this, and walk, gracefully smiling, into Mrs. Smith's drawing-rooms, where the brown holland bags have been removed from the chandeliers; a man from Kirkman's is thumping on the piano, and Mrs. Smith is standing simpering in the middle of the room, dressed in red, with a bird of paradise in her turban, a tremulous fan in one hand, and the other clutching hold of her little fat gold watch and seals;—the man who, after making his bow to Mrs. Smith, can advance to Miss Jones, in blue crape, and lead her to a place among six other pairs of solemn-looking persons, and whisper *fadaisies* to her (at which she cries, "O fie, you naughty man! how can you?"), and look at Miss Smith's red shoulders struggling out of her gown, and her mottled elbows that a pair of crumpled kid gloves leave in a state of delicious nature; and, after having gone through certain mysterious quadrille figures with her, lead her back to her mamma, who has just seized a third glass of muddy negus from the black footman;—the man who can do all this may do it, and go hang, for me! And many such men there be, my Gustavus, in yonder dusky London city. Be it ours, my dear friend, when the day's labor and repast are done, to lie and ruminate calmly; to watch the bland cigar-smoke as it rises gently ceiling-wards; to be idle in body as well as mind; not to kick our heels madly in quadrilles, and puff and pant in senseless gallopades; let us appreciate the joys of idleness; let us give a loose to silence; and having enjoyed this, the best dessert after a goodly dinner, at close of eve, saunter slowly home.

* * * *

As the dinner above described drew no less than three franc pieces out of my purse, I determined to economize for the next few days, and either to be invited out to dinner, or else to partake of some repast at a small charge, such as one may have here. I had on the day succeeding the troufled partridge a dinner for a shilling, viz.:—

> Bifsteck aux pommes (heu quantum mutatus ab illo!)
> Galantine de volaille,
> Fromage de Gruyère,
> Demie-bouteille du vin très-vieux de mâcon ou chablis,
> Pain à discrétion.

This dinner, my young friend, was taken about half past two o'clock in the day, and was, in fact, a breakfast,—a breakfast taken at a two-franc house, in the Rue Heure Vivienne; it was certainly a sufficient dinner: I certainly was not hungry for all the rest of the day. Nay, the wine was decently good, as almost all wine is in the morning, if one had the courage or the power to drink it. You see many honest English families marching into these two-franc eating-houses at five o'clock, and fancying they dine in great luxury. Returning to England, however, they inform their friends that the meat in France is not good; that the fowls are very small, and black; the kidneys very tough: the partridges and fruit have no taste in them; and the soup is execrably thin. A dinner at Williams's, in the Old Bailey, is better than the best of these; and therefore had the English Cockney better remain at Williams's, than judge the great nation so falsely.

The worst of these two-franc establishments is a horrid air of shabby elegance which distinguishes them. At some of them they will go the length of changing your knife and fork with every dish; they have grand chimney-glasses, and a fine lady at the counter, and fine arabesque paintings on the walls; they give you your soup in a battered dish of plated ware, which has served its best time, most likely, in a first-rate establishment, and comes here to *étaler* its second-hand splendor amongst amateurs of a lower grade. I fancy the very meat that is served to you has undergone the same degradation, and that some of the mouldy cutlets that are offered to the two-franc epicures lay once plump and juicy in Vérey's larder. Much better is the sanded floor and the iron fork! Homely neatness is the charm of poverty: elegance should belong to wealth alone. There is a very decent place where you dine for thirty-two sous in the Passage Choiseuil. You get your soup in china bowls; they don't change your knife and fork, but they give you very fit portions of meat and potatoes, and mayhap a herring with mustard sauce, a dish of apple fritters, a dessert of stewed prunes, and a pint of drinkable wine, as I have proved only yesterday.

After two such banyan days, I allowed myself a little feasting; and as nobody persisted in asking me to dinner, I went off to the Trois Frères by myself, and dined in that excellent company.

I would recommend a man who is going to dine by himself here, to reflect well before he orders soup for dinner.

My notion is, that you eat as much after soup as without it, but you *don't eat with the same appetite.*

Especially if you are a healthy man, as I am,—deuced hungry at five o'clock. My appetite runs away with me; and if I order soup (which is always enough for two), I invariably swallow the whole of it; and the greater portion of my *petit pain*, too, before my second dish arrives.

The best part of a pint of Julienne or purée à la Condé, is very well for a man who has only one dish besides to devour; but not for you and me, who like our fish and our *rôti* of game or meat as well.

Oysters you may eat. They do, for a fact, prepare one to go through the rest of a dinner properly. Lemon and cayenne pepper is the word, depend on it, and a glass of white wine braces you up for what is to follow.

French restaurateur dinners are intended, however, for two people, at least; still better for three; and require a good deal of thought before you can arrange them for one.

Here, for instance, is a recent *menu:*—

Trois Frères Provençeaux.	f.	c.
Pain	0	25
Beaune première	3	0
Purée à la créci	0	75
Turbot aux capres	1	75
Quart poulet aux truffes	2	25
Champignons à la Provençale	1	25
Gélée aux pommes	1	25
Cognac	0	30
	10	80

A heavy bill for a single man; and a heavy dinner, too; for I have said before I have a great appetite, and when a thing is put before me I eat it. At Brussels I once ate fourteen dishes; and have seen a lady, with whom I was in love, at the table of a German grand duke, eat seventeen dishes. This is a positive, though disgusting fact. Up to the first twelve dishes she had a very good chance of becoming Mrs. Titmarsh, but I have lost sight of her since.

Well, then, I say to you, if you have self-command enough to send away half your soup, order some; but you are a poor creature if you do, after all. If you are a man, and have *not* that self-command, don't have any. The Frenchmen cannot live without it, but I say to you that you are better than a Frenchman. I would lay even money that you who are reading this are more than five feet seven in height, and weigh eleven stone; while a Frenchman is five feet four and does not weigh nine. The Frenchman has after his soup a dish of vegetables, where you have one of meat. You are a different and superior animal, — a French-beating animal (the history of hundreds of years has shown you to be so); you must have to keep up that superior weight and sinew, which is the secret of your superiority, — as for public institutions, bah! — you must have, I say, simpler, stronger, succulenter food.

Eschew the soup, then, and have the fish up at once. It is the best to begin with fish, if you like it, as every epicure and honest man should, simply boiled or fried in the English fashion, and not tortured and bullied with oil, onions, wine, and herbs, as in Paris it is frequently done.

Turbot with lobster-sauce is too much; turbot *à la*

Hollandaise vulgar; sliced potatoes swimming in melted butter are a mean concomitant for a noble, simple, liberal fish: turbot with capers is the thing. The brisk little capers relieve the dulness of the turbot; the melted butter is rich, bland, and calm, — it *should be*, that is to say; not that vapid, watery mixture that I see in London; not oiled butter, as the Hollanders have it, but melted with plenty of thickening matter: I don't know how to do it, but I know it when it is good.

They melt butter well at the Rocher de Caucale, and at the Frères.

Well, this turbot was very good; not so well, of course, as one gets it in London, and dried rather in the boiling; which can't be helped, unless you are a Lucullus or a Cambaçeres of a man, and can afford to order one for yourself. This *grandeur d'âme* is very rare; my friend, Tom Willows, is almost the only man I know who possessed it. Yes, * * *, one of the wittiest men in London, I once knew to take the whole *intérieur* of a diligence (six places), because he was a little unwell. Ever since I have admired that man. He understands true economy; a mean, extravagant man would have contented himself with a single place, and been unwell in consequence. How I am rambling from my subject, however. The fish was good, and I ate up every single scrap of it, sucking the bones and fins curiously. That is the deuce of an appetite, it *must* be satisfied; and if you were to put a roast donkey before me, with the promise of a haunch of venison afterwards, I believe I should eat the greater part of the long-eared animal.

A pint of *purée à la créci*, a *pain de gruau*, a slice of turbot, — a man should think about ordering his bill, for he has had enough dinner; but no, we are creatures of superstition and habit, and must have one regular course of meat. Here comes the *poulet à la Marengo:* I hope they've given me the wing.

No such thing. The *poulet à la Marengo aux truffes* is bad, — too oily by far; the truffles are not of this year as they should be, for there are cart-loads in town: they are poor in flavor, and have only been cast into the dish a minute before it was brought to table, and what is the consequence? They do not flavor the meat in the least; some faint trufflesque savor you may get as you are crunching each individual root, but that is all, and that all not worth the having; for as nothing is finer than a good truffle, in like manner nothing is meaner than a bad one. It is merely pompous, windy, and pretentious, like those scraps of philosophy with which a certain eminent novelist decks out his meat.

A mushroom, thought I, is better a thousand times than these tough, flavorless roots. I finished every one of them, however, and the fine, fat capon's thigh, which they surrounded. It was a disappointment not to get a wing, to be sure. They *always* give me legs; but after all, with a little good-humor and philosophy, a leg of a fine Mans capon may be found very acceptable. How plump and tender the rogue's thigh is! his very drumstick is as fat as the calf of a London footman; and the sinews which puzzle one so over the lean, black hen-legs in London, are miraculously whisked away from the limb before me. Look at it now! Half a dozen cuts with the knife, and yonder lies the bone, — white, large, stark naked, without a morsel of flesh left upon it, solitary in the midst of a pool of melted butter.

How good the Burgundy smacks after it! I always drink Burgundy at this house, and that not of the best.

It is my firm opinion that a third-rate Burgundy, and a third-rate claret, — Beaune and Larose for instance, are *better* than the best. The Bordeaux enlivens, the Burgundy invigorates: stronger drink only inflames; and where a bottle of good Beaune only causes a man to feel a certain manly warmth of benevolence, — a glow something like that produced by sunshine and gentle exercise, — a bottle of Chambertin will set all your frame in a fever, swells the extremities, and causes the pulses to throb. Chambertin should *never* be handed round more than twice; and I recollect to this moment the headache I had after drinking a bottle and a half of Romanée-Gélée, for which this house is famous. Somebody else *paid* for the — (no other than you, O Gustavus! with whom I hope to have many a tall dinner on the same charges) — but 't was in our hot youth, ere experience had taught us that moderation was happiness, and had shown us that it is absurd to be guzzling wine at fifteen francs a bottle.

By the way, I may here mention a story relating to some of Blackwood's men, who dined at this very house. Fancy the fellows trying claret, which they voted sour; then Burgundy, at which they made wry faces, and finished the evening with brandy and *lunel!* This is what men call eating a French dinner. Willows and I dined at the Rocher, and an English family there feeding ordered — mutton-chops and potatoes. Why not, in these cases, stay at home? Chops is better chops in England (the best chops in the world are to be had at the Reform Club) than in France. What would literary men mean by ordering lunel? I always rather liked the descriptions of eating in the *Noctes.* They were gross in all cases, absurdly erroneous, in many; but there was a manliness about them, and strong evidence of a great, though misdirected and uneducated, genius for victuals.

Mushrooms, thought I, are better than these tasteless truffles, and so ordered a dish to try. You know what a *Provençale* sauce is, I have no doubt? — a rich, savory mixture, of garlic and oil; which, with a little cayenne pepper and salt, impart a pleasant taste to the plump little mushrooms, that can't be described but may be thought of with pleasure.

The only point was, how will they agree with me to-morrow morning? for the fact is, I had eaten an immense quantity of them, and began to be afraid! Suppose we go and have a glass of punch and a cigar? O, glorious garden of the Palais Royal! your trees are leafless now, but what matters? Your alleys are damp, but what of that? All the windows are blazing with light and merriment; at least two thousand happy people are pacing up and down the colonnades; cheerful sounds of money chinking are heard as you pass the changers' shops; bustling shouts of *garçon*, and *V'là mousieur!* come from the swinging doors of the restaurateurs. Look at that group of soldiers gaping at Véfour's window, where lie lobsters, pine-apples, fat truffle-stuffed partridges, which make me almost hungry again. I wonder whether those three fellows with mustachios and a toothpick apiece have had a dinner, or only a toothpick. When the Trois Frères used to be on the first floor, and had a door leading into the Rue de Valois, as well as one into the garden, I recollect seeing three men with toothpicks mount the stair from the street, descend the stair into the garden, and give themselves as great airs as if they had dined for a napoleon a head. The rogues are lucky if they have had a sixteen sous dinner; and the next time I dine abroad, I am resolved to have one myself. I never understood why Gil Blas grew so mighty squeamish in the affair of the cat and the hare. Hare is best, but why should not cat be good ?

Being on the subject of bad dinners, I may as well ease my mind of one that occurred to me some few days back. When walking in the Boulevard, I met my friend, Captain Hopkinson, of the half-pay, looking very hungry, and indeed going to dine. In most cases one respects the dictum of a half-pay officer regarding a dining-house. He knows as a general rule where the fat of the land lies, and how to take his share of that fat in the most economical manner.

" I tell you what I do," says Hopkinson ; " I allow myself fifteen franc a week for dinner (I count upon being asked out twice a week), and so have a three-franc dinner at Richard's, where, for the extra franc, they give me an excellent bottle of wine, and make me comfortable."

" Why should n't they ? " I thought. " Here is a man who has served his king and country, and no doubt knows a thing when he sees it." We made a party of four, therefore, and went to the captain's place to dine.

We had a private room *au second;* a very damp and dirty private room, with a faint odor of stale punch, and dingy glasses round the walls.

We had a soup of purée aux crouton ; a very dingy, dubious soup, indeed ; thickened, I fancy, with brown paper, and flavored with the same.

At the end of the soup Monsieur Landlord came up stairs very kindly, and gave us each a pinch of snuff out of a gold snuff-box.

We had four portions of anguille à la tartare, very good and fresh (it is best in these places to eat fresh-water fish). Each portion was half the length of a man's finger. Dish one was despatched in no time, and we began drinking the famous wine that our guide recommended. I have cut him ever since. It was four-sous wine, — weak, vapid, watery stuff, of the most unsatisfactory nature.

We had four portions of gigot aux haricots, — four flaps of bleeding, tough meat, cut unnaturally (that is, with the grain: the French gash the meat in parallel lines with the bone). We ate these up as we might, and the landlord was so good as to come up again and favor us with a pinch from his gold box.

With wonderful unanimity, as we were told the place was famous for civet de liévre, we ordered civet de liévre for four.

It came up, but we could n't, — really we could n't. We were obliged to have extra dishes, and pay extra. Gustavus had a mayonnaise of crayfish, and half a fowl; I fell to work upon my cheese as usual, and availed myself of the discretionary bread. We went away disgusted, wretched, unhappy. We had had for our three francs bad bread, bad meat, bad wine. And there stood the landlord at the door (and be hanged to him!) grinning and offering his box.

We don't speak to Hopkinson any more now when we meet him. How can you trust or be friendly with a man who deceives you in this miserable way?

What is the moral to be drawn from this dinner? It is evident. Avoid pretence; mistrust shabby elegance; cut your coat according to your cloth; if you have but a few shillings in your pocket, aim only at those humble and honest meats which your small store will purchase. At the Café Foy, for the same money, I might have had

	f.	s.
A delicious entrecote and potatoes	1	5
A pint of excellent wine	0	15
A little bread (meaning a good deal) . . .	0	5
A dish of stewed kidneys	1	0
	3	0

Or at Paolo's.

A bread (as before)	0	5
A heap of macaroni, or ravioli	0	15
A Milanese cutlet	1	0
A pint of wine	0	10

And ten sous for any other luxury your imagination could suggest. The ravioli and the cutlets are admirably dressed at Paolo's. Does any healthy man need more?

These dinners, I am perfectly aware, are by no means splendid; and I might, with the most perfect ease, write you out a dozen bills of fare, each more splendid and piquant than the other, in which all the luxuries of the season should figure. But the remarks here set down are the result of experience, not fancy, and intended only for persons in the middling classes of life. Very few men can afford to pay more than five francs daily for dinner. Let us calmly, then, consider what enjoyment may be had for those five francs; how, by economy on one day, we may venture upon luxury the next; how, by a little forethought and care, we may be happy on all days. Who knew and studied this cheap philosophy of life better than old Horace, before quoted? Sometimes (when in luck) he cherupped over cups that were fit for an archbishop's supper; sometimes he philosophized over his own *ordinaire* at his own farm. How affecting is the last ode of the first book:—

TO HIS SERVING-BOY.

Persicos odi,
Puer, apparatus;
Displicent nexæ
Philyrâ coronæ:
Mitte sectari
Rosa quo locorum
Sera moretur.

Simplici myrto
Nihil allabores
Sedulus curæ:
Neque te ministrum
Dedecet myrtus,
Neque me sub arctâ
Vite bibentem.

AD MINISTRAM.

Dear Lucy, you know what my wish is,—
I hate all your Frenchified fuss:
Your silly entrées and made dishes
Were never intended for us.
No footman in lace and in ruffles
Need dangle behind my arm-chair;
And never mind seeking for truffles,
Although they be ever so rare.

But a plain leg of mutton, my Lucy,
I pr'ythee get ready at three:
Have it smoking, and tender, and juicy,
And what better meat can there be?
And when it has feasted the master,
'T will amply suffice for the maid;
Meanwhile I will smoke my canaster,
And tipple my ale in the shade.

Not that this is the truth entirely and forever. Horatius Flaccus was too wise to dislike a good thing; but it is possible that the Persian apparatus was on that day beyond his means, and so he contented himself with humble fare.

A gentleman, by the by, has just come to Paris, to whom I am very kind; and who will, in all human probability, between this and next month, ask me to a dinner at the Rocher de Caucale. If so, something may occur worth writing about; or if you are anxious to hear more on the subject, send me over a sum to my address, to be laid out for you exclusively in eating. I give you my honor I will do you justice, and account for every farthing of it.

One of the most absurd customs at present in use is that of giving your friend, — when some piece of good luck happens to him, such as an appointment as Chief Judge of Owhyhee, or King's Advocate to Timbuctoo, — of giving your friend, because, forsooth, he may have been suddenly elevated from £200 a-year to £2,000, an enormous dinner of congratulation.

Last year, for instance, when our friend, Fred Jowling, got his place of Commissioner at Quashumaboo, it was considered absolutely necessary to give the man a dinner, and some score of us had to pay about fifty shillings a-piece for the purpose. I had, so help me, Moses! but three guineas in the world at that period; and out of this sum the *bienséances* compelled me to sacrifice five sixths, to feast myself in company of a man gorged with wealth, rattling sovereigns in his pocket as if they had been so much dross, and capable of treating us all without missing the sum he might expend on us.

Jow himself allowed, as I represented the case to him, that the arrangement *was* very hard; but represented, fairly enough, that this was one of the sacrifices that a man of the world, from time to time, is called to make. "You, my dear Titmarsh," said he, know very well that I don't care for these grand entertainments" (the rogue, he is a five-bottle man, and just the most finished *gourmet* of my acquaintance!); "you know that I am perfectly convinced of your friendship for me, though you join in the dinner or not, but,—it would look rather queer if you backed out,—*it would look rather queer.*" Jow said this in such an emphatic way, that I saw I must lay down my money; and accordingly Mr. Lovegrove of Blackwall, for a certain quantity of iced punch, champagne, cider cup, fish, flesh, and fowl, received the last of my sovereigns.

At the beginning of the year Bolter got a place too,—Judge-Advocate in the Topinambo Islands, of £3,000 a-year, which he said was a poor remuneration in consideration of *the practice* which he gave up in town. He may have practised on his laundress, but for anything else I believe the man never had a client in his life.

However, on his way to Topinambo—by Marseilles, Egypt, the Desert, the Persian Gulf, and so on—Bolter arrived in Paris; and I saw from his appearance, and the manner of shaking hands with me, and the peculiar way in which he talked about the Rocher de Caucale, that he expected we were to give him a dinner, as we had to Jowling.

There were four friends of Bolter's in the capital besides myself, and among us the dinner-question was mooted: we agreed that it should be a simple dinner of ten francs a head, and this was the bill of fare:—

1. Oysters (common), nice.
2. Oysters, green of Marenne (very good).
3. Potage, purée de gibier (very fair).

As we were English, they instantly then served us,—

4. Sole en matelotte Normande (comme ça).
5. Turbot à la crême au gratin (excellent).
6. Jardinière cutlets (particularly seedy).

7. Poulet à la Marengo (very fair, but why the deuce is one always to be pestered by it ?).

8.
9. } (Entrées of some kind, but a blank in my memory).

10. A rôt of chevreuil.

11. Ditto of eperlans (very hot, crisp, and nice).

12. Ditto of partridges (quite good and plump).

13. Pointes d'asperges.

14. Champignons à la Provençale (the most delicious mushrooms I ever tasted).

15. Pine-apple jelly.

16. Blanc, or red mange.

17. Pencacks. Let everybody who goes to the Rocher order these pancakes; they are arranged with jelly inside, rolled up between various *couches* of vermicilli, flavored with a *leetle* wine; and, by everything sacred, the most delightful meat possible.

18. Timballe of macaroni.

The jellies and sucreries should have been mentioned in the dessert, and there were numberless plates of trifles, which made the table look very pretty, but need not be mentioned here.

The dinner was not a fine one, as you see. No rarities, no troufles even, no mets de primeur, though there were peas and asparagus in the market at a pretty fair price. But with rarities no man has any business except he have a colossal fortune. Hot-house strawberries, asparagus, &c., are, as far as my experience goes, most *fade*, mean, and tasteless meats. Much better to have a simple dinner of twenty dishes, and content therewith, than to look for impossible splendors and Apician morsels.

In respect of wine. Let those who go to the Rocher take my advice and order Madeira. They have here some pale old East India very good. How they got it is a secret, for the Parisians do not know good Madeira when they see it. Some very fair strong young wine may be had at the Hôtel des Americains, in the Rue St. Honoré; as, indeed, all West India produce, — pine-apple rum, for instance. I may say, with confidence, that I never knew what rum was until I tasted this at Paris.

But to the Rocher. The Madeira was the best wine served; though some Burgundy, handed round in the course of dinner, and a bottle of Montrachet, similarly poured out to us, were very fair. The champagne was decidedly not good, — poor, inflated, thin stuff. They say the drink we swallow in England is not genuine wine, but brandy-loaded and otherwise doctored for the English market; but, ah, what superior wine! *Au reste*, the French will not generally pay the money for the wine; and it therefore is carried from an ungrateful country to more generous climes, where it is better appreciated. We had claret and speeches after dinner; and very possibly some of the persons present made free with a jug of hot water, a few lumps of sugar, and the horrid addition of a glass of cognac. There can be no worse practice than this. After a dinner of eighteen dishes, in which you have drunk at least thirty-six glasses of wine, — when the stomach is full, the brain heavy, the hands and feet inflamed, — when the claret begins to pall, — you, forsooth, must gorge yourself with brandy-and-water, and puff filthy cigars. For shame! Who ever does it? Does a gentleman drink brandy-and-water? Does a man who mixes in the society of the loveliest half of humanity befoul himself by tobacco smoke? Fie, fie! avoid the practice. I indulge in it always myself; but that is no reason why you, a young man entering into the world, should degrade yourself in any such way. No, no, my dear lad, never refuse an evening party, and avoid tobacco as you would the upas plant.

By the way, not having my purse about me when the above dinner was given, I was constrained to borrow from Bolter, whom I knew more intimately than the rest; and nothing grieved me more than to find, on calling at his hotel four days afterwards, that he had set off by the mail post for Marseilles. Friend of my youth, dear, dear Bolton! if haply this trifling page should come before thine eyes, weary of perusing the sacred rolls of Themis in thy far-off island in the Indian Sea, thou wilt recall our little dinner in the little room of the Cancalian Coffee-House, and think for a while of thy friend!

Let us now mention one or two places that the Briton, on his arrival here, should frequent or avoid. As a quiet, dear house, where there are some of the best rooms in Paris — always the best meat, fowls, vegetables, &c. — we may specially recommend Monsieur Voisin's café, opposite the church of the Assumption. A very decent and lively house of restauration is that at the corner of the Rue du Faubourg Montmartre, on the Boulevard. I never yet had a good dinner in my life at Véfour's; *something* is always *manqué* at the place. The Grand Vattel is worthy of note, as cheap, pretty, and quiet. All the English houses gentlemen may frequent who are so inclined; but though the writer of this has many times dined for sixteen sous at Catcomb's, cheek by jowl with a French chasseur or a laborer, he has, he confesses, an antipathy to enter into the confidence of a footman or groom of his own country.

A gentleman who purchases pictures in this town was lately waited upon by a lady, who said she had in her possession one of the greatest rarities in the world, — a picture, admirable, too, as a work of art, — no less than an original portrait of Shakespeare, by his comrade, the famous John Davis. The gentleman rushed off immediately to behold the wonder, and saw a head, rudely but vigorously painted on panel, about twice the size of life, with a couple of hooks drawn through the top part of the board, under which was written,

THE WILLIAM SHAKESPEARE,

BY JOHN DAVIS.

"Voyez vous, Monsieur," said the lady; "il n'y a plus de doute. Le portrait de Shakespeare du célèbre Davis, et signé même de lui!"

I remember it used to hang up in a silent little street in the Latin quarter, near an old convent, before a quaint old quiet tavern that I loved. It was pleasant to see the old name written up in a strange land, and the well-known friendly face greeting one. There was a quiet little garden at the back of the tavern, and famous good roast-beef, clean rooms, and English beer. Where are you now, John Davis? Could not the image of thy august patron preserve thy house from ruin, or rally the faithful around it? Are you unfortunate, Davis? Are you a bankrupt? Let us hope not. I swear to thee, that when, one sunny afternoon, I first saw the ensign of thy tavern, I loved thee for the choice, and douced my cap on entering the porch, and looked around, and thought all friends were here.

In the queer old pleasant novel of the *Spiritual Quixote*, honest Tugwell, the Sancho of the story, relates a Warwickshire legend, which at the time Graves wrote was not much more than a hundred years old; and by which it appears that the owner of New Place was a famous jesting gentleman, and used to sit at his gate of summer evenings, cutting the queerest, merriest jokes with all the passers-by. I have heard from a Warwickshire clergyman that the legend still exists in the country; and Ward's *Diary* says, that Master Shakespeare died of a surfeit, brought on by carousing with a literary friend who had come to visit him from London. And wherefore not? Better to die of good wine and good company than of slow disease and doctor's doses. Some geniuses live on sour misanthropy, and some on meek milk-and-water. Let us not deal too hardly with those that are of a jovial sort, and indulge in the decent practice of the cup and the platter.

A word or two, by way of conclusion, may be said about the numerous pleasant villages in the neighborhood of Paris, or rather of the eating and drinking to be found in the taverns of those suburban spots. At Versailles, Monsieur Duboux, at the Hôtel des Reservoirs, has a good cook and cellars, and will gratify you with a heavier bill than is paid at Vérey's and the Rocher. On the beautiful terrace of Saint Germain, looking over miles of river and vineyard, of fair villages basking in the meadows, and great tall trees stretching wide round about; you may sit in the open air of summer evenings and see the white spires of Saint Denis rising in the distance, and the gray arches of Marly to the right, and before you the city of Paris with innumerable domes and towers.

Watching these objects, and the setting sun gorgeously illumining the heavens and them, you may have an excellent dinner served to you by the *chef* of Messire Gallois, who at present owns the pavilion where Louis XIV. was born. The *maître d'hôtel* is from the Rocher, and told us that he came out to St. Germain for the sake of the air. The only drawback to the entertainment is, that the charges are as atrociously high in price as the dishes provided are small in quantity; and dining at this pavilion on the 15th of April, at a period when a *botte* of asparagus at Paris cost only three francs, the writer of this and a chosen associate had to pay seven francs for about the third part of a *botte* of asparagus, served up to them by Messire Gallois.

Facts like these ought not to go unnoticed. Therefore, let the readers of *Fraser's Magazine* who propose a visit to Paris, take warning by the unhappy fate of the person now addressing them, and avoid the place or not, as they think fit. A bad dinner does no harm to any human soul, and the philosopher partakes of such with easy resignation; but a bad and dear dinner is enough to raise the anger of any man, however naturally sweet-tempered, and he is bound to warn his acquaintance of it.

With one parting syllable in praise of the Marroniers at Bercy, where you get capital eels, fried gudgeons fresh from the Seine, and excellent wine of the ordinary kind, this discourse is here closed. "*En telle ou meilleure pensée, Beuueurs très illustres (car à vous non à aultres sont dédiés ces escriptz) reconfortez vostre malheur, et beuuez fraiz si faire se peult.*"

MEN AND COATS.

HERE is some peculiar influence, which no doubt the reader has remarked in his own case, for it has been sung by ten thousand poets, or versifying persons, whose ideas you adopt, if perchance, as is barely possible, you have none of your own, — there is, I say, a certain balmy influence in the spring-time, which brings a rush of fresh dancing blood into the veins of all nature, and causes it to wear a peculiarly festive and sporting look. Look at the old Sun, — how pale he was all the winter through! Some days he was so cold and wretched he would not come out at all, — he would not leave his bed till eight o'clock, and retired to rest, the old sluggard! at four; but, lo! comes May, and he is up at five, — he feels, like the rest of Us, the delicious vernal influence; he is always walking abroad in the fresh air, and his jolly face lights up anew! Remark the trees; they have dragged through the shivering winter time without so much as a rag to cover them, but about May they feel obligated to follow the mode, and come out in a new suit of green. The meadows, in like manner, appear invested with a variety of pretty spring fashions, not only covering their backs with a bran-new, glossy suit, but sporting a world of little coquettish, ornamental gimcracks that are suited to the season. This one covers his robe with the most delicate twinkling white daisies; that tricks himself out with numberless golden cowslips, or decorates his bosom with a bunch of dusky violets. Birds sing and make love; bees wake and make honey; horses and men leave off their shaggy winter clothing and turn out in fresh coats. The only animal that does not feel the power of spring, is that selfish, silent, and cold-blooded beast, the oyster, who shuts himself up for the best months of the year, and with whom the climate disagrees.

Some people have wondered how it is that what is called "the season" in London should not begin until spring. What an absurd subject for wondering at! How *could* the London season begin at any other time? How could the great, black, bilious, overgrown city, stifled by gas, and fogs, and politics, ever hope to have a season at all, unless nature with a violent effort came to its aid about Easter time, and infused into it a little spring blood? The town of London feels then the influences of the spring, and salutes it after its fashion. The parks are green for about a couple of months. Lady Smigsmag, and other leaders of the *ton*, give their series of grand parties; Gunter and Grange come forward with iced-creams and champagnes; ducks and green-pease burst out; the river Thames blossoms with whitebait; and Alderman Birch announces the arrival of fresh, lively turtle. If there are no birds to sing and make love, as in country places, at least there are coveys of opera girls that frisk and hop about airily, and Rubini and Lablache to act as a couple of nightingales. "A lady of fashion remarked," says Dyson, in the *Morning Post*, "that for all persons pretending to hold a position in genteel society," — I forget the exact words, but the sense of them remains indelibly engraven upon my mind, — "for any one pretending to take a place in genteel society two things are *indispensable.* And what are these? — a BOUQUET AND AN EMBROIDERED POCKET-HANDKERCHIEF." This is a self-evident truth. Dyson does not furnish the bouquets, — he is not a market-gardener, — he is not the goddess Flora; but, a town-man, he knows what the season requires, and furnishes his contribution to it. The lilies of the field are not more white and graceful than his embroidered nose ornaments, and with a little *eau des cent-milles fleurs,* not more fragrant. Dyson knows that pocket-handkerchiefs are necessary, and has "an express from Longchamps" to bring them over.

Whether they are picked from ladies' pockets by Dyson's couriers, who then hurry breathless across the Channel with them, no one need ask. But the gist of Dyson's advertisement, and of all the preceding remarks, is this great truth, which need not be carried out further by any illustrations from geography or natural history, — that in the spring-time all nature renews itself. There is not a country newspaper published in England that does not proclaim the same fact. Madame Hoggin informs the nobility and gentry of Penzance that her new and gigantic stock of Parisian fashions has just arrived from London. Mademoiselle M'Whirter begs to announce to the *haut-ton* in the environs of John-o'-Groats that she has this instant returned from Paris, with her dazzling and beautiful collection of spring fashions.

In common with the birds, the trees, the meadows, — in common with the Sun, with Dyson, with all nature, in fact, I yielded to the irresistible spring impulse, — *homo sum, nihil humani a me alienum,* &c., — I acknowledged the influence of the season, and ordered a new coat, waistcoat and tr—— in short, a new suit. Now, having worn it for a few days, and studied the effect which it has upon the wearer, I thought that perhaps an essay upon new clothes and their influence might be attended with some profit both to the public and the writer.

One thing is certain. A man does not have a new suit of clothes every day; and another general proposition may be advanced, that a man in sporting a coat for the first time is either

agreeably affected, or
disagreeably affected, or
not affected at all, —

which latter case I don't believe. There is no man, however accustomed to new clothes, but must feel some sentiment of pride in assuming them, — no philosopher, however calm, but must remark the change of raiment. Men consent to wear old clothes forever, — nay, feel a pang at parting with them for new; but the first appearance of a new garment is always attended with exultation.

Even the feeling of shyness, which makes a man ashamed of his splendor, is a proof of his high sense of it. What causes an individual to sneak about in corners and shady places, to avoid going out in new clothes of a Sunday, lest he be mistaken for a snob? Sometimes even to go the lengths of ordering his servant to powder his new coat with sand, or to wear it for a couple of days, and remove the gloss thereof? Are not these manœuvres proofs of the effects of new coats upon mankind in general?

As this notice will occupy at least ten pages (for a reason that may be afterwards mentioned), I intend, like the great philosophers who have always sacrificed themselves for the public good, imbibing diseases, poisons, and medicines, submitting to operations, inhaling asphysifications, &c., in order that they might note in themselves the particular phenomena of the case, — in like manner, I say, I intend to write this essay in five several coats, viz: —

1. My old single-breasted black frock-coat, with patches at the elbows, made to go into mourning for William IV.

2. My double-breasted green ditto, made last year but one, and still very good, but rather queer about the lining, and snowy in the seams.

3. My grand black dress-coat, made by Messrs. Sparding and Spohrer, of Conduit Street, in 1836. A little scouring and renovating have given it a stylish look even now; and it was always a splendid cut.

4. My worsted-net-jacket that my uncle Harry gave me on his departure for Italy. This jacket is wadded inside with a wool like that one makes Welsh wigs of; and though not handsome, amazing comfortable, with pockets all over.

5. My new frock-coat.

Now, will the reader be able to perceive any difference in the style of writing of each chapter? I fancy I see it myself clearly; and am convinced that the new frock-coat chapter will be infinitely more genteel, spruce, and glossy, than the woollen-jacket chapter; which, again, shall be more comfortable than the poor, seedy, patched William-the-Fourth's black-frock chapter. The double-breasted green one will be dashing, manly, free-and-easy; and though not fashionable, yet with a well-bred look. The grand black-dress chapter will be solemn and grave, devilish tight about the waist, abounding in bows and shrugs, and small talk; it will have a great odor of bohea and pound-cake; perhaps there will be a faint whiff of negus; and the tails will whisk up in a quadrille at the end, or sink down, mayhap, on a supper-table bench before a quantity of trifles, lobster-salads, and champagnes; and near a lovely blushing white satin skirt, which is continually crying out, "O you ojous creature!" or, "O you naughty, satirical man, you!" "And do you really be lieve Miss Moffat dyes her hair?" "And have you read that sweet thing in the *Keepsake* by Lord Diddle?" "Well, only one *leetle*, leetle drop, for mamma will scold"; and "O you horrid Mr. Titmarsh, you have filled my glass, I declare!" Dear white satin skirt, what pretty shoulders and eyes you have! what a nice white neck, and bluish-mottled, round, innocent arms! how fresh you are and candid! and ah, my dear, what a fool you are!

* * * * *

I don't have so many coats now-a-days as in the days of hot youth, when the figure was more elegant, and credit, mayhap, more plenty; and, perhaps, this accounts for the feeling of unusual exultation that comes over me as I assume this one. Look at the skirts how they are shining in the sun, with a delicate gloss upon them,—that evanescent gloss that passes away with the first freshness of the coat, as the bloom does from the peach. A friend meets you,—he salutes you cordially, but looks puzzled for a moment at the change in your appearance. "I have it!" says Jones. "Hobson, my boy, I congratulate you,—a new coat, and very neat cut,—puce-colored frock, brown silk lining, brass buttons, and velvet collar,—quite novel, and quiet and genteel at the same time." You say, "Pooh, Jones! do you think so, though?" and at the same time turn round just to give him a view of the back, in which there is not a single wrinkle. You find suddenly that you must buy a new stock; that your old Berlin gloves will never do; and that a pair of three-

and-sixpenny kids are absolutely necessary. You find your boots are cruelly thick, and fancy that the attention of the world is accurately divided between the new frock-coat and the patch on your great toe. It is very odd that that patch did not annoy you yesterday in the least degree, — that you looked with a good-natured grin at the old sausage-fingered Berlin gloves, bulging out at the end and concaved like spoons. But there *is* a change in the man, without any doubt. Notice Sir M—— O'D——; those who know that celebrated military man by sight are aware of one peculiarity in his appearance, — his hat is never brushed. I met him one day with the beaver brushed quite primly; and looking hard at the baronet to ascertain the cause of this phenomenon, saw that he had a new coat. Even his great spirit was obliged to yield to the power of the coat, — he made a genteel effort, — he awoke up from his habitual Diogenic carelessness; and I have no doubt that had Alexander, before he visited the cynic, ordered some one to fling a new robe into his barrel, I have no doubt but that he would have found the fellow prating and boasting with all the airs of a man of fashion, and talking of tilburies, opera girls, and the last ball at Devonshire House, as if the brute had been used for all his life to no other company. Fie upon the swaggering, vulgar bully! I have always wondered how the Prince of Macedon, a gentleman by birth, with an excellent tutor to educate him, could have been imposed upon by the grovelling, obscene, envious tub-man, and could have uttered the speech we know of. It was a humbug, depend upon it, attributed to his majesty by some maladroit *bon-mot* maker of the court, and passed subsequently for genuine Alexandrine.

It is hardly necessary for the moralist earnestly to

point out to persons moving in a modest station of life the necessity of not having coats of too fashionable and rakish a cut. Coats have been, and will be in the course of this disquisition, frequently compared to the flowers of the field: like them they bloom for a season, like them they grow seedy and they fade.

Can you afford always to renew your coat when this fatal hour arrives? Is your coat like the French monarchy, and does it never die? Have, then, clothes of the newest fashion, and pass on to the next article in the Magazine, — unless, always, you prefer the style of this one.

But while a shabby coat, worn in a manly way, is a bearable, nay, sometimes a pleasing object, reminding one of "a good man struggling with the storms of fate," whom Mr. Joseph Addison has represented in his tragedy of *Cato*, — while a man of a certain character may look august and gentlemanlike in a coat of a certain cut, — it is quite impossible for a person who sports an ultra-fashionable costume to wear it with decency beyond a half-year say. *My* coats always last me two years, and any man who knows me knows how *I* look; but I defy Count d'Orsay thus publicly to wear a suit for seven hundred and thirty days consecutively, and look respectable at the end of that time. In like manner, I would defy, without any disrespect, the Marchioness of X——, or her Grace the Duchess of Z——, to sport a white satin gown constantly for six months and look decent. There is *propriety* in dress. Ah, my poor Noll Goldsmith, in your famous plum-colored velvet! I can see thee strutting down Fleet Street, and stout old Sam rolling behind as Maister Boswell pours some Caledonian jokes into his ear, and grins at the poor vain poet. In what a pretty condition will Goldy's puce-colored velvet be about two months hence, when it is covered with dust and grease, and he comes in his slatternly finery to borrow a guinea of his friend!

A friend of the writer's once made him a present of two very handsome gold pins; and what did the author of this notice do? Why, with his usual sagacity, he instantly sold the pins for five-and-twenty shillings, the cost of the gold, knowing full well that he could not afford to live up to such fancy articles. If you sport handsome gold pins, you must have everything about you to match. Nor do I in the least agree with my friend Bosk, who has a large amethyst brooch, and fancies that, because he sticks it in his shirt, his atrocious shabby stock and surtout may pass muster. No, no! let us be all peacock, if you please; but one peacock's feather in your tail is a very absurd ornament, and of course all moderate men will avoid it. I remember, when I travelled with Captain Cook in the South Sea Islands, to have seen Quashamaboo with nothing on him but a remarkably fine cocked-hat, his queen sported a red coat, and one of the princesses went frisking about in a pair of leather-breeches, much to our astonishment.

This costume was not much more absurd than poor Goldsmith's, who might be very likely seen drawing forth from the gold-embroidered pocket of his plum-colored velvet, a pat of butter wrapped in a cabbage-leaf, a pair of farthing rushlights, an onion or two, and a bit of bacon.

I recollect meeting a great, clever, ruffianly boor of a man, who had made acquaintance with a certain set of very questionable aristocracy, and gave himself the air of a man of fashion. He had a coat made of the very pattern of Lord Toggery's, — a green frock, a green velvet collar, a green lining: a plate of spring-cabbage is not of a brisker, brighter hue. This man, who had been a shop-keeper's apprentice originally, now declared that every man who was a gentleman wore white kid gloves, and for a certain period sported a fresh pair every day.

One hot, clear, sunshiny, July day, walking down the Haymarket at two o'clock, I heard a great yelling and shouting of blackguard boys, and saw that they were hunting some object in their front.

The object approached us, — it was a green object, — a green coat, collar, and lining, and a pair of pseudo-white kid gloves. The gloves were dabbled with mud and blood, the man was bleeding at the nose, and slavering at the mouth, and yelling some unintelligible verses of a song, and swaying to and fro across the sunshiny street, with the blackguard boys in chase.

I turned round the corner of Vigo Lane with the velocity of a cannon-ball, and sprung panting into a baker's shop. It was Mr. Bludyer, our London Diogenes. Have a care ye gay, dashing Alexanders! how ye influence such men by too much praise, or debauch them by too much intimacy. How much of that man's extravagance, and absurd aristocratic airs, and subsequent *roueries*, and cutting of old acquaintance, is to be attributed to his imitation of Lord Toggery's coat!

Actors of the lower sort affect very much braiding and fur collars to their frock-coats; and a very curious and instructive sight it is to behold these personages with pale, lean faces, and hats cocked on one side, in a sort of pseudo-military trim. One sees many such sauntering under Drury Lane Colonnade, or about Bow Street, with sickly smiles on their faces. Poor fellows, poor fellows! how much of their character is embroidered in that seedy braiding of their coats! Near five o'clock, in the neighborhood of Rupert Street and the Haymarket, you may still occasionally see the old, shabby, manly, gentlemanly, half-pay frock: but the braid is now growing scarce in London; and your military man, with reason perhaps, dresses more like a civilian; and understanding life better, and the means of making his half-crown go as far as five shillings in former days, has usually a club to dine at, and leaves Rupert Street eating-houses to persons of a different grade, — to some of those dubious dandies whom one sees swaggering in Regent Street in the afternoon, or to those gay, spruce gentlemen whom you encounter in St. Paul's Churchyard at ten minutes after five, on their way westward from the City. Look at the same hour at the Temple, and issuing thence and from Essex Street, you behold many scores of neat barristers, who are walking to the joint and half a pint of Marsala at the Oxford and Cambridge Club. They are generally tall, slim, proper, well-dressed men, but their coats are too prim and professionally cut. Indeed, I have generally remarked that their clerks, who leave chambers about the same time, have a far more rakish and fashionable air; and if, my dear madam, you will condescend to take a beefsteak at the Cock, or at some of the houses around Covent Garden, you will at once allow that this statement is perfectly correct.

I have always had rather a contempt for a man who, on arriving at home, deliberately takes his best coat from his back and adopts an old and shabby one. It is a mean precaution. Unless very low in the world indeed, one should be above a proceeding so petty. Once I knew a French lady very smartly dressed in a black velvet pelisse, a person whom I admired very much, — and indeed for the matter of that she was very fond of me, but that is neither here nor there, — I say I knew a French lady of some repute who used to wear a velvet pelisse, and how do you think the back of it was arranged?

Why, pelisses are worn, as you know, very full behind; and Madame de Tournuronval had actually a strip of black satin let into the hinder part of her dress, over which the velvet used to close with a spring when she walked or stood, so that the satin was invisible. But when she sat on a chair, especially one of the cane-bottomed species, Euphemia gave a loose to her spring, the velvet divided on each side, and she sat down on the satin.

Was it an authorized stratagem of millinery? Is a woman under any circumstances permitted to indulge in such a manœuvre? I say, No. A woman with such a gown is of a mean, deceitful character. Of a woman who has a black satin patch behind her velvet gown, it is right that one should speak ill behind the back; and when I saw Euphemia Tournuronval spread out her wings (*non usitatæ pennæ*, but what else to call them?) — spread out her skirts and insure them from injury by means of this dastardly *ruse*, I quitted the room in disgust, and never was intimate with her as before. A widow I know she was; I am certain she looked sweet upon me; and she said she had a fortune, but I don't believe it. Away with parsimonious ostentation! That woman, had I married her, would either have turned out a swindler, or we should have had *bouilli* five times a week for dinner, — *bouilli* off silver, and hungry lackeys in lace looking on at the windy meal!

The old coat plan is not so base as the above female arrangement; but say what you will, it is not high-minded and honorable to go out in a good coat, to flaunt the streets in it with an easy, *dégagé* air, as if you always wore such, and returning home assume another under pretext of dressing for dinner. There is no harm in putting on your old coat of a morning, or in wearing one always. Common reason points out the former precaution, which is at once modest and manly. If your coat pinches you, there is no harm in changing it; if you are going out to dinner, there is no harm in changing it for a better. But I say the plan of habitual changing is a base one, and only fit for a man at last extremities; or for a clerk in the city, who hangs up his best garment on a peg, both at the office and at home; or for a man who smokes, and has to keep his coat for tea-parties, — a paltry precaution, however, this. If you like smoking, why should n't you? If you *do* smell a little of tobacco, where 's the harm? The smell is not pleasant, but it does not kill anybody. If the lady of the house do not like it, she is quite at liberty not to invite you again. *Et puis?* Bah! Of what age are you and I? Have we lived? Have we seen men and cities? Have we their manners noted, and understood their idiosyncrasy? Without a doubt! And what is the truth at which we have arrived? This, — that a pipe of tobacco is many an hour in the day, and many a week in the month, a thousand times better and more agreeable society than the best Miss, the loveliest Mrs., the most beautiful Baroness, Countess, or what not. Go to tea-parties, those who will; talk fiddle-faddle, such as like; many men there are who do so, and are a little partial to music, and know how to twist the leaf of the song that Miss Jemima is singing exactly at the right moment. Very good. These are the enjoyments of dress-coats; but *men*, — are they to be put off with such fare forever? No! One goes out to dinner, because one likes eating and drinking; because the very act of eating and drinking opens the heart, and causes the tongue to wag. But evening parties! O, milk and water, bread and butter! No, no, the age is wiser! The manly youth frequents his club for common society, has a small circle of amiable ladies for friendly intercourse, his book and his pipe always.

Do not be angry, ladies, that one of your most ardent and sincere admirers should seem to speak disparagingly of your merits, or recommend his fellows to shun the society in which you ordinarily assemble. No, Miss, I am the man who respect you truly, — the man who respect and love you when you are most lovely and respectable, — in your families, my dears. A wife, a mother, a daughter, — has God made anything more beautiful? A friend, — can one find a truer, kinder, a more generous and enthusiastic one, than a woman often will be? All that has to do with your hearts is beautiful, and in everything with which they meddle, a man must be a brute not to love and honor you.

But Miss Rudge in blue crape, squeaking romances at a harp, or Miss Tobin dancing in a quadrille, or Miss Blogg twisting round the room in the arms of a lumbering Lifeguardsman; — what are these? — so many vanities. With the operations here described the heart has nothing to do. Has the intellect? O, ye gods! think of Miss Rudge's intellect while singing, —

"Away, away to the mountain's brow,
Where the trees are gently waving;
Away, away to the fountain's flow,
Where the streams are softly la-a-ving!"

These are the words of a real song that I have heard many times, and rapturously applauded too. Such a song, such a poem, — such a songster!

No, madam, if I want to hear a song sung I will pay eight and sixpence and listen to Tamburini and Persiani. I will not pay, gloves, three-and-six; cab, there and back, four shillings; silk stockings every now and then, say a shilling a time; I will not pay to hear Miss Rudge screech such disgusting twaddle as the above. If I want to see dancing, there is Taglioni for my money; or across the water, Mrs. Serle and her forty pupils; or at Covent Garden, Madame Vedy, beautiful as a houri, dark-eyed and agile as a gazelle. I can see all these in comfort, and they dance a great deal better than Miss Blogg and Captain Haggerty, the great red-whiskered monster, who always wears nankeens because he thinks his legs are fine. If I want conversation, what has Miss Flock to say to me, forsooth, between the figures of a cursed quadrille that we are all gravely dancing? By heavens, what an agony it is! Look at the he-dancers, they seem oppressed with dreadful care. Look at the cavalier seul! if the operation lasted long the man's hair would turn white, — he would go mad! And is it for this that men and women assemble in multitudes, for this sorry pastime?

No! dance as you will, Miss Smith, and swim through the quadrille like a swan, or flutter through the gallop like a sylphide, and have the most elegant fresh toilettes, the most brilliantly polished white shoulders, the blandest eyes, the reddest, simperingest mouth, the whitest neck, the — in fact, I say, be as charming as you will, *that* is not the place to which, if you are worth anything, you are most charming. You are beautiful; you are very much *décolletée;* your eyes are always glancing down at a pretty pearl necklace, round a pearly neck, or on a fresh, fragrant bouquet, stuck — fiddlestick! What is it that the men admire in you ? — the animal, Miss, — the white, plump, external Smith, which men with their eye-glasses, standing at various parts of the room, are scanning pertly and curiously, and of which they are speaking brutally. A pretty admiration, truly ! But is it possible that these men can admire anything else in you who have so much that is really admirable ? Cracknell, in the course of the waltz, has just time to pant into your ear, " Were you at Ascot Races ? " Kidwinter, who dances two sets of quadrilles with you, whispers to you, " Do you pwefer thtwawbewy ithe aw wathbewy ithe ? " and asks the name of " that gweat enawmuth fat woman in wed thatin and bird of pawadithe ? " to which you reply, " Law, sir, it 's mamma ! " The rest of the evening passes away in conversation similarly edifying. What can any of the men admire in you, you little silly creature, but the animal ? There is your mother, now, in red and a bird of paradise, as Kidwinter says. She has a large fan, which she flaps to and fro across a broad chest ; and has one eye directed to her Amelia, dancing with Kidwinter before mentioned ; another watching Jane, who is dancing *vis-à-vis* with Major Cutts ; and a third complacently cast upon Edward, who is figuring with Miss Binx in the other quadrille. How the dear fellow has grown, to be sure ; and how like his papa at his age — heigho ! There is mamma, the best woman breathing ; but fat, and even enormous, as has been said of her. Does anybody gaze on *her ?* And yet she was once as slim and as fair as you, O simple Amelia !

Does anybody care for her ? Yes, one. Your father cares for her ; SMITH cares for her ; and in his eyes she is still the finest woman of the room ; and he remembers when he danced down seven-and-forty couples of a country-dance with her, two years before you were born or thought of. But it was all chance that Miss Hopkins turned out to be the excellent creature she was. Smith did not know any more than that she was gay, plump, good-looking, and had five thousand pounds. Hit or miss, he took her, and has had assuredly no cause to complain; but she might have been a Borgia or Joan of Naples, and have had the same smiling looks and red cheeks, and five thousand pounds, which won his heart in the year 1814.

The system of evening parties, then, is a false and absurd one. Ladies may frequent them professionally with an eye to a husband, but a man is an ass who takes a wife out of such assemblies, having no other means of judging of the object of his choice. You are not the same person in your white crape and satin slip as you are in your morning dress. A man is not the same in his tight coat and feverish glazed pumps, and stiff white waistcoat, as he is in his green double-breasted frock, his old black ditto, or his woollen jacket. And a man is doubly an ass who is in the habit of frequenting evening parties, unless he is forced thither in search of a lady to whom he is attached, or unless he is compelled to go by his wife. A man who loves dancing may be set down to be an ass; and the fashion is greatly going out with the increasing good sense of the age. Do not say that he who lives at home, or frequents clubs in lieu of balls, is a brute, and has not a proper respect for the female sex; on the contrary, he may respect it most sincerely. He feels that a woman appears to most advantage, not among those whom she cannot care about, but among those whom she loves. He thinks her beautiful when she is at home making tea for her old father. He believes her to be charming when she is singing a simple song at her piano, but not when she is screeching at an evening party. He thinks by far the most valuable part of her is her heart; and a kind, simple heart, my dear, shines in conversation better than the best of wit. He admires her best in her intercourse with her family and her friends, and detests the miserable, twaddling slipslop that he is obliged to hear from and utter to her in the course of a ball; and avoids and despises such meetings.

He keeps his evening coat, then, for *dinners*. And if this friendly address to all the mothers who read this miscellany may somewhat be acted upon by them; if heads of families, instead of spending hundreds upon chalking floors, and Gunter, and cold suppers, and Weippert's band, will determine upon giving a series of plain, neat, nice dinners, of not too many courses, but well cooked, of not too many wines, but good of their sort, and according to the giver's degree, they will see that the young men will come to them fast enough; that they will marry their daughters quite as fast, without injuring their health, and that they will make a saving at the year's end. I say that young men, young women, and heads of families, should bless me for pointing out this obvious plan to them, so natural, so hearty, so hospitable, so different to the present artificial mode.

A grand ball in a palace is splendid, generous, and noble, — a sort of procession in which people may figure properly. A family dance is a pretty and pleasant amusement; and (especially after dinner) it does the philosopher's heart good to look upon merry young people who know each other, and are happy, natural, and familiar. But a Baker Street hop is a base invention, and as such let it be denounced and avoided.

A dressing-gown has great merits, certainly, but it is dangerous. A man who wears it of mornings generally takes the liberty of going without a neckcloth, or of not shaving, and is no better than a driveller. Sometimes, to be sure, it is necessary, in self-defence, not to shave, as a precaution against yourself that is to say; and I know no better means of ensuring a man's remaining at home than neglecting the use of the lather and razor for a week, and encouraging a crop of bristles. When I wrote my tragedy, I shaved off for the last two acts my left eyebrow, and never stirred out of doors until it had grown to be a great deal thicker than its right-hand neighbor. But this was an extreme precaution, and unless a man has very strong reasons indeed for stopping at home, and a very violent propensity to gadding, his best plan is to shave every morning neatly, to put on his regular coat, and go regularly to work, and to avoid a dressing-gown as the father of all evil. Painters are the only persons who can decently appear in dressing-gowns; but these are none of your easy morning-gowns; they are commonly of splendid stuff, and put on by the artist in order to render himself remarkable and splendid in the eyes of his sitter. Your loose-wadded German schlafrock, imported of late years into our country, is the laziest, filthiest invention; and I always augur as ill of a man whom I see appearing at breakfast in one, as of a woman who comes down stairs in curl-papers.

By the way, in the third act of *Macbeth*, Mr. Macready makes his appearance in the court-yard of Glamis Castle in an affair of brocade that has always struck me as absurd and un-Macbethlike. Mac in a dressing-gown (I mean 'Beth, not 'Ready), — Mac in list slippers, — Mac in a cotton nightcap, with a tassel bobbing up and down,

— I say the thought is unworthy, and am sure the worthy thane would have come out, if suddenly called from bed, by any circumstance, however painful, in a *good stout jacket*. It is a more manly, simple, and majestic wear than the lazy dressing-gown; it more becomes a man of Macbeth's mountainous habits; it leaves his legs quite free, to run whithersoever he pleases, — whether to the stables, to look at the animals, — to the farm, to see the pig that has been slaughtered that morning, — to the garden, to examine whether that scoundrel of a John Hoskins has dug up the potato-bed, — to the nursery, to have a romp with the little Macbeths that are spluttering and quarrelling over their porridge, — or whither you will. A man in a jacket is fit company for anybody; there is no shame about it as about being seen in a changed coat; it is simple, steady, and straightforward. It is, as I have stated, all over pockets, which contain everything you want; in one, your buttons, hammer, small nails, thread, twine, and cloth-strips for the trees on the south wall; in another, your dog-whip and whistle, your knife, cigar-case, gingerbread for the children, paper of Epsom salts for John Hoskins's mother, who is mortal bad, — and so on: there is no end to the pockets, and to the things you put in them. Walk about in your jacket, and meet what person you will, you assume at once an independent air; and, thrusting your hands into the receptacle that flaps over each hip, look the visitor in the face, and talk to the ladies on a footing of perfect equality. Whereas, look at the sneaking way in which a man caught in a dressing-gown, in loose bagging trousers most likely (for the man who has a dressing-gown, has, two to one, no braces), and in shuffling slippers, — see how he whisks his dressing-gown over his legs, and looks ashamed and uneasy. His lanky hair hangs over his blowsy, fat, shining, unhealthy face; his bristly, dumpling-shaped double chin peers over a flaccid shirt collar; the sleeves of his gown are in rags, and you see underneath a pair of black wristbands, and the rim of a dingy flannel waistcoat.

A man who is not strictly neat in his person is not an honest man. I shall not enter into this very ticklish subject of personal purification and neatness, because this essay will be read by hundreds of thousands of ladies as well as men; and for the former I would wish to provide nothing but pleasure. Men may listen to stern truths; but for ladies one should only speak verities that are sparkling, rosy, brisk, and agreeable. A man who wears a dressing-gown is not neat in his person; his moral character takes invariably some of the slatternliness and looseness of his costume; he becomes enervated, lazy, incapable of great actions; A man IN A JACKET is a man. All great men wore jackets. Walter Scott wore a jacket, as everybody knows; Byron wore a jacket (not that I count a man who turns down his collars for much); I have a picture of Napoleon in a jacket, at St. Helena; Thomas Carlyle wears a jacket; Lord John Russell always mounts a jacket on arriving at the Colonial Office; and if I have a single fault to find with that popular writer, the author of —— never mind what, you know his name as well as I, — it is that he is in the habit of composing his works in a large, flowered damask dressing-gown, and morocco slippers; whereas, in a jacket he would write you off something, not so flowery, if you please, but of honest texture, — something, not so long, but terse, modest, and comfortable, — no great, long, strealing tails of periods, — no staring peonies and hollyhocks of illustrations, — no flaring cords and tassels of episodes, — no great, dirty, wadded sleeves of sentiment, ragged at the elbows and cuffs, and mopping up everything that comes in their way, — cigar-ashes, ink, candle-wax, cold brandy-and-water, coffee, or whatever aids to the brain he may employ as a literary man; not to mention the quantity of tooth-powder, whisker-dye, soapsuds, and pomatum, that the same garment receives in the course of the toilets at which it assists. Let all literary men, then, get jackets. I prefer them without tails; but do not let this interfere with another man's pleasure: he may have tails if he likes, and I for one will never say him nay.

Like all things, however, jackets are subject to abuse; and the pertness and conceit of those jackets cannot be sufficiently reprehended which one sees on the backs of men at watering-places, with a telescope poking out of one pocket, and a yellow bandana flaunting from the other. Nothing is more contemptible than Tims in a jacket, with a blue bird's-eye neck-handkerchief tied sailor-fashion, puffing smoke like a steamer, with his great broad orbicular stern shining in the sun. I always long to give the wretch a smart smack upon that part where his coat-tails ought to be, and advise him to get into a more decent costume. There is an age and a figure for jackets; those who are of a certain build should not wear them in public. Witness fat officers of the dragoon-guards that one has seen bumping up and down the Steyne, at Brighton, on their great chargers, with a laced and embroidered coat, a cartridge-box, or whatever you call it, of the size of a twopenny loaf, placed on the small of their backs, — if their backs may be said to have a small, — and two little twinkling abortions of tails pointing downwards to the enormity jolting in the saddle. Officers should be occasionally measured, and after passing a certain width, should be drafted into other regiments, or allowed, — nay ordered to wear frock-coats.

The French tailors make frock-coats very well, but the people who wear them have the disgusting habit of wearing stays, than which nothing can be more unbecoming the dignity of man. Look what a waist the Apollo has, not above four inches less in the girth than the chest is. Look, ladies, at the waist of the Venus, and pray, — pray do not pinch in your dear little ribs in that odious and unseemly way. In a young man a slim waist is very well; and if he looks like the Eddystone lighthouse, it is as nature intended him to look. A man of certain age may be built like a tower, stalwart and straight. Then a man's middle may expand from the pure cylindrical to the barrel shape; well, let him be content. Nothing is so horrid as a fat man with a band; an hour-glass is a most mean and ungracious figure. Daniel Lambert is ungracious, but not mean. One meets with some men who look in their frock-coats perfectly sordid, sneaking, and ungentlemanlike, who if you see them dressed for an evening have a slim, easy, almost fashionable, appearance. Set these persons down as fellows of poor spirit and milksops. Stiff white ties and waistcoats, prim straight tails, and a gold chain, will give any man of moderate lankiness an air of factitious gentility; but if you want to understand the individual, look at him in the daytime; see him walking with his hat on. There is a great deal in the build and wearing of hats, a great deal more than at first meets the eye. I know a man who in a particular hat looked so extraordinarily like a man of property, that no tradesman on earth could refuse to give him credit. It was one of André's, and cost a guinea and a half ready money; but the person in question was frightened at the enormous charge, and afterwards purchased beavers in the city at the cost of seventeen-and-sixpence. And what was the consequence? He fell off in public estimation, and very soon after he came out in his city hat it began to be whispered abroad that he was a ruined man.

A blue coat is, after all, the best; but a gentleman of my acquaintance has made his fortune by an Oxford mixture, of all colors in the world, with a pair of white buckskin gloves. He looks as if he had just got off his horse, and as if he had three thousand a-year in the country. There is a kind of proud humility in an Oxford mixture. Velvet collars, and all such gimcracks, had best be avoided by sober people. This paper is not written for drivelling dandies, but for honest men. There is a great deal of philosophy and forethought in Sir Robert Peel's dress; he does not wear those white waistcoats for nothing. I say that O'Connell's costume is likewise that of a profound rhetorician, slouching and careless as it seems. Lord Melbourne's air of reckless, good-humored, don't-care-a-damn-ativeness is not obtained without an effort. Look at the Duke as he passes along in that stern little straight frock and plaid breeches; look at him, and off with your hat! How much is there in that little gray coat of Napoleon's! A spice of clap-trap and dandyism, no doubt; but we must remember the country which he had to govern. I never see a picture of George III. in his old stout Windsor uniform without feeling a respect; or of George IV., breeches and silk stockings, a wig, a sham smile, a frogged frock-coat and a fur collar, without that proper degree of reverence which such a costume should inspire. The coat is the expression of the man, — *οἱηπερ φυλλων*, &c.; and as the peach-tree throws out peach-leaves, the pear-tree pear ditto, as old George appeared invested in the sober old garment of blue and red, so did young George in oiled wigs, fur collars, stays, and braided surtouts, according to his nature.

* * * * *

Enough, — enough; and may these thoughts arising in the writer's mind from the possession of a new coat, which circumstance caused him to think not only of new coats but of old ones, and of coats neither old nor new, — and not of coats merely, but of men, — may these thoughts so inspired answer the purpose for which they have been set down on paper, and which is not a silly wish to instruct mankind, — no, no; but an honest desire to pay a deserving tradesman whose confidence supplied the garment in question.

Pentonville, April 25, 1841.

BLUEBEARD'S GHOST.

FOR some time after the fatal accident which deprived her of her husband, Mrs. Bluebeard was, as may be imagined, in a state of profound grief.

There was not a widow in all the country who went to such an expense for black bombazine. She had her beautiful hair confined in crimped caps, and her weepers came over her elbows. Of course she saw no company except her sister Anne (whose company was anything but pleasant to the widow); as for her brothers, their odious mess-table manners had always been disagreeable to her. What did she care for jokes about the major, or scandal concerning the Scotch surgeon of the regiment? If they drank their wine out of black bottles or crystal, what did it matter to her? Their stories of the stable, the parade, and the last run with the hounds, were perfectly odious to her; besides she could not bear their impertinent mustachios, and filthy habit of smoking cigars.

They were always wild, vulgar young men, at the best; but now — *now*, oh! their presence to her delicate soul was horror! How could she bear to look on them after what had occurred? She thought of the best of husbands ruthlessly cut down by their cruel, heavy, cavalry sabres; the kind friend, the generous landlord, the spotless justice of peace, in whose family differences these rude cornets of dragoons had dared to interfere, whose venerable blue hairs they had dragged down with sorrow to the grave!

She put up a most splendid monument to her departed lord over the family vault of the Bluebeards. The rector, Dr. Sly, who had been Mr. Bluebeard's tutor at college, wrote an epitaph in the most pompous yet pathetic Latin: "Siste, viator! mœrens conjux, heu! quanto minus est cum reliquis versari quam tui meminisse"; in a word, everything that is usually said in epitaphs. A bust of the departed saint, with Virtue mourning over it, stood over the epitaph, surrounded by medallions of his wives, and one of these medallions had as yet no name in it, nor (the epitaph said) could the widow ever be consoled until her own name was inscribed there. "For then I shall be with him. In cœlo quies," she would say, throwing up her fine eyes to heaven, and quoting the enormous words of the hatchment which was put up in the church, and over Bluebeard's hall, where the butler, the housekeeper, the footman, the housemaid, and scullions, were all in the profoundest mourning. The keeper went out to shoot birds in a crape band; nay, the very scarecrows in the orchard and fruit-garden were ordered to be dressed in black.

Sister Anne was the only person who refused to wear black. Mrs. Bluebeard would have parted with her, but she had no other female relative. Her father, it may be remembered by readers of the former part of her Memoirs, had married again, and the mother-in-law and Mrs. Bluebeard, as usual, hated each other furiously. Mrs. Shacabac had come to the hall on a visit of condolence; but the widow was so rude to her on the second day of the visit that the step-mother quitted the house in a fury. As for the Bluebeards, of course *they* hated the widow. Had not Mr. Bluebeard settled every shilling upon her? and, having no children by his former marriage, her property, as I leave you to fancy, was pretty handsome. So sister Anne was the only female relative whom Mrs. Bluebeard would keep near her; and, as we all know, a woman *must* have a female relative under any circumstances of pain, or pleasure, or profit, — when she is married, or when she is widowed, or when she is in a delicate situation. But let us continue our story.

"I will never wear mourning for that odious wretch, sister!" Anne would cry.

"I will trouble you, Miss Anne, not to use such words in my presence regarding the best of husbands, or to quit the room at once!" the widow would answer.

"I'm sure it's no great pleasure to sit in it. I wonder you don't make use of the closet, sister, where the *other* Mrs. Bluebeards are."

"Impertinence! they were all embalmed by M. Gannal. How dare you report the monstrous calumnies regarding the best of men? Take down the family Bible, and read what my blessed saint says of his wives, — read it written in his own hand: —

"'*Friday, June* 20. — Married my beloved wife, Anna Maria Scrogginsia.

"'*Saturday, August* 1. — A bereaved husband has scarcely strength to write down in this chronicle that the dearest of wives, Anna Maria Scrogginsia, expired this day of sore throat.'.

"There! can anything be more convincing than that? Read again: —

"'*Tuesday, Sept.* 1. — This day I led to the hymeneal altar my soul's blessing, Louisa Matilda Hopkinson. May this angel supply the place of her I have lost!

"'*Wednesday, October* 5. — O, Heavens! pity the distraction of a wretch who is obliged to record the ruin of his dearest hopes and affections! This day my adored Louisa Matilda Hopkinson gave up the ghost! A complaint of the head and shoulders was the sudden cause of the event which has rendered the unhappy subscriber the most miserable of men.

"'BLUEBEARD.'

"Every one of the women are calendared in this delightful, this pathetic, this truly virtuous and tender way; and can you suppose that a man who wrote such sentiments could be a *murderer*, miss?"

"Do you mean to say that he did not *kill* them, then?" said Anne.

"Gracious, goodness, Anne, kill them! they died all as naturally as I hope you will. My blessed husband was an angel of goodness and kindness to them. Was it *his* fault that the doctors could not cure their maladies? No, that it was n't! and when they died the inconsolable husband had their bodies embalmed in order that on this side of the grave he might never part from them."

"And why did he take you up in the tower, pray? and why did you send me in such a hurry to the leads? and why did he sharpen his long knife, and roar out to you to COME DOWN?"

"Merely to punish me for my curiosity, — the dear, good, kind, excellent creature!" sobbed the widow, overpowered with affectionate recollections of her lord's attentions to her.

"I wish," said sister Anne, sulkily, "that I had not been in such a hurry in summoning my brothers."

"Ah!" screamed Mrs. Bluebeard, with a harrowing

scream, "don't, — don't recall that horrid, fatal day, miss! If you had not misled your brothers, my poor, dear, darling Bluebeard would still be in life, still — still the soul's joy of his bereaved Fatima!"

Whether it is that all wives adore husbands when the latter are no more, or whether it is that Fatima's version of the story is really the correct one, and that the common impression against Bluebeard is an odious prejudice, and that he no more murdered his wives than you and I have, remains yet to be proved, and, indeed, does not much matter for the understanding of the rest of Mrs. B.'s adventures. And though people will say that Bluebeard's settlement of his whole fortune on his wife, in event of survivorship, was a mere act of absurd mystification, seeing that he was fully determined to cut her head off after the honeymoon, yet the best test of his real intentions is the profound grief which the widow manifested for his death, and the fact that he left her mighty well to do in the world.

If any one were to leave you or me a fortune, my dear friend, would we be too anxious to rake up the how and the why? Pooh! pooh! we would take it and make no bones about it, and Mrs. Bluebeard did likewise. Her husband's family, it is true, argued the point with her, and said, "Madam, you must perceive that Mr. Bluebeard never intended the fortune for you, as it was his fixed intention to chop off your head! It is clear that he meant to leave his money to his blood relations, therefore you ought in equity to hand it over." But she sent them all off with a flea in their ears, as the saying is, and said, "Your argument may be a very good one, but I will, if you please, keep the money." And she ordered the mourning as we have before shown, and indulged in grief, and exalted everywhere the character of the deceased. If any one would but leave me a fortune what a funeral and what a character I would give him!

Bluebeard Hall is situated, as we all very well know, in a remote country district, and, although a fine residence, is remarkably gloomy and lonely. To the widow's susceptible mind, after the death of her darling husband, the place became intolerable. The walk, the lawn, the fountain, the green glades of park over which frisked the dappled deer, all, — all recalled the memory of her beloved. It was but yesterday that, as they roamed through the park in the calm summer evening, her Bluebeard pointed out to the keeper the fat buck he was to kill. "Ah!" said the widow, with tears in her fine eyes, "the artless stag was shot down, the haunch was cut and roasted, the jelly had been prepared from the currant-bushes in the garden that he loved, but my Bluebeard never ate of the venison! Look, Anna sweet, pass we the old oak hall; 't is hung with trophies won by him in the chase, with pictures of the noble race of Bluebeard! Look! by the fireplace there is the gig-whip, his riding-whip, the spud with which you know he used to dig the weeds out of the terrace-walk; in that drawer are his spurs, his whistle, his visiting-cards, with his dear, dear name engraven upon them! There are the bits of string that he used to cut off the parcels and keep because string was always useful; his button-hook, and there is the peg on which he used to hang his h—h—*hat!*"

Uncontrollable emotions, bursts of passionate tears, would follow these tender reminiscences of the widow; and the long and short of the matter was, that she was determined to give up Bluebeard Hall and live elsewhere; her love for the memory of the deceased, she said, rendered the place too wretched.

Of course an envious and sneering world said that she was tired of the country and wanted to marry again; but she little heeded its taunts, and Anne, who hated her step-mother and could not live at home, was fain to accompany her sister to the town where the Bluebeards have had for many years a very large, genteel, old-fashioned house. So she went to the town-house, where they lived and quarrelled pretty much as usual; and though Anne often threatened to leave her and go to a boarding-house, of which there were plenty in the place, yet after all to live with her sister, and drive out in the carriage with the footman and coachman in mourning, and the lozenge on the panels, with the Bluebeard and Shacabac arms quartered on it, was far more respectable, and so the lovely sisters continued to dwell together.

For a lady under Mrs. Bluebeard's circumstances the town-house had other and peculiar advantages. Besides being an exceedingly spacious and dismal brick building, with a dismal iron railing in front, and long dismal thin windows with little panes of glass, it looked out into the churchyard where, time out of mind, between two yew-trees, one of which is cut into the form of a peacock, while the other represents a dumb-waiter, it looked into the churchyard where the monument of the late Bluebeard was placed over the family vault. It was the first thing the widow saw from her bedroom window in the morning, and 't was sweet to watch at night from the parlor the pallid moonlight lighting up the bust of the departed, and Virtue throwing great black shadows athwart it. Polyanthuses, rhododendra, ranunculuses, and other flowers with the largest names and of the most delightful odors, were planted within the little iron railing that in closed the last resting-place of the Bluebeards; and the beadle was instructed to half-kill any little boys who might be caught plucking these sweet testimonials of a wife's affection.

Over the sideboard in the dining-room hung a full-length of Mr. Bluebeard, by Ticklegill, R.A., in a militia uniform, frowning down upon the knives and forks and silver trays. Over the mantel-piece he was represented in a hunting costume on his favorite horse; there was a sticking-plaster silhouette of him in the widow's bedroom, and a miniature in the drawing-room, where he was drawn in a gown of black and gold, holding a gold-tasselled trencher cap with one hand, and with the other pointing to a diagram of Pons Asinorum. This likeness was taken when he was a fellow-commoner at St. John's College, Cambridge, and before the growth of that blue beard which was the ornament of his manhood, and a part of which now formed a beautiful blue neck-chain for his bereaved wife.

Sister Anne said the town-house was even more dismal than the country-house, for there was pure air at the Hall, and it was pleasanter to look out on a park than on a churchyard, however fine the monuments might be. But the widow said she was a light-minded hussy, and persisted as usual in her lamentations and mourning. The only male whom she would admit within her doors was the parson of the parish, who read sermons to her; and, as his reverence was at least seventy years old, Anne, though she might be ever so much minded to fall in love, had no opportunity to indulge her inclination; and the town-people, scandalous as they might be, could not find a word to say against the *liaison* of the venerable man and the heart-stricken widow.

All other company she resolutely refused. When the players were in the town, the poor manager, who came to beg her to bespeak a comedy, was thrust out of the gates by the big butler. Though there were balls, card-parties, and assemblies, Widow Bluebeard would never subscribe to one of them; and even the officers, those all-conquering heroes who make such ravages in ladies' hearts, and to whom all ladies' doors are commonly open, could never get an entry into the widow's house. Captain Whiskerfield strutted for three weeks up and down before her house, and had not the least effect upon her. Captain O'Grady (of an Irish regiment) attempted to bribe the servants, and one night actually scaled the garden wall; but all that he got was his foot in a man-trap, not to mention being dreadfully scarified by the broken glass; and so *he* never made love any more. Finally, Captain Blackbeard, whose whiskers vied in magnitude with those of the deceased Bluebeard himself, although he attended church regularly every week, — he who had not darkened the doors of a church for ten years before, — even Captain Blackbeard got nothing by his piety; and the widow never once took her eyes off her book to look at him. The barracks were in despair; and Captain Whiskerfield's tailor, who had supplied him with new clothes in order to win the widow's heart, ended by clapping the Captain into jail.

His reverence the parson highly applauded the widow's conduct to the officers; but, being himself rather of a social turn, and fond of a good dinner and a bottle, he represented to the lovely mourner that she should endeavor to divert her grief by a little respectable society, and recommended that she should from time to time entertain a few grave and sober persons whom he would present to her. As Dr. Sly had an unbounded influence over the fair mourner, she acceded to his desires; and accordingly he introduced to her house some of the most venerable and worthy of his acquaintance, — all married people, however, so that the widow should not take the least alarm.

It happened that the doctor had a nephew, who was a lawyer in London, and this gentleman came dutifully in the long vacation to pay a visit to his reverend uncle. "He is none of your roystering, dashing young fellows," said his reverence; "he is the delight of his mamma and sisters; he never drinks anything stronger than tea; he never missed church thrice a Sunday for these twenty years; and I hope, my dear and amiable madam, that you will not object to receive this pattern of young men for the sake of your most devoted friend, his uncle."

The widow consented to receive Mr. Sly. He was not a handsome man certainly. "But what does that matter?" said the doctor; "he is *good*, and virtue is better than all the beauty of all the dragoons in the Queen's service."

Mr. Sly came there to dinner, and he came to tea; and he drove out with the widow in the carriage with the lozenge on it; and at church he handed the psalm-book; and, in short, he paid her every attention which could be expected from so polite a young gentleman.

At this the town began to talk, as people in towns will. "The doctor kept all bachelors out of the widow's house," said they, "in order that that ugly nephew of his may have the field entirely to himself." These speeches were of course heard by sister Anne, and the little minx was not a little glad to take advantage of them, in order to induce her sister to see some more cheerful company.

The fact is, the young hussy loved a dance or a game at cards much more than a humdrum conversation over a tea-table; and so she plied her sister day and night with hints as to the propriety of opening her house, receiving the gentry of the county, and spending her fortune.

To this point the widow at length, though with many sighs and vast unwillingness, acceded; and she went so far as to order a very becoming half-mourning, in which all the world declared she looked charming. "I carry," said she, "my blessed Bluebeard in my heart, — *that* is in the deepest mourning for him, and when the heart grieves there is no need of outward show."

So she issued cards for a little quiet tea and supper, and several of the best families in the town and neighborhood attended her entertainment. It was followed by another and another; and at last Captain Blackbeard was actually introduced, though, of course, he came in plain clothes.

Dr. Sly and his nephew never could abide the captain. "They had heard some queer stories," they said, "about proceedings in barracks. Who was it that drank three bottles at a sitting? who had a mare that ran for the plate? and why was it that Dolly Coddlins left the town so suddenly?" Mr. Sly turned up the whites of his eyes as his uncle asked these questions, and sighed for the wickedness of the world. But for all that he was delighted, especially at the anger which the widow manifested when the Dolly Coddlins' affair was hinted at. She was furious, and vowed she would never see the wretch again. The lawyer and his uncle were charmed. O shortsighted lawyer and parson, do you think Mrs. Bluebeard would have been so angry if she had not been jealous ? — do you think she would have been jealous if she had not . . . . had not what? She protested that she no more cared for the captain than she did for one of her footmen; but the next time he called she would not condescend to say a word to him.

"My dearest Miss Anne," said the captain, as he met her in Sir Roger de Coverley (she was herself dancing with Ensign Trippet), "what is the matter with your lovely sister?"

"Dolly Coddlins is the matter," said Miss Anne. "Mr. Sly has told all"; and she was down the middle in a twinkling.

The captain blushed so at this monstrous insinuation that any one could see how incorrect it was. He made innumerable blunders in the dance, and was all the time casting such ferocious glances at Mr. Sly (who did not dance, but sat by the widow and ate ices), that his partner thought he was mad, and that Mr. Sly became very uneasy.

When the dance was over, he came to pay his respects to the widow, and, in so doing, somehow trod so violently on Mr. Sly's foot that that gentleman screamed with pain, and presently went home. But though he was gone the widow was not a whit more gracious to Captain Blackbeard. She requested Mr. Trippet to order her carriage that night, and went home without uttering one single word to Captain Blackbeard.

The next morning, and with a face of preternatural longitude, the Rev. Dr. Sly paid a visit to the widow. "The wickedness and bloodthirstiness of the world," said he, "increase every day. O my dear madam, what monsters do we meet in it, — what wretches, what assassins, are allowed to go abroad! Would you believe it, that this morning, as my nephew was taking his peaceful morning meal, one of the ruffians from the barracks presented himself with a challenge from Captain Blackbeard?"

"Is he hurt?" screamed the widow.

"No, my dear friend, my dear Frederick is not hurt. And oh, what a joy it will be to him to think you have that tender solicitude for his welfare!"

"You know I have always had the highest respect for him," said the widow; who, when she screamed, was in truth thinking of somebody else. But the doctor did not choose to interpret her thoughts in that way, and gave all the benefit of them to his nephew.

"That anxiety, dearest madam, which you express for him emboldens me, encourages me, authorizes me, to press a point upon you which I am sure must have entered your thoughts ere now. The dear youth in whom you have shown such an interest lives but for you! Yes, fair lady, start not at hearing that his sole affections are yours; and with what pride shall I carry to him back the news that he is not indifferent to you!"

"And they going to fight?" continued the lady, in a breathless state of alarm. "For Heaven's sake, dearest doctor, prevent the horrid, horrid meeting. Send for a magistrate's warrant; do anything; but do not suffer those misguided young men to cut each other's throats!"

"Fairest lady, I fly!" said the doctor, and went back to lunch quite delighted with the evident partiality Mrs. Bluebeard showed for his nephew. And Mrs. Bluebeard, not content with exhorting him to prevent the duel, rushed to Mr. Pound, the magistrate, informed him of the facts, got out warrants against both Mr. Sly and the captain, and would have put them into execution; but it was discovered that the former gentleman had abruptly left town, so that the constable could not lay hold of him.

It somehow, however, became to be generally known that the widow Bluebeard had declared herself in favor of Mr. Sly, the lawyer; that she had fainted when told her lover was about to fight a duel; finally, that she had accepted him, and would marry him as soon as the quarrel between him and the captain was settled. Dr. Sly, when applied to, hummed and ha'd, and would give no direct answer; but he denied nothing, and looked so knowing, that all the world was certain of the fact; and the county paper next week stated: —

"We understand that the lovely and wealthy Mrs. Bl—b—rd is about once more to enter the bands of wedlock with our distinguished townsman, Frederick S—y, Esq., of the Middle Temple, London. The learned gentleman left town in consequence of a dispute with a gallant son of Mars, which was likely to have led to warlike results, had not a magistrate's warrant intervened, when the captain was bound over to keep the peace."

In fact, as soon as the captain was so bound over, Mr. Sly came back, stating that he had quitted the town not to avoid a duel, — far from it, but to keep out of the way of the magistrates, and give the captain every facility. *He* had taken out no warrant; *he* had been perfectly ready to meet the captain; if others had been more prudent, it was not his fault. So he held up his head, and cocked his hat with the most determined air; and all the lawyers' clerks in the place were quite proud of their hero.

As for Captain Blackbeard, his rage and indignation may be imagined; a wife robbed from him, his honor put in question by an odious, lanky, squinting lawyer! He fell ill of a fever incontinently; and the surgeon was obliged to take a quantity of blood from him, ten times the amount of which he swore he would have out of the veins of the atrocious Sly.

The announcement in the *Mercury*, however, filled the widow with almost equal indignation. "The widow of the gallant Bluebeard," she said, "marry an odious wretch who lives in dingy chambers in the Middle Temple! Send for Dr. Sly." The doctor came; she rated him soundly, asked him how he dared set abroad such calumnies concerning her; ordered him to send his nephew back to London at once; and, as he valued her esteem, as he valued the next presentation to a fat living which lay in her gift, to contradict everywhere, and in the fullest terms, the wicked report concerning her.

"My dearest madam," said the doctor, pulling his longest face, "you shall be obeyed. The poor lad shall be acquainted with the fatal change in your sentiments!"

"Change in my sentiments, Dr. Sly!"

"With the destruction of his hopes, rather let me say; and Heaven grant that the dear boy have strength to bear up against the misfortune which comes so suddenly upon him!"

The next day sister Anne came with a face full of care to Mrs. Bluebeard. "O that unhappy lover of yours!" said she.

"Is the captain unwell?" exclaimed the widow.

"No, it is the other," answered sister Anne. "Poor, poor Mr. Sly! He made a will leaving you all, except five pounds a-year to his laundress: he made his will, locked his door, took heart-rending leave of his uncle at night, and this morning was found hanging at his bedpost when Sambo, the black servant, took him up his water to shave. 'Let me be buried,' he said, 'with the pincushion she gave me and the locket containing her hair.' *Did* you give him a pincushion, sister? *did* you give him a locket with your hair?"

"It was only silver-gilt!" sobbed the widow; "and now, O Heavens! I have killed him!" The heart-rending nature of her sobs may be imagined; but they were abruptly interrupted by her sister.

"Killed him? — no such thing! Sambo cut him down when he was as black in the face as the honest negro himself. He came down to breakfast, and I leave you to fancy what a touching meeting took place between the nephew and the uncle."

"So much love!" thought the widow. "What a pity he squints so! If he would but get his eyes put straight, I might perhaps ——" She did not finish the sentence: ladies often leave this sort of sentence in a sweet confusion.

But hearing some news regarding Captain Blackbeard, whose illness and blood-letting were described to her most pathetically, as well as accurately, by the Scotch surgeon of the regiment, her feelings of compassion towards the lawyer cooled somewhat; and when Dr. Sly called to know if she would condescend to meet the unhappy youth, she said, in rather a *distrait* manner, that she wished him every happiness; that she had the highest regard and respect for him; that she besought him not to think any more of committing the dreadful crime which would have made her unhappy forever; *but* that she thought, for the sake of both parties, they had better not meet until Mr. Sly's feelings had grown somewhat more calm.

"Poor fellow! poor fellow!" said the doctor, "may he be enabled to bear his frightful calamity! I have taken away his razors from him, and Sambo my man, never lets him out of his sight."

The next day Mrs. Bluebeard thought of sending a friendly message to Dr. Sly's, asking for news of the health of his nephew; but, as she was giving her orders on that subject to John Thomas the footman, it happened that the captain arrived, and so Thomas was sent down stairs again. And the captain looked so delightfully interesting with his arm in a sling, and his beautiful black whiskers curling round a face which was paler than usual, that at the end of two hours the widow forgot the message altogether, and, indeed, I believe, asked the captain whether he would not stop and dine. Ensign Trippet came, too, and the party was very pleasant; and the military gentlemen laughed hugely at the idea of the lawyer having been cut off the bedpost by the black servant, and were so witty on the subject, that the widow ended by half believing that the bedpost and hanging scheme on the part of Mr. Sly was only a feint, — a trick to win her heart. Though this, to be sure, was not agreed to by the lady without a pang, for, *entre nous*, to hang one's self for a lady is no small compliment to her attractions, and, perhaps, Mrs. Bluebeard was rather disappointed at the notion that the hanging was not a *bonâ fide* strangulation.

However, presently her nerves were excited again; and she was consoled or horrified, as the case may be (the reader must settle the point according to his ideas and knowledge of woman-kind), — she was at any rate dreadfully excited by the receipt of a billet in the well-known clerk-like hand of Mr. Sly. It ran thus: —

"I saw you through your dining-room windows. You were hob-nobbing with Captain Blackbeard. You looked rosy and well. You smiled. You drank off the champagne at a single draught.

"I can bear it no more. Live on, smile on, and be happy. My ghost shall repine, perhaps, at your happiness with another, — but in life I should go mad were I to witness it.

"It is best that I should be gone.

"When you receive this, tell my uncle to drag the fish-pond at the end of Bachelor's Acre. His black servant Sambo accompanies me, it is true. But Sambo shall perish with me should his obstinacy venture to restrain me from my purpose. I know the poor fellow's honesty well, but I also know my own despair.

"Sambo will leave a wife and seven children. Be kind to those orphan mulattoes for the sake of

"FREDERICK."

The widow gave a dreadful shriek, and interrupted the two captains, who were each just in the act of swallowing a bumper of claret. "Fly — fly — save him," she screamed; "save him, monsters, ere it is too late! Drowned! — Frederick! — Bachelor's Wa—." Syncope took place, and the rest of the sentence was interrupted.

Deucedly disappointed at being obliged to give up their wine, the two heroes seized their cocked hats, and went towards the spot which the widow in her wild exclamations of despair had sufficiently designated.

Trippet was for running to the fish-pond at the rate of ten miles an hour. "Take it easy, my good fellow," said Captain Blackbeard; "running is unwholesome after dinner. And, if that squinting scoundrel of a lawyer *does* drown himself, I sha'n't sleep any the worse." So the two gentlemen walked very leisurely on towards the Bachelor's Walk; and, indeed, seeing on their way thither Major Macabaw looking out of the window at his quarters and smoking a cigar, they went up stairs to consult the major, as also a bottle of Schiedam he had.

"They come not!" said the widow, when restored to herself. "O Heavens! grant that Frederick is safe! Sister Anne, go up to the leads and look if anybody is coming." And up, accordingly, to the garrets sister Anne mounted. "Do you see anybody coming, sister Anne?"

"I see Dr. Drench's little boy," said sister Anne; "he is leaving a pill and draught at Miss Molly Grub's."

"Dearest sister Anne, don't you see any one coming?" shouted the widow once again.

"I see a flock of dust, — no! a cloud of sheep. Pshaw! I see the London coach coming in. There are three outsides, and the guard has flung a parcel to Mrs. Jenkins's maid."

"Distraction! Look once more, sister Anne."

"I see a crowd, — a shutter, — a shutter with a man on it, — a beadle, — forty little boys, — Gracious goodness! what *can* it be?" and down stairs tumbled sister Anne, and was looking out of the parlor-window by her sister's side, when the crowd she had perceived from the garret passed close by them.

At the head walked the beadle, slashing about at the little boys.

Two scores of these followed and surrounded

A SHUTTER carried by four men.

On the shutter lay *Frederick!* He was ghastly pale; his hair was draggled over his face; his clothes stuck tight to him on account of the wet; streams of water gurgled down the shutter-sides. But he was not dead! He turned one eye round towards the window where Mrs.

Bluebeard sat, and gave her a look which she never could forget.

Sambo brought up the rear of the procession. He was quite wet through; and if anything would have put his hair out of curl, his ducking would have done so. But, as he was not a gentleman, he was allowed to walk home on foot, and as he passed the widow's window, he gave her one dreadful glance with his goggling black eyes, and moved on, pointing with his hands to the shutter.

John Thomas, the footman, was instantly despatched to Dr. Sly's to have news of the patient. There was no shilly-shallying now. He came back in half an hour to say that Mr. Frederick flung himself into Bachelor's Acre fish-pond with Sambo, had been dragged out with difficulty, had been put to bed, and had a pint of white wine whey, and was pretty comfortable. "Thank Heaven!" said the widow, and gave John Thomas a seven-shilling piece, and sat down with a lightened heart to tea. "What a heart!" said she to sister Anne. "And O, what a pity it is that he squints!"

Here the two captains arrived. They had not been to the Bachelor's Walk; they had remained at Major Macabaw's consulting the Schiedam. They had made up their minds what to say. "Hang the fellow! he will never have the pluck to drown himself," said Captain Blackbeard. "Let us argue on that, as we may safely."

"My sweet lady," said he, accordingly, "we have had the pond dragged. No Mr. Sly. And the fisherman who keeps the punt assures us that he has not been there all day."

"Audacious falsehood!" said the widow, her eyes flashing fire. "Go, heartless man! who dares to trifle thus with the feelings of a respectable and unprotected woman. Go, sir, you 're only fit for the love of a — Dolly — Coddlins!" She pronounced the *Coddlins* with a withering sarcasm that struck the captain aghast; and, sailing out of the room, she left her tea untasted, and did not wish either of the military gentlemen good-night.

But, gentles, an' ye know the delicate fibre of woman's heart, ye will not in very sooth believe that such events as those we have described — such tempests of passion — fierce winds of woe — blinding lightnings of tremendous joy and tremendous grief — could pass over one frail flower and leave it all unscathed. No! Grief kills as joy doth. Doth not the scorching sun nip the rose-bud as well as the bitter wind? As Mrs. Sigourney sweetly sings: —

> "Ah! the heart is a soft and a delicate thing;
> Ah! the heart is a lute with a thrilling string;
> A spirit that floats on a gossamer's wing!"

Such was Fatima's heart. In a word, the preceding events had a powerful effect upon her nervous system, and she was ordered much quiet and sal-volatile by her skilful medical attendant, Dr. Glauber.

To be so ardently, passionately loved as she was, to know that Frederick had twice plunged into death from attachment to her, was to awaken in her bosom "a thrilling string," indeed! Could she witness such attachment, and not be touched by it? She *was* touched by it, — she was influenced by the virtues, by the passion, by the misfortunes of Frederick; but then he was so abominably ugly that she could not — she could not consent to become his bride!

She told Dr. Sly so. "I respect and esteem your nephew," said she; "but my resolve is made. I will continue faithful to that blessed saint whose monument is ever before my eyes" (she pointed to the churchyard as she spoke). "Leave this poor tortured heart in quiet. It has already suffered more than most hearts could bear. I will repose under the shadow of that tomb until I am called to rest within it, — to rest by the side of my Bluebeard!"

The ranunculuses, rhododendra, and polyanthuses, which ornamented that mausoleum, had somehow been suffered to run greatly to seed during the last few months, and it was with no slight self-accusation that she acknowledged this fact on visiting the "garden of the grave," as she called it; and she scolded the beadle soundly for neglecting his duty towards it. He promised obedience for the future, dug out all the weeds that were creeping round the family vault, and (having charge of the key) entered that awful place, and swept and dusted the melancholy contents of the tomb.

Next morning the widow came down to breakfast looking very pale. She had passed a bad night; she had had awful dreams; she had heard a voice call her thrice at midnight. "Pooh! my dear, it 's only nervousness," said sceptical sister Anne.

Here John Thomas, the footman, entered, and said the beadle was in the hall looking in a very strange way. He had been about the house since day-break, and insisted on seeing Mrs. Bluebeard. "Let him enter," said that lady, prepared for some great mystery. The beadle came; he was pale as death; his hair was dishevelled, and his cocked hat out of order. "What have you to say?" said the lady, trembling.

Before beginning, he fell down on his knees.

"Yesterday," said he, "according to your ladyship's orders, I dug up the flower-beds of the family-vault, dusted the vault and the — the coffins (added he, trembling) inside. Me and John Sexton did it together, and polished up the plate quite beautiful."

"For Heaven's sake, don't allude to it," cried the widow, turning pale.

"Well, my lady, I locked the door, came away, and found in my hurry — for I wanted to beat two little boys what was playing at marbles on Alderman Paunch's monyment — I found, my lady, I 'd forgot my cane.

"I could n't get John Sexton to go back with me till this morning, and I did n't like to go alone, and so we went this morning; and what do you think I found? I found his honor's coffin turned round, and the cane broke in two. Here 's the cane!"

"Ah!" screamed the widow, "take it away, — take it away!"

"Well, what does this prove," said sister Anne, "but that somebody moved the coffin, and broke the cane?"

"Somebody! *who 's somebody?*" said the beadle, staring round about him. And all of a sudden he started back with a tremendous roar, that made the ladies scream and all the glasses on the sideboard jingle, and cried, "*That 's the man!*"

He pointed to the portrait of Bluebeard, which stood over the jingling glasses on the sideboard. "That 's the man I saw last night walking round the vault, as I 'm a living sinner. I saw him a-walking round and round, and, when I went up to speak to him, I 'm blessed if he did n't go in at the iron gate, which opened afore him like — like winking, and then in at the vault door, which I 'd double-locked, my lady, and bolted inside, I 'll take my oath on it!"

"Perhaps you had given him the key?" suggested sister Anne.

"It 's never been out of my pocket. "Here it is," cried the beadle; "I 'll have no more to do with it"; and he flung down the ponderous key, amidst another scream from widow Bluebeard.

"At what hour did you see him?" gasped she.

"At twelve o'clock, of course."

"It must have been at that very hour," said she, "I heard the voice."

"What voice?" said Anne.

"A voice that called 'Fatima! Fatima! Fatima!' three times as plain as ever voice did."

"It did n't speak to me," said the beadle; "it only nodded its head, and wagged its head and beard."

"W—w—was it a *bl—ue beard?*" said the widow.

"Powder-blue, ma'am, as I 've a soul to save!"

Doctor Drench was of course instantly sent for. But what are the medicaments of the apothecary in a case where the grave gives up its dead? Dr. Sly arrived, and he offered ghostly — ah! too ghostly — consolation. He said he believed in them. His own grandmother had appeared to his grandfather several times before he married again. He could not doubt that supernatural agencies were possible, even frequent.

"Suppose he were to appear to me alone," ejaculated the widow, "I should die of fright."

The doctor looked particularly arch. "The best way in these cases, my dear madam," said he, "the best way for unprotected ladies is to get a husband. I never heard of a first husband's ghost appearing to a woman and her second husband in my life. In all history there is no account of one."

"Ah! why should I be afraid of seeing my Bluebeard again?" said the widow; and the doctor retired quite pleased, for the lady was evidently thinking of a second husband.

"The captain would be a better protector for me certainly than Mr. Sly," thought the lady, with a sigh; "but Mr. Sly will certainly kill himself, and will the captain be a match for two ghosts? Sly will kill himself; but ah! the captain won't"; and the widow thought with pangs of bitter mortification of Dolly Coddlins. How — how should these distracting circumstances be brought to an end?

She retired to rest that night not without a tremor, — to bed, but not to sleep. At midnight a voice was heard in her room, crying, "Fatima! Fatima! Fatima!" in awful accents. The doors banged to and fro, the bells began to ring, the maids went up and down stairs skurrying and screaming, and gave warning in a body. John Thomas, as pale as death, declared that he found Bluebeard's yeomanry sword, that hung in the hall, drawn, and on the ground; and the sticking-plaster miniature in Mr. Bluebeard's bedroom was found turned topsy-turvy!

"It is some trick," said the obstinate and incredulous sister Anne. "To-night I will come and sleep with you, sister." And the night came, and the two sisters retired together.

'T was a wild night. The wind howling without went crashing through the old trees of the old rookery round about the old church. The long bedroom windows went thump, thumping; the moon could be seen through them lighting up the graves with their ghastly shadows; the yew-tree, cut into the shape of a bird, looked particularly dreadfully, and bent and swayed as if it would peck something off that other yew-tree which was of the shape of a dumb-waiter. The bells at midnight began to ring as usual, the doors clapped, jingle—jingle down came a suit of armor in the hall, and a voice came and cried, "Fatima! Fatima! Fatima! look, look, look; the tomb, the tomb, the tomb!"

She looked. The vault door was open, and there in the moonlight stood Bluebeard, exactly as he was represented in the picture, in his yeomanry dress, his face frightfully pale, and his great blue beard curling over his chest, as awful as Mr. Muntz's.

Sister Anne saw the vision as well as Fatima. We shall spare the account of their terrors and screams. Strange to say, John Thomas, who slept in the attic above his mistress's bedroom, declared he was on the watch all night, and had seen nothing in the churchyard, and heard no sort of voices in the house.

And now the question came, What could the ghost want by appearing? "Is there anything," exclaimed the unhappy and perplexed Fatima, "that he would have me do? It is well to say 'now, now, now,' and to shew himself; but what is it that makes my blessed husband so uneasy in his grave?" And all parties consulted agreed that it was a very sensible question.

John Thomas, the footman, whose excessive terror at the appearance of the ghost had procured him his mistress's confidence, advised Mr. Screw, the butler, who communicated with Mrs. Baggs, the housekeeper, who condescended to impart her observations to Mrs. Bustle, the lady's-maid,—John Thomas, I say, decidedly advised that my lady should consult a cunning man. There was such a man in town; he had prophesied who should marry his (John Thomas's) cousin; he had cured Farmer Horn's cattle, which were evidently bewitched; he could raise ghosts, and make them speak, and he therefore was the very person to be consulted in the present juncture.

"What nonsense is this you have been talking to the maids, John Thomas, about the conjurer who lives in — in ——"

"In Hangman's Lane, ma'am, where the gibbet used to stand," replied John, who was bringing in the muffins. "It 's no nonsense, my lady. Every word as that man says comes true, and he knows everything."

"I desire you will not frighten the girls in the servants' hall with any of those silly stories," said the widow; and the meaning of this speech may, of course, at once be guessed. It was that the widow meant to consult the conjurer that very night. Sister Anne said that she would never, under such circumstances, desert her dear Fatima. John Thomas was summoned to attend the ladies with a dark lantern, and forth they set on their perilous visit to the conjurer at his dreadful abode in Hangman's Lane.

* * * * *

What took place at that frightful interview has never been entirely known. But there was no disturbance in the house on the night after. The bells slept quite quietly, the doors did not bang in the least, twelve o'clock struck, and no ghost appeared in the churchyard, and the whole family had a quiet night. The widow attributed this to a sprig of rosemary which the wizard gave her, and a horseshoe which she flung into the garden round the family vault, and which would keep *any* ghost quiet.

It happened the next day that, going to her milliner's, sister Anne met a gentleman who has been before mentioned in this story, Ensign Trippet by name; and, indeed, if the truth must be known, it somehow happened that she met the ensign somewhere every day of the week.

"What news of the ghost, my dearest Miss Shacabac?" said he (you may guess on what terms the two young people were by the manner in which Mr. Trippet addressed the lady); "has Bluebeard's ghost frightened your sister to any more fits, or set the bells a-ringing?"

Sister Anne, with a very grave air, told him that he must not joke on so awful a subject, that the ghost had been laid for a while, that a cunning man had told her sister things so wonderful that *any* man must believe in them; that, among other things, he had shown to Fatima her future husband.

"Had," said the ensign, "he black whiskers and a red coat?"

"No," answered Anne, with a sigh, "he had red whiskers and a black coat?"

"It can't be that rascal Sly!" cried the ensign. But Anne only sighed more deeply, and would not answer yes or no. "You may tell the poor captain," she said, "there is no hope for him, and all he has left is to hang himself."

"He shall cut the throat of Sly first, though," replied Mr. Trippet, fiercely. But Anne said things were not decided as yet. Fatima was exceedingly restive, and unwilling to acquiesce in the idea of being married to Mr. Sly; she had asked for further authority. The wizard said he could bring her own husband from the grave to point out her second bridegroom, who shall be, can be, must be, no other than Frederick Sly.

"It is a trick," said the ensign; but Anne was too much frightened by the preceding evening's occurrences to say so. "To-night," she said, "the grave will tell all."

And she left Ensign Trippet in a very solemn and affecting way.

* * * * *

At midnight three figures were seen to issue from Widow Bluebeard's house, and pass through the churchyard turnstile, and so away among the graves.

"To call up a ghost is bad enough," said the wizard; "to make him speak is awful. I recommend you, ma'am, to beware, for such curiosity has been fatal to many. There was one Arabian necromancer of my acquaintance who tried to make a ghost speak, and was torn in pieces on the spot. There was another person who *did* hear a ghost speak certainly, but came away from the interview deaf and dumb. There was another ——"

"Never mind," says Mrs. Bluebeard, all her old curiosity aroused, "see him and hear him I will. Have n't I seen him and heard him, too, already? When he 's audible *and* visible, *then 's* the time."

"But when you heard him," said the necromancer, "he was invisible, and when you saw him he was inaudible; so make up your mind what you will ask him, for ghosts will stand no shilly-shallying. I knew a stuttering man who was flung down by a ghost, and ——"

"I *have* made up my mind," said Fatima, interrupting him.

"To ask him what husband you shall take," whispered Anne.

Fatima only turned red, and sister Anne squeezed her hand; they passed into the graveyard in silence.

There was no moon; the night was pitch dark. They threaded their way through the graves, stumbling over them here and there. An owl was toowhooing from the church tower, a dog was howling somewhere, a cock began to crow, as they will sometimes at twelve o'clock at night.

"Make haste," said the wizard. "Decide whether you will go on or not."

"Let us go back, sister," said Anne.

"I *will* go on," said Fatima. "I should die if I gave it up, I feel I should."

"Here 's the gate; kneel down," said the wizard. The women knelt down.

"Will you see your first husband or your second husband?"

"I will see Bluebeard first," said the widow; "I shall know then whether this be a mockery, or you have the power you pretend to."

At this the wizard uttered an incantation, so frightful and of such incomprehensible words, that it is impossible for any mortal man to repeat them. And at the end of what seemed to be a versicle of his chant he called Bluebeard. There was no noise but the moaning of the wind in the trees, and the toowhooing of the owl in the tower.

At the end of the second verse he paused again, and called *Bluebeard.* The cock began to crow, the dog began to howl, a watchman in the town began to cry out the hour, and there came from the vault within a hollow groan, and a dreadful voice said, "Who wants me?"

Kneeling in front of the tomb, the necromancer began the third verse. As he spoke, the former phenomena were still to be remarked. As he continued, a number of ghosts rose from their graves, and advanced round the kneeling figures in a circle. As he concluded, with a loud bang the door of the vault flew open, and there in blue light stood Bluebeard in his blue uniform, waving his blue sword, and flashing his blue eyes round about!

"Speak now, or you are lost," said the necromancer to Fatima. But, for the first time in her life, she had not a word to say. Sister Anne, too, was dumb with terror. And, as the awful figure advanced towards them as they were kneeling, the sister thought all was over with them, and Fatima once more had occasion to repent her fatal curiosity.

The figure advanced, saying, in dreadful accents, "Fatima! Fatima! Fatima! wherefore am I called from my grave?" when all of a sudden down dropped his sword, down the ghost of Bluebeard went on his knees, and, clasping his hands together, roared out "Murder, mercy!" as loud as man could roar.

Six other ghosts stood round the kneeling group. "Why do you call me from the tomb?" said the first; "Who dares disturb my grave?" said the second; "Seize him and away with him," cried the third. "Murder, mercy!" still roared the ghost of Bluebeard, as the white-robed spirits advanced and caught hold of him.

"It 's only Tom Trippet," said a voice at Anne's ear.

"And your very humble servant," said a voice well known to Mrs. Bluebeard; and they helped the ladies to rise, while the other ghosts seized Bluebeard. The necromancer took to his heels and got off; he was found to be no other than Mr. Claptrap, the manager of the theatre.

It was some time before the ghost of Bluebeard could recover from the fainting fit into which he had been plunged when seized by the opposition ghosts in white; and while they were ducking him at the pump his bluebeard came off, and he was discovered to be — who do you think? Why Mr. Sly, to be sure; and it appears that John Thomas, the footman, had lent him the uniform, and had clapped the doors, and rung the bells, and spoken down the chimney; and it was Mr. Claptrap who gave Mr. Sly the blue fire and the theatre gong; and he went to London next morning by the coach; and, as it was discovered that the story concerning Miss Coddlins was a shameful calumny, why, of course, the widow married Captain Blackbeard. Dr. Sly married them, and has always declared that he knew nothing of his nephew's doings, and wondered that he has not tried to commit suicide since his last disappointment.

Mr. and Mrs. Trippet are likewise living happily together, and this, I am given to understand, is the ultimate fate of a family in whom we were all very much interested in early life.

You will say that the story is not probable. Psha! Is n't it written in a book? and is it a whit less probable than the first part of the tale?

DICKENS IN FRANCE.

EEING placarded on the walls a huge announcement that "NICHOLAS NICKLEBY, ou les Voleurs de Londres," was to be performed at the Ambigu-Comique Théâtre on the Boulevard, and having read in the "Journal des Débats" a most stern and ferocious criticism upon the piece in question, and upon poor Monsieur Dickens, its supposed author, it seemed to me by no means unprofitable to lay out fifty sous in the purchase of a stall at the theatre, and to judge with my own eyes of the merits and demerits of the play.

Who does not remember (except those who never saw the drama, and therefore of course cannot be expected to have any notion of it) — who does not, I say, remember the pathetic acting of Mrs. Keeley in the part of Smike, as performed at the Adelphi; the obstinate good-humor of Mr. Wilkinson, who, having to represent the brutal Squeers, was, according to his nature, so chuckling, oily, and kind-hearted, that little boys must have thought it a good joke to be flogged by him; finally, the acting of the admirable Yates in the kindred part of Mantalini? Can France, I thought, produce a fop equal to Yates? Is there any vulgarity and assurance on the Boulevard that can be compared to that of which, in the character of

Mantalini, he gives a copy so wonderfully close to nature? Never then were fifty sous more cheerfully, — nay, eagerly paid, than by your obedient servant.

After China, this is the most ignorant country, thought I, in the whole civilized world (the company was dropping into the theatre, and the musicians were one by one taking their seats); these people are so immensely conceited, that they think the rest of Europe beneath them; and though they have invaded Spain, Italy, Russia, Germany, not one in ten thousand can ask for a piece of bread in the national language of the countries so conquered. But see the force of genius; after a time it conquers everything, even the ignorance and conceit of Frenchmen! The name of Nicholas Nickleby crosses the Channel in spite of them. I shall see honest John Browdie and wicked Ralph once more, honest and wicked in French. Shall we have the Kenwigses, and their uncle, the delightful collector; and will he, in Portsmouth church, make that famous marriage with Juliana Petowker? Above all, what will *Mrs.* Nickleby say? — the famous Mrs. Nickleby, who has lain undescribed until Boz seized upon her and brought that great truth to light, and whom yet every man possesses in the bosom of his own family. Are there Mrs. Nicklebies, — or, to speak more correctly, are there Mistresses Nickleby in France? We shall see all this at the rising of the curtain; and, hark! the fiddlers are striking up.

Presently the prompter gives his three heart-thrilling slaps, and the great painted cloth moves upwards: it is always a moment of awe and pleasure. What is coming? First you get a glimpse of legs and feet; then suddenly the owners of the limbs in question in steady attitudes, looking as if they had been there one thousand years before; now behold the landscape, the clouds; the great curtain vanishes altogether, the charm is dissolved, and the disenchanted performers begin.

ACT I.

You see a court of a school, with great iron bars in front, and a beauteous sylvan landscape beyond. Could you read the writing on the large board over the gate, you would know that the school was the "Paradis des Enfans," kept by Mr. Squeers. Somewhere by that bright river, which meanders through the background, is the castle of the stately Earl of Clarendon, — no relation to a late ambassador at Madrid.

His lordship is from home; but his young and lovely daughter, Miss Annabella, is in Yorkshire, and at this very moment is taking a lesson of French from Mr. Squeers's *sous-maître*, Neekolass Neeklbee. Nicholas is, however, no vulgar usher; he is but lately an orphan; and his uncle, the rich London banker, Monsieur Ralph, taking charge of the lad's portionless sister, has procured for Nicholas this place of usher at a school in le Yorksheer.

A rich London banker procuring his nephew a place in a school at eight guineas per annum! Sure there must be some roguery in this; and the more so when you know that Monsieur Squeers, the keeper of the academy, was a few years since a vulgar rope-dancer and tumbler at a fair. But peace! let these mysteries clear up, as, please Heaven, before five acts are over they will. Meanwhile, Nicholas is happy in giving his lessons to the lovely Meess Annabel. Lessons, indeed! Lessons of what? Alack, alack! when two young, handsome, ardent, tender-hearted people pore over the same book, we know what happens, be the book what it may. French or Hebrew, there is always one kind of language in the leaves, as those can tell who have conned them.

Meanwhile, in the absence of his usher, Monsieur Squeers keeps school. But one of his scholars is in the court-yard, — a lad beautifully dressed, fat, clean, and rosy. A gentleman by the name of Browdie, by profession a drover, is with the boy, employed at the moment (for he is at leisure, and fond of music) in giving him a lesson on *the clarionet.*

The boy thus receiving lessons is called facetiously by his master *Prospectus*, and why? Because he is so excessively fat and healthy, and well clothed, that his mere appearance in the court-yard is supposed to entice parents and guardians to place their children in a seminary where the scholars were in such admirable condition.

And here I cannot help observing in the first place, that Squeers, exhibiting in this manner a sample-boy, and pretending that the whole stock was like him (whereas they are a miserable, half-starved set), must have been an abominable old scoundrel; and secondly (though the observation applies to the French nation merely, and may be considered more as political than general), that, by way of a fat specimen, never was one more unsatisfactory than this. Such a poor shrivelled creature I never saw; it is like a French fat pig, as lanky as a greyhound! Both animals give one a thorough contempt for the nation.

John Browdie gives his lesson to Prospectus, who informs him of some of the circumstances narrated above; and having concluded the lesson, honest John produces a piece of *pudding* for his pupil. Ah, how Prospectus devours it! for though the only well-fed boy in the school, he is, we regret to say, a gormandizer by disposition.

While Prospectus eats, another of Mr. Squeers's scholars is looking unnoticed on, — another boy, a thousand times more miserable. See yon poor shivering child, trembling over his book in a miserable hutch at the corner of the court! He is in rags, he is not allowed to live with the other boys; at play they constantly buffet him, at lesson-time their blunders are visited upon his poor shoulders.

Who is this unhappy boy? Ten years since a man by the name of Becher brought him to the Paradis des Enfans, and paying in advance five years of his pension, left him under the charge of Monsieur Squeers. No family ever visited the child; and when at the five years' end the *instituteur* applied at the address given him by Becher for the further payment of his pupil's expenses, Monsieur Squeers found that Becher had grossly deceived him, that no such persons existed, and that no money was consequently forthcoming, hence the misfortunes which afterwards befell the hapless orphan. None cared for him, — none knew him. 'T is possible that even the name he went by was fictitious. That name was Smike, pronounced Smeek.

Poor Smeek! he had, however, found one friend, — the kind-hearted *sous-maître* Neeklbee, — who gave him half of his own daily pittance of bread and pudding, encouraged him to apply to his books, and defended him as much as possible from the assaults of the schoolboys and Monsieur Squeers.

John Browdie had just done giving his lesson of clarionet to Prospectus when Neeklbee arrived at the school. There was a difference between John and Nicholas; for the former, seeing the young usher's frequent visits at Clarendon Castle, foolishly thought he was enamored of Meess Jenny, the fermier's daughter, on whom John, too, had fixed an eye of affection. Silly John! Nicholas's heart was fixed (hopelessly, as the young man thought) upon higher objects. However, the very instant that Nickleby entered the court-yard of the school, John took up his stick, and set off for London, whither he was bound, with a drove of oxen.

Nickleby had not arrived a whit too soon to protect his poor friend, Smeek. All the boys were called into the court-yard by Monsieur Squarrs, and made to say their lessons. When it came to poor Smeek's turn, the timid lad trembled, hesitated, and could not do his spelling.

Inflamed with fury, old Squarrs rushed forward, and would have assomméd his pupil, but human nature could bear this tyranny no longer. Nickleby, stepping forward, defended the poor prostrate child; and when Squeers raised his stick to strike — pouf! pif! un, deux, trois, et la! — Monsieur Nicholas flanquéd him several coups de poing, and sent him bientôt grovelling à terre.

You may be sure that there was now a pretty hallooing among the boys; all jumped, kicked, thumped, bumped, and scratched their unhappy master (and serve him right, too!), and when they had finished their fun, vlan! flung open the gates of the Infants' Paradise, and run away home.

Neeklbee, seeing what he had done, had nothing left but to run away, too. He penned a hasty line to his lovely pupil Miss Annabel, to explain that though his departure was sudden his honor was safe, and seizing his stick quitted the school.

There was but one pupil left in it, and he, poor soul, knew not whither to go. But when he saw Nicholas, his sole friend, departing, he mustered courage, and then made a step forward, — and then wondered if he dared, — and then, when Nicholas was at a little distance from him, ran, ran as if his life (as indeed it did) depended upon it.

This is the picture of Neeklbee and poor Smeek. They are both dressed in the English fashion, and you must fancy the curtain falling amidst thunders of applause.

[*End of Act I.*

"Ah, ah, ah! ouf, pouf." "Dieu, qu'il fait chaud!" "Orgeat, limonade, bière!" "L'Entracte, journal de tous les spectacles!" "LA MARSEILLAI-AI-AISE!" With such cries from pit and boxes the public wiles away the weary ten minutes between the acts. The three *bonnes* in the front boxes, who had been escorted by a gentleman in a red cap, and jacket, and earrings, begin sucking oranges with great comfort, while their friend amuses himself with a piece of barley-sugar. The *petite-*

maîtresse in the private box smoothes her *bandeaux* of hair and her little trim, white cuffs, and looks at her *chiffons*. The friend of the tight black velvet spencer meanwhile pulls his yellow kid gloves tighter on his hands, and looks superciliously round the house with his double-glass. Fourteen people, all smelling of smoke, all bearded, and all four feet high, pass over your body to their separate stalls. The prompter gives his thumps, whack — whack — whack! the music begins again, the curtain draws, and, lo! we have

ACT II.

The tavern of Les Armes du Roi appears to be one of the most frequented in the city of London. It must be in the Yorkshire road, that is clear; for the first person whom we see there is John Browdie; to him presently comes Prospectus, then Neeklbee, then poor Smeek, each running away individually from the Paradis des Enfans.

It is likewise at this tavern that the great banker Ralph does his business, and lets you into a number of his secrets. Hither, too, comes Milor Clarendon, a handsome peer, forsooth, but a sad reprobate, I fear. Sorrow has driven him to these wretched courses. Ten years since he lost a son, a lovely child of six years of age; and, hardened by the loss, he has taken to gambling, to the use of the *vins de France* which take the reason prisoner, and to other excitements still more criminal. He has cast his eyes upon the lovely Kate Nickleby (he, the father of Miss Annabel!), and asks the banker to sup with him, to lend him ten thousand pounds, and to bring his niece with him. With every one of these requests the capitalist promises to comply. The money he produces forthwith, the lady he goes to fetch. Ah, milor!

beware, — beware, your health is bad, your property is ruined, — death and insolvency stare you in the face, — but what cares Lor Clarendon? He is desperate; he orders a splendid repast in a private apartment, and while they are getting it ready, he and the young lords of his acquaintance sit down and crack a bottle in the coffee-room. A gallant set of gentlemen, truly; all in short coats with capes to them, in tights and Hessian boots, such as our nobility are in the custom of wearing.

"I bet you cinq cents guinées, Lor Beef," says Milor Clarendon (whom the wine has begun to excite), "that I will have the lovely Kate Nicklbee at supper with us to-night."

"Done!" says Lor Beef. But why starts yon stranger who has just come into the hotel? Why, forsooth? because he is Nicholas Nickleby, Kate's brother; and a pretty noise he makes when he hears of his lordship's project!

"You have Meess Neeklbee at your table, sir? You are a liar!"

All the lords start up.

"Who is this very strange person?" says Milor Clarendon, as cool as a cucumber.

"Dog! give me your name!" shouts Nicholas.

"Ha! ha! ha!" says my lord, scornfully.

"John," says Nickleby, seizing hold of a waiter, "tell me that man's name."

John the waiter looks frightened, and hums and has, when, at the moment, who should walk in but Mr. Ralph the banker, and his niece.

Ralph. "Nicholas! — confusion!"

Kate. "My brother!"

Nicholas. "Avaunt, woman! Tell me, sirrah, by what right you bring my sister into such company, and who is the villain to whom you have presented her?"

Ralph. "Lord *Clarendon*."

Nicholas. "The father of Meess Annabel? Gracious heaven!"

What followed now need not be explained. The young lords and the banker retire abashed to their supper, while Meess Kate, and Smike, who has just arrived, fall into the arms of Nicholas.

Such, ladies and gentlemen, is the second act, rather feeble in interest, and not altogether probable in action. That five people running away from Yorkshire should all come to the same inn in London, arriving within five minutes of each other, — that Mr. Ralph, the great banker, should make the hotel his place of business, and openly confess in the coffee-room to his ex-agent Becher that he had caused Becher to make away with or murder the son of Lord Clarendon, — finally, that Lord Clarendon himself, with an elegant town mansion, should receive his distinguished guests in a tavern, of not the first respectability, — all these points may, perhaps, strike the critic from their extreme improbability. But, bless your soul! if *these* are improbabilities, what will you say to the revelations of the

THIRD ACT.

That scoundrel Squarrs before he kept the school was, as we have seen, a tumbler and *saltimbanque*, and, as such, member of the great fraternity of cadgers, beggars, *gueux*, thieves, that have their club in London. It is held in immense Gothic vaults under ground: here the beggars consort their plans, divide their spoil, and hold their orgies.

In returning to London Monsieur Squarrs instantly resumes his acquaintance with his old comrades, who appoint him, by the all-powerful interest of a *peculiar person*, head of the community of cadgers.

That person is no other than the banker Ralph, who, in secret, directs this godless crew, visits their haunts, and receives from them a boundless obedience. A villain himself, he has need of the aid of villany. He pants for vengeance against his nephew, he has determined that his niece shall fall a prey to Milor Clarendon, — nay, more, he has a dark suspicion that Smike, — the orphan boy, — the homeless fugitive from Yorkshire, — is no other than the child who ten years ago — But, hush!

Where is his rebellious nephew and those whom he protects? The quick vigilance of Ralph soon discovered them; Nicholas, having taken the name of Edward Browne, was acting at a theatre in the neighborhood of the Thames. Haste, Squarrs, take a couple of trusty beggars with you, and hie thee to Wapping; seize young Smike and carry him to Cadger's Cavern, — haste, then! The mind shudders to consider what is to happen.

In Nicholas's room at the theatre we find his little family assembled, and with them honest John Browdie, who has forgotten his part on learning that Nicholas was attached, not to the *fermière*, but to the mistress; to them comes — gracious heavens! — Meess Annabel. "Fly," says she, "fly! I have overheard a plot concocted between my father and your uncle; the sheriff is to seize you for the abduction of Smeek and the assault upon Squarrs," &c. &c. &c.

In short, it is quite impossible to describe this act, so much is there done in it. Lord Clarendon learns that he has pledged his life interest in his estates to Ralph.

His Lordship *dies*, and Ralph seizes a paper, which proves beyond a doubt that young Smike is no other than Clarendon's long-lost son.

L'infame Squarrs with his satellites carry off the boy; Browdie pitches Squarrs into the river; the sheriff carries Nickleby to prison; and VICE TRIUMPHS in the person of the odious Ralph. But vice does not always triumph; wait awhile and you will see. For in the

FOURTH ACT

John Browdie, determined to rescue his two young friends, follows Ralph like his shadow; he dogs him to a rendezvous of the beggars, and overhears all his conversation with Squarrs. The boy is in the Cadger's Cavern, hidden a thousand feet below the Thames; there is to be a grand jollification among the rogues that night, — a dance and a feast. "*I*," says John Browdie, *will be there.*" And, wonderful to say, who should pass but his old friend Prospectus, to whom he gave lessons on the clarionet.

Prospectus is a cadger now, and is to play his clarionet that night at Cadger's Hall. Browdie will join him, — he is dressed up like a blind beggar, and strange sights, Heaven knows, meet his eyes in Cadger's Hall.

Here they come trooping in by scores, — the halt and the lame, black sweepers, one-legged fiddlers, the climber mots, the fly-fakers, the kedgoree coves, —in a word, the rogues of London, to their Gothic hall, a thousand miles below the level of the sea. Squarrs is their nominal head; but their real leader is the tall man yonder in the black mask, he whom nobody knows but Browdie, who has found him out at once, — 't is Ralph!

"Bring out the prisoner," says the black mask; "he has tried to escape, — he has broken his oaths to the cadgers, let him meet his punishment."

And without a word more, what do these cadgers do? They take poor Smike and *bury him alive;* down he goes into the vault, a stone is rolled over him, the cadgers go away, — so much for Smike.

But in the mean time Master Browdie has not been idle. He has picked the pocket of one of the cadgers of a portfolio containing papers that prove Smike to be Lord Clarendon beyond a doubt; he lags behind until all the cadgers are gone, and with the help of Nicholas (who, by the by, has found his way somehow into the place), he pushes away the stone, and brings the fainting boy to the world.

These things are improbable, you certainly may say, but are they impossible? If they are possible, then they may come to pass; if they may come to pass then, they may be supposed to come to pass: and why should they not come to pass? That is my argument: let us pass on to the

FIFTH ACT.

Aha! Master Ralph, you think you will have it all your own way, do you? The lands of Clarendon are yours, provided there is no male heir, and you have done for *him*. The peerage, to be sure (by the laws of England), is to pass to the husband of Meess Annabella. Will she marry Ralph, or not? Yes: then well and good; he is an earl for the future and the father of a new race of Clarendon. No: then, in order to spell her still more, he has provided amongst the beggars a lad who is to personate the young mislaid Lord Clarendon, who is to come armed with certain papers that make his right unquestionable, and who will be a creature of Ralph's, to be used or cast away at will.

Ralph pops the question; the lady repels him with scorn. "Quit the house, Meess," says he; "it is not yours, but mine. Give up that vain title which you have adopted since your papa's death; you are no countess,—your brother lives. Ho! John, Thomas, Samuel! introduce his lordship, the Comte de Clarendon."

And who slips in? Why, in a handsome new dress, in the English fashion, Smike, to be sure,—the boy whom Ralph has murdered,—the boy who had risen from the tomb,—the boy who had miraculously discovered the papers in Cadger's Hall and (by some underhand work that went on behind the scenes, which I don't pretend to understand) had substituted himself for the substitute which that wicked banker had proposed to bring forward! A rush of early recollections floods the panting heart of the young boy. Can it be? Yes, — no; sure these halls are familiar to him? That conservatory, has he not played with the flowers there, — played with his blessed mother at his side? That portrait! Stop! a — a — a — a — ah! it is, — it is my sister Anna — Anna — bella!

Fancy the scene as the two young creatures rush with a scream into each other's arms. Fancy John Browdie's hilarity: he jumps for joy, and throws off his beggar's cloak and beard. Nicholas clasps his hands, and casts his fine eyes heavenward. But, above all, fancy the despair of that cursed banker Ralph as he sees his victim risen from the grave, and all his hopes dashed down into it. O Heaven, Thy hand is here! How must the banker then have repented of his bargain with the late Lord Clarendon, and that he had not had his lordship's life insured! Perdition! to have been out-tricked by a boy and a country boor! Is there no hope? * * *

Hope? Psha! man, thy reign of vice is over, — it is the fifth act. Already the people are beginning to leave the house, and never more again canst thou expect to lift thy head.

"Monsieur Ralph," Browdie whispers, "after your pretty doings in Cadger's Hall, had you not best be thinking of leaving the country, as Nicholas Nickleby's uncle, I would fain not see you, crick! You understand?" (pointing to his jugular).

"I do," says Ralph, gloomily, "and will be off in two hours." And Lord Smike takes honest Browdie by one hand, gently pressing Kate's little fingers with the other, and the sheriff, and the footmen, and attendants form a tableau, and the curtain begins to fall, and the blushing Annabel whispers to happy Nicholas, — "Ah! my friend, I can give up with joy to my brother *ma couronne de comtesse.* What care I for rank or name with you? the name that I love above all others is that of LADY ANNABEL NICKLEBY." [*Exeunt omnes.*

The musicians have hurried off long before this. In one instant the stage lamps go out, and you see fellows starting forward to cover the boxes with canvas. Up goes the chandelier amongst the gods and goddesses painted on the ceiling. Those in the galleries, meanwhile, bellow out "SAINT-ERNEST!" he it is who acted John Browdie. Then there is a yell of "SMEEK! SMEEK!" Blushing and bowing, Madame Prosper comes forward; by heavens! a pretty woman, with tender eyes and a fresh, clear voice. Next the gods call for "CHILLY!" who acted the villain: but by this time you are bustling and struggling among the crowd in the lobbies, where there is the usual odor of garlic and tobacco. Men in sabots come tumbling down from the galleries; cries of "*Auguste, solo! Eugenie! prends ton parapluie.*" "*Monsieur, vous me marchez sur les pieds,*" are heard in the crowd, over which the brazen helmets of the Pompier's tower are shining. A cabman in the Boulevard, who opens his vehicle eagerly as you pass by, growls dreadful oaths when, seated inside, you politely request him to drive to the Barrière de l'Etoile. "*Ah, ces Anglais,*" says he, "*ça demeure dans les déserts, — dans les déserts, grand Dieu, avec les loups; ils prennent leur* beautyfine *thé avec leurs tartines le soir, et puis ils se couchent dans les déserts, ma parole d'honneur; comme des Arabes.*"

If the above explanation of the plot of the new piece of *Nicholas Nickleby* has appeared intolerably long to those few persons who have perused it, I can only say for their comfort that I have not told one half of the real plot of the piece in question; nay, very likely have passed over all the most interesting part of it. There, for instance, was the assassination of the virtuous villain Becher, the dying scene with my lord, the manner in which Nicholas got into the Cadger's Cave, and got out again. Have I breathed a syllable upon any of these points? No; and never will to my dying day. The imperfect account of *Nicholas Nickleby* given above is all that the most impatient reader (let him have fair warning) can expect to hear from his humble servant. Let it be sufficient to know that the piece in itself contains a vast number of beauties entirely passed over by the unworthy critic, and only to be appreciated by any gentleman who will take the trouble to step across the Channel, and thence from his hotel to the ambiguously-comic theatre. And let him make haste, too; for who knows what may happen? Human life is proverbially short. Theatrical pieces bloom and fade like the flowers of the field, and very likely, long before this notice shall appear in print (as let us heartily, from mercenary considerations, pray that it will), the drama of *Nicholas Nickleby* may have disappeared altogether from the world's ken, like Carthage, Troy, Swallow Street, the Marylebone bank, Babylon, and other fond magnificences elevated by men, and now forgotten and prostrate.

As for the worthy Boz, it will be seen that *his* share in the piece is perfectly insignificant, and that he has no more connection with the noble geniuses who invented the drama than a pig has with a gold-laced hat that a nobleman may have hung on it, or a starting-post on the race-course with some magnificent, thousand-guinea, fiery horses who may choose to run from it. How poor do his writings appear after those of the Frenchman! How feeble, mean, and destitute of imagination! *He* never would have thought of introducing six lords, an ex-kidnapper, a great banker, an idiot, a schoolmaster, his usher, a cattle-driver, coming for the most part a couple of hundred miles, in order to lay open all their secrets in the coffee-room of the King's Arms hotel! He never could have invented the great subterraneous cavern, *cimetière et salle de bal*, as Jules Janin calls it! The credit of all this falls upon the French adaptors of Monsieur Dickens's romance; and so it will be advisable to let the public know.

But as the French play-writers are better than Dickens, being incomparably more imaginative and poetic, so, in progression, is the French critic, Jules Janin, above named, a million times superior to the French playwrights, and, after Janin, Dickens disappears altogether. He is cut up, disposed of, done for. J. J. has hacked him into small pieces, and while that wretched romancer is amusing himself across the Atlantic, and fancying, perhaps, that he is a popular character, his business has been done for ever and ever in Europe. What matters that he is read by millions in England and billions in America? that everybody who understands English had a corner in his heart for him? The great point is, *what does Jules Janin think?* and that we shall hear presently; for though I profess the greatest admiration for Mr. Dickens, yet there can be no reason why one should deny one's self the little pleasure of acquainting him that *some* ill-disposed persons in the world are inclined to abuse him. Without this privilege what is friendship good for?

Who is Janin? He is the critic of France. J. J., in fact, — the man who writes a weekly *fueilleton* in the "Journal des Débats" with such indisputable brilliancy and wit, and such a happy mixture of effrontery, and honesty, and poetry, and impudence, and falsehood, and impertinence, and good feeling, that one can't fail to be charmed with the compound, and to look rather eagerly for the Monday's paper; Jules Janin is the man, who, not knowing a single word of the English language, as he actually professes in the preface, *has helped to translate* the *Sentimental Journey*. He is the man, who, when he was married (in a week when news were slack no doubt), actually *criticised his own marriage ceremony*, letting all the public see the proof-sheets of his bridal, as was the custom among certain ancient kings, I believe. In fact, a more modest, honest, unassuming, blushing, truth-telling, gentlemanlike J. J. it is impossible to conceive.

Well, he has fallen foul of Monsieur Dickens, this fat French moralist; he says Dickens is *immodest*, and Jules cannot abide immodesty; and a great and conclusive proof this is upon a question which the two nations have been in the habit of arguing, namely, which of the two is the purer in morals? and may be argued clear thus: —

1. We in England are accustomed to think Dickens modest, and allow our children to peruse his works.

2. In France, the man who wrote the history of "The Dead Donkey and the Guillotined Woman,"* and afterwards his own epithalamium in the newspaper, is revolted by Dickens.

3. Therefore Dickens *must* be immodest, and grossly

* Some day the writer meditates a great and splendid review of J. J.'s work.

immodest, otherwise a person so confessedly excellent as J. J. would never have discovered the crime.

4. And therefore it is pretty clear that the French morals are of a much higher order than our own, which remark will apply to persons and books, and all the relations of private and public life.

Let us now see how our fat Jules attacks Dickens. His remarks on him begin in the following jocular way: —

"THÉÂTRE DE L'AMBIGU-COMIQUE.

"*Nicolas Nickleby*, Mélodrame, en Six Actes.

"A genoux devant celui-là qui s'appelle Charles Dickens! à genoux! Il a accompli à lui seul ce que n'ont pu faire à eux deux Lord Byron et Walter Scott! Joignez-y, si vous voulez, Pope et Milton et tout ce que la littérature Anglaise a produit de plus solennel et de plus charmant. Charles Dickens! mais il n'est question que de lui en Angleterre. Il en est la gloire, et la joie, et l'orgueil! Savez-vous combien d'acheteurs possède ce Dickens; j'ai dit *d'acheteurs*, de gens qui tirent leur argent du leur bourse pour que cet argent passe de leur main dans la main du libraire? — Dix mille acheteurs. Dix mille? que disons-nous, dix mille! vingt mille! — Vingt mille? Quoi! vingt mille acheteurs? — Fi donc, vingt mille! quarante mille acheteurs. — Eh quoi! il a trouvé quarante mille acheteurs, vous vous moquez de nous sans doute? — Oui, mon brave homme on se moque de vous, car ce n'est pas vingt mille et quarante mille et soixante mille acheteurs qu'a rencontrés ce Charles Dickens, c'est cent mille acheteurs. Cent mille, pas un de moins. Cent mille esclaves, cent mille tributaires, cent mille! Et mes grands écrivains modernes s'estiment bien heureux et bien fiers quand leur livre le plus vanté parvient, au bout de six mois de célébrité, à son huitième cent!"

There is raillery for you! there is a knowledge of English literature, — of "Pope et Milton, si solennel et si charmant!" Milton, above all; his little comédie "Samson l'Agoniste" is one of the gayest and most graceful trifles that ever was acted on the stage. And to think that Dickens has sold more copies of his work than the above two eminent hommes-de-lettres, and Scott and Byron into the bargain! It is a fact, and J. J. vouches for it. To be sure, J. J. knows no more of English literature than I do of hieroglyphics, — to be sure, he has not one word of English. N'importe: he has had the advantage of examining the books of Mr. Dickens's publishers, and has discovered that they sell of Boz's works "*cent mille, pas un de moins.*" Janin will not allow of one less. Can you answer numbers? And there are our grands écrivains modernes, who are happy if they sell eight hundred in six months. Byron and Scott doubtless, "le solennel Pope, et le charmant Milton," as well as other geniuses not belonging to the three kingdoms. If a man is an arithmetician as well as a critic, and we join together figures of speech and Arabic numerals, there is no knowing what he may not prove.

"*Or,*" continues J. J.: —

"Or, parmi les chefs-d'œuvre de sa façon que dévore l'Angleterre, ce Charles Dickens a produit un gros mélodrame en deux gros volumes, intitulé *Nicolas Nickleby.* Ce livre a été traduit chez nous par un homme de beaucoup d'esprit, qui n'est pas fait pour ce triste métier-là. Si vous saviez ce que peut-être un pareil chef-d'œuvre, certes vouz prendriez en pitié les susdits cent mille souscripteurs de Charles Dickens. Figurez-vous donc un amas d'inventions puériles, où l'horrible et le niais se donnent la main, dans une ronde infernale; ici passent en riant de bonnes gens si bons qu'ils en sont tout-à-fait bêtes; plus loin bondissent et blasphèment toutes sortes de bandits, de fripons, de voleurs et de misérables si affreux qu'on ne sait pas comment pourrait vivre, seulement vingt-quatre heures, une société ainsi composée. C'est le plus nauséabond mélange qu'on puisse imaginer de lait chaud et de bierre tournée, d'œufs frais et de bœuf salé, de haillons et d'habits brodés, d'écus d'or et de gros sous, de roses et de pissenlits. On se bat, on s'embrasse, on s'injurie, on s'enivre, on meurt de faim. Les filles de la rue et les lords de la Chambre haute, les portefaix et les poëtes, les écoliers et les voleurs, se promènent, bras dessus bras dessous, au milieu de ce tohubohu insupportable. Aimez-vous la fumée de tabac, l'odeur de l'ail, le goût du porc frais, l'harmonie que fait un plat d'étain frappé contre une casserole de cuivre non étamé? Lisez-moi consciencieusement ce livre de Charles Dickens. Quelles plaies! quelles pustules! et que de saintes vertus! Ce Dickens a réuni en bloc toutes les descriptions de Guzman d'Alfarache et tous les rêves de Grandisson. Oh! qu'êtes-vous devenus, vous les lectrices tant soit peu prudes des romans de Walter Scott? Oh! qu'a-t-on fait de vous, les lectrices animées de *Don Juan* et de *Lara?* O vous, les chastes enthousiastes de la *Clarisse Harlowe*, voilez-vous la face de honte! A cent mille exemplaires le Charles Dickens!"

To what a pitch of *dévergondago* must the English ladies have arrived, when a fellow who can chronicle his own marriage, and write "The Dead Donkey and the Guillotined Woman,"—when even a man like that, whom nobody can accuse of being squeamish, is obliged to turn away with disgust at their monstrous immodesty!

J. J. is not difficult; a little harmless gallantry and trifling with the seventh commandment does not offend him,—far from it. Because there are no love-intrigues in Walter Scott, Jules says that Scott's readers are *tant soit peu prudes!* There *ought* to be, in fact, in life and in novels, a little, pleasant, gentlemanlike, anti-seventh-commandment excitement. Read "The Dead Donkey and the Guillotined Woman," and you will see how the thing may be agreeably and genteelly done. See what he says of "Clarisse," — it is *chaste;* of "Don Juan," — it is not indecent, it is not immoral, it is only ANIMÉE! Animée! O ciel! what a word! Could any but a Frenchman have had the grace to hit on it? "Animation" our Jules can pardon; prudery he can excuse, in his good-humored, contemptuous way; but Dickens, — this Dickens, — O fie! And, perhaps, there never was a more succinct, complete, elegant, just, and satisfactory account given of a book than that by our friend Jules of "Nicholas Nickleby." "It is the most disgusting mixture imaginable of warm milk and sour beer, of fresh eggs and salt beef, of rags and laced clothes, of gold crowns and coppers, of roses and dandelions."

There is a receipt for you! or take another, which is quite as pleasant: —

II.

"The fumes of tobacco, the odor of garlic, the taste of fresh pork, the harmony made by striking a pewter plate against an untinned copper saucepan. Read me conscientiously this book of Charles Dickens; what sores! what pustules!" &c.

Try either mixture (and both are curious), — for fresh pork is an ingredient in one, salt beef in another; tobacco and garlic in receipt No. 2 agreeably take the places of warm milk and sour beer in formula No. 1; and whereas, in the second prescription, a pewter plate and *untinned* copper saucepan (what a devilish satire in that epithet *untinned!*), a gold crown and a few half-pence, answer in the first. Take either mixture, and the result is a Dickens. Hang thyself, thou unhappy writer of *Pickwick;* or, blushing at this exposition of thy faults, turn red man altogether, and build a wigwam in a wilderness, and live with 'possums up gum-trees. Fresh pork and warm milk; sour beer and salt b—— Faugh! how could you serve us so atrociously?

And this is one of the "chefs-d'œuvre *de sa façon* que dévore l'Angleterre." The beastly country! How Jules lashes the islanders with the sting of that epigram,—*chefs-d'œuvre de leur façon!*

* * * * *

Look you, J. J., it is time that such impertinence should cease. Will somebody,—out of three thousand literary men in France, there are about three who have a smattering of the English,—will some one of the three explain to J. J. the enormous folly and falsehood of all that the fellow has been saying about Dickens and English literature generally? We have in England literary *chefs-d'œuvre de notre façon*, and are by no means ashamed to devour the same. "Le charmant Milton" was not, perhaps, very skilled for making epigrams and chansons-à-boire, but, after all, was a person of merit, and of his works have been sold considerably more than eight hundred copies. "Le solennel Pope" was a writer not undeserving of praise. There must have been something worthy in Shakespeare,—for his name has penetrated even to France, where he is not unfrequently called "le Sublime Williams." Walter Scott, though a prude, as you say, and not having the agreeable *laisser-aller* of the author of the *Dead Donkey*, &c., could still turn off a romance pretty creditably. He and "le Sublime Williams" between them have turned your French literature topsy-turvy; and many a live donkey of your crew is trying to imitate their paces and their roars, and to lord it like those dead lions. These men made *chefs-d'œuvre de nôtre façon*, and we are by no means ashamed to acknowledge them.

But what right have you, O blundering ignorances! to pretend to judge them and their works,—you, who might as well attempt to give a series of lectures upon the literature of the Hottentots, and are as ignorant of English as the author of the *Random Recollections?* Learn modesty, Jules; Listen to good advice; and when you say to other persons, *lisez moi ce livre consciencieusement*, at least do the same thing, O critic! before you attempt to judge and arbitrate.

And I am ready to take an affidavit in the matter of this criticism of *Nicholas Nickleby*, that the translator of Sterne, who does not know English, has not read Boz in the original,—has not even read him in the translation, and slanders him out of pure invention. Take these concluding opinions of J. J. as a proof of the fact:—

"De ce roman de *Nicolas Nickleby* a été tiré le mélodrame qui va suivre. Commencez d'abord par entasser les souterrains sur les ténèbres, le vice sur le sang, le mensonge sur l'injure, *l'adultère sur l'inceste*, battez-moi tout ce mélange, et vous verrez ce que vous allez voir.

"Dans un comté Anglais, dans une école, ou plutôt dans une horrible prison habitée par le froid et la faim, un nommé Squeers entraîne, sous prétexte de les élever dans la belle discipline, tous les enfans qu'on lui confie. Ce misérable Squeers spécule tout simplement sur la faim, sur la soif, sur les habits de ces pauvres petits. On n'entend que le bruit des verges, les soupirs des battus, les cris des battans, les blasphèmes du maître. C'est affreux à lire et à voir. Surtout ce qui fait peur (je parle du livre en question), c'est la misère d'un pauvre petit nommé Smilke, dont cet affreux Squeers est le bourreau. Quand parut le livre de Charles Dickens, on raconte que plus d'un maître de pension de l'Angleterre se récria contre la calomnie. Mais, juste ciel! si la cent millième partie d'une pareille honte était possible; s'il était vrai qu'un seul marchand de chair humaine ainsi bâti pût exister de l'autre côté du détroit, ce serait le déshonneur d'une nation tout entière. Et si en effet la chose est impossible, que venez-vous donc nous conter, que le roman, tout comme la comédie, est la peinture des mœurs?

"Or ce petit malheureux couvert de haillons et de plaies, le jouet de M. Squeers, c'est tout simplement le fils unique de Lord Clarendon, un des plus grands seigneurs de l'Angleterre. Voilà justement ce que je disais tout à l'heure. Dans ces romans qui sont le rebut d'une imagination en délire, il n'y a pas de milieu. Ou bien vous êtes le dernier des mendians chargés d'une besace vide, ou bien, salut à vous! vous êtes duc et pair du royaume et chevalier de la Jarretière! Ou le manteau royal ou le haillon. Quelquefois, pour varier la thèse, on vous met par dessus vos haillons le manteau de pourpre. — Votre tête est pleine de vermine, à la bonne heure! mais laissez faire le romancier, il posera tout à l'heure sur vos immondes cheveux la couronne ducale. Ainsi procèdent M. Dickens et le Capitaine Marryat et tous les autres."

Here we have a third receipt for the confection of *Nicholas Nickleby*, — darkness and caverns, vice and blood, incest and adultery, "*battez mois tout ça*," and the thing is done. Considering that Mr. Dickens has not said a word about darkness, about caverns, about blood (further than a little harmless claret drawn from Squeers's nose), about the two other crimes mentioned by J. J., — is it not *de luxe* to put them into the Nickleby-receipt? Having read the romances of his own country, and no others, J. J. thought he was safe, no doubt, in introducing the last-named ingredients; but in England the people is still *tant soit peu prudes*, and will have none such fare. In what a luxury of filth, too, does this delicate critic indulge! *votre tête est pleine de vermine* (a flattering supposition for the French reader, by the way, and remarkable for its polite propriety). Your head is in this condition; but never mind; let the romancer do his work, and he will presently place upon *your filthy hair* (kind again) the ducal coronet. This is the way with Monsieur Dickens, Captain Marryat, and *the others.*

With whom, in Heaven's name? What has poor Dickens ever had to do with ducal crowns, or with the other ornaments of the kind which Monsieur Jules distributes to his friends? Tell lies about men, friend Jules, if you will, but not *such* lies. See, for the future, that they have a greater likelihood about them; and try if, at least when you are talking of propriety and decency of behavior, to have your words somewhat more cleanly, and your own manners as little offensive as possible.

And with regard to the character of Squeers, the impossibility of it, and the consequent folly of placing such a portrait in a work that pretends to be a painting of manners, that, too, is a falsehood like the rest. Such a disgrace to human nature not only existed, but existed in J. J.'s country of France. Who does not remember the history of the Boulogne schoolmaster, a year since, whom the newspapers called the "French Squeers"; and about the same time, in the neighborhood of Paris, there was a case still more atrocious, of a man and his wife who farmed some score of children, subjected them to ill-treatment so horrible, that only J. J. himself, in his nastiest fit of indignation, could describe it; and ended by murdering one or two, and starving all. The whole story was in the *Débats*, J. J.'s own newspaper, where the accomplished critic may read it.

JOHN LEECH'S PICTURES OF LIFE AND CHARACTER.

WE, who recall the consulship of Plancus, and quite respectable old-fogeyfied times, remember, amongst other amusements which we had as children, the pictures at which we were permitted to look. There was Boydell's Shakespeare, black and ghastly gallery of murky Opies, glum Northcotes, straddling Fuselis! there were Lear, Oberon, Hamlet, with starting muscles, rolling eyeballs, and long pointing quivering fingers; there was little Prince Arthur (Northcote) crying, in white satin, and bidding good Hubert not put out his eyes; there was Hubert crying; there was little Rutland being run through the poor little body by bloody Clifford; there was Cardinal Beaufort (Reynolds) gnashing his teeth, and grinning and howling demoniacally on his death-bed (a picture frightful to the present day); there was Lady Hamilton (Romney) waving a torch and dancing before a black background,— a melancholy museum indeed. Smirke's delightful Seven Ages only fitfully relieved its general gloom. We did not like to inspect it unless the elders were present, and plenty of lights and company were in the room.

Cheerful relatives used to treat us to Miss Linwood's. Let the children of the present generation thank their stars *that* tragedy is put out of their way. Miss Linwood's was worsted work. Your grandmother or grand-aunts took you there, and said the pictures were admirable. You saw "The Woodman" in worsted, with his axe and dog, trampling through the snow; the snow bitter cold to look at, the woodman's pipe wonderful; a gloomy piece, that made you shudder. There were large dingy pictures of woollen martyrs, and scowling warriors with limbs strongly knitted; there was especially, at the end of a black passage, a den of lions, that would frighten any boy not born in Africa, or Exeter Change, and accustomed to them.

Another exhibition used to be West's Gallery, where the pleasing figures of Lazarus in his grave-clothes, and Death on the Pale Horse, used to impress us children. The tombs of Westminster Abbey, the vaults at St. Paul's, the men in armor at the Tower, frowning ferociously out of their helmets, and wielding their dreadful swords; that superhuman Queen Elizabeth at the end of the room, a livid sovereign with glass eyes, a ruff, and a dirty satin petticoat, riding a horse covered with steel: who does not remember these sights in London in the consulship of Plancus? and the waxwork in Fleet Street, not like that of Madame Tussaud's, whose chamber of death is gay and brilliant, but a nice old gloomy waxwork, full of murderers; and as a chief attraction, the dead baby and the Princess Charlotte lying in state.

Our story-books had no pictures in them for the most part. Frank (dear old Frank!) had none; nor the Parent's Assistant; nor the Evenings at Home; nor our copy of the *Ami des Enfans:* there were a few just at the end of the Spelling Book; besides the allegory at the beginning, of Education leading up Youth to the temple of Industry, where Dr. Dilworth and Professor Walkinghame stood with crowns of laurel; there were, we say, just a few pictures at the end of the Spelling Book, little oval gray woodcuts of Bewick's, mostly of the Wolf and the Lamb, the Dog and the Shadow, and Brown, Jones, and Robinson with long ringlets and little tights; but for pictures, so to speak, what had we? The rough old wood-blocks in the old harlequin-backed fairy-books had served hundreds of years; before *our* Plancus, in the time of Priscus Plancus, — in Queen Anne's time, who knows? We were flogged at school; we were fifty boys in our boarding-house, and had to wash in a leaden trough, under a cistern, with lumps of fat yellow soap floating about in the ice and water. Are *our* sons ever flogged? Have they not dressing-rooms, hair-oil, hipbaths, and Baden towels? And what picture-books the young villains have! What have these children done that they should be so much happier than we were?

We had the Arabian Nights and Walter Scott, to be sure. Smirke's illustrations to the former are very fine. We did not know how good they were then; but we doubt whether we did not prefer the little old Miniature Library Nights with frontispieces by Uwins; for *these* books the pictures don't count. Every boy of imagination does his own pictures to Scott and the Arabian Nights best.

Of funny pictures there were none especially intended for us children. There was Rowlandson's Dr. Syntax: Doctor Syntax, in a fuzz-wig, on a horse with legs like sausages, riding races, making love, frolicking with rosy exuberant damsels. Those pictures were very funny, and that aqua-tinting and the gay-colored plates very pleasant to witness; but if we could not read the poem in those days, could we digest it in this? Nevertheless, apart from the text which we could not master, we remember Dr. Syntax pleasantly, like those cheerful painted hieroglyphics in the Nineveh Court at Sydenham. What matter for the arrow-head, illegible stuff? give us the placid grinning kings, twanging their jolly bows over their rident horses, wounding those good-humored enemies, who tumble gayly off the towers, or drown, smiling in the dimpling waters, amidst the anerithmon gelasma of the fish.

After Dr. Syntax, the apparition of Corinthian Tom, Jerry Hawthorne, and the facetious Bob Logic must be recorded, — a wondrous history indeed theirs was! When the future student of our manners comes to look over the pictures and the writing of these queer volumes, what will he think of our society, customs, and language in the consulship of Plancus? We have still in our mind's eye some of the pictures of that sportive gallery: the white coat, Prussian-blue pantaloons, Hessian boots, and hooked nose of Corinthian Tom; Jerry's green cut-away and leather gaiters; Bob Logic's green spectacles, and high-waisted surtout. "Corinthian," it appears, was the phrase applied to men of fashion and *ton* in Plancus's time: they were the brilliant predecessors of the "swell" of the present period, — brilliant, but somewhat barbarous it must be confessed. The Corinthians were in the habit of drinking a great deal too much in Tom Cribb's parlor; they used to go and see "life" in the ginshops; of nights, walking home (as well as they could), they used to knock down "Charleys," poor harmless old watchmen with lanterns, guardians of the streets of Rome, Planco Consule. They perpetrated a vast deal of boxing; they put on the "mufflers" in Jackson's rooms; they "sported their prads" in the Ring in the Park; they attended cock-fights, and were enlightened patrons of dogs and destroyers of rats. Besides these sports, the *délassemens* of gentlemen mixing with the people, our patricians, of course, occasionally enjoyed the society of their own class. What a wonderful picture that used to be of Corinthian Tom dancing with Corinthian Kate at Almack's! What a prodigious dress Kate wore! With what graceful *abandon* the pair flung their arms about as they swept through the mazy quadrille, with all the noblemen standing round in their stars and uniforms! You may still, doubtless, see the pictures at the British Museum, or find the volumes in the corner of some old country-house library. You are led to suppose that the English aristocracy of 1820 *did* dance and caper in that way, and box and drink at Tom Cribb's, and knock down watchmen; and the children of to-day, turning to their elders, may say, "Grandmamma, did you wear such a dress as that when you danced at Almack's? There was very little of it, grandmamma. Did grandpapa kill many watchmen when he was a young man, and frequent thieves, gin-shops, cock-fights, and the ring before you married him? Did he use to talk the extraordinary slang and jargon which is printed in this book? He is very much changed. He seems a gentlemanly old boy enough now."

In the above-named consulate, when *we* had grandfathers alive, there would be in the old gentleman's library in the country two or three old mottled portfolios, or great swollen scrap-books of blue paper, full of the comic prints of grandpapa's time, ere Plancus ever had the fasces borne before him. These prints were signed Gillray, Bunbury, Rowlandson, Woodward, and some actually George Cruikshank, for George is a veteran now, and he took the etching needle in hand as a child. He caricatured "Boney," borrowing not a little from Gillray in his first puerile efforts. He drew Louis XVIII. trying on Boney's boots. Before the century was actually in its teens we believe that George Cruikshank was amusing the public.

In those great colored prints in our grandfather's portfolios in the library, and in some other apartments of the house, where the caricatures used to be pasted in those days, we found things quite beyond our comprehension. Boney was represented as a fierce dwarf, with goggle eyes, a huge lace hat, and tricolored plume, a crooked sabre, reeking with blood, — a little demon, revelling in lust, murder, massacre. John Bull was shown kicking him a good deal; indeed, he was prodigiously kicked all through that series of pictures; by Sydney Smith and our brave allies the gallant Turks; by the excellent and patriotic Spaniards; by the amiable and indignant Russians, — all nations had boots at the service of poor Master Boney. How Pitt used to defy him! How good old George, King of Brobdignag, laughed at Gulliver-Boney, sailing about in his tank to make sport for their majesties! This little fiend, this beggar's brat, cowardly, murderous, and atheistic as he was (we remember in those old portfolios, pictures representing Boney and his family in rags, gnawing raw bones in a Corsican hut; Boney murdering the sick at Jaffa; Boney with a hookah and a large turban, having adopted the Turkish religion, &c.), — this Corsican monster, nevertheless, had some devoted friends in England, according to the Gillray chronicle, — a set of villains who loved atheism, tyranny, plunder, and wickedness, in general, like their French friend. In the pictures, these men were all represented as dwarfs, like their ally. The miscreants got into power at one time, and, if we remember right, were called the Broadbacked Administration. One with shaggy eyebrows and a bristly beard, the hirsute ringleader of the rascals, was, it appears, called Charles James Fox; another miscreant, with a blotched countenance, was a certain Sheridan; other imps were hight Erskine, Norfolk (Jockey of), Moira, Henry Petty. As in our childish innocence we used to look at these demons, now sprawling and tipsy in their cups; now scaling heaven, from which the angelic Pitt hurled them down; now cursing the light (their atrocious ringleader Fox was represented with hairy cloven feet, and a tail and horns); now kissing Boney's boot, but inevitably discomfited by Pitt and the other good angels, we hated these vicious wretches, as good children should; we were on the side of Virtue and Pitt and Grandpapa. But if our sisters wanted to look at the portfolios, the good old grandfather used to hesitate. There were some prints among them very odd indeed; some that girls could not understand; some that boys, indeed, had best not see. We swiftly turn over those prohibited pages. How many of them were in the wild, coarse, reckless, ribald, generous book of old English humor!

How savage the satire was, — how fierce the assault, — what garbage hurled at opponents, — what foul blows were hit, — what language of Billingsgate flung! Fancy a party in a country house now looking over Woodward's facetiæ, or some of the Gillray comicalities, or the slatternly Saturnalia of Rowlandson! Whilst we live we must laugh, and have folks to make us laugh. We cannot afford to lose Satyr, with his pipe and dances and gambols. But we have washed, combed, clothed, and taught the rogue good manners; or rather, let us say, he has learned them himself; for he is of nature soft and kindly, and he has put aside his mad pranks and tipsy habits; and, frolicsome always, has become gentle and harmless, smitten into shame by the pure presence of our women and the sweet confiding smiles of our children. Among the veterans, the old pictorial satirists, we have mentioned the famous name of one humorous designer who is still alive and at work. Did we not see, by his own hand, his own portrait of his own famous face, and whiskers, in the "Illustrated London News" the other day? There was a print in that paper of an assemblage of Teatotallers in Sadler's Wells Theatre, and we straightway recognized the old Roman hand, — the old Roman's of the time of Plancus, — George Cruikshank's. There were the old bonnets and droll faces and shoes, and short trousers, and figures of 1820, sure enough. And there was George (who has taken to the water-doctrine, as all the world knows) handing some teatotalleresses over a plank to the table where the pledge was being administered. How often has George drawn that picture of Cruikshank! Where have n't we seen it? How fine it was, facing the effigy of Mr. Ainsworth in "Ainsworth's Magazine," when George illustrated that periodical! How grand and severe he stands in that design in G. C.'s "Omnibus," where he represents himself tonged like St. Dunstan, and tweaking a wretch of a publisher by the nose! The collectors of George's etchings, — O the charming etchings! O the dear old German popular tales! — the capital "Points of Humor," — the delightful Phrenology and scrap-books, of the good time, *our* time, — Plancus's in fact, — the collectors of the Georgian etchings, we say, have at least a hundred pictures of the artist.

Why, we remember him in his favorite Hessian boots in "Tom and Jerry" itself; and in woodcuts as far back as the Queen's trial. He has rather deserted satire and comedy of late years, having turned his attention to the serious, and warlike, and sublime. Having confessed our age and prejudices, we prefer the comic and fanciful to the historic, romantic, and at present didactic George. May respect, and length of days, and comfortable repose attend the brave, honest, kindly, pure-minded artist, humorist, moralist! It was he first who brought English pictorial humor and children acquainted. Our young people and their fathers and mothers owe him many a pleasant hour and harmless laugh. Is there no way in which the country could acknowledge the long services and brave career of such a friend and benefactor?

Since George's time humor has been converted. Comus and his wicked satyrs and leering fauns have disappeared, and fled into the lowest haunts; and Comus's lady (if she had a taste for humor, which may be doubted) might take up our funny picture-books without the slightest precautionary squeamishness. What can be purer than the charming fancies of Richard Doyle? In all Mr. Punch's huge galleries can't we walk as safely as through Miss Pinkerton's school-rooms? And as we look at Mr. Punch's pictures, at the Illustrated News pictures, at all the pictures in the book-shop windows at this Christmas season, as oldsters, we feel a certain pang of envy against the youngsters, — they are too well off. Why had n't *we* picture-books? Why were we flogged so? A plague on the lictors and their rods in the time of Plancus!

And now, after this rambling preface, we are arrived at the subject in hand, — Mr. John Leech and his "Pictures of Life and Character," in the collection of Mr.

Punch. This book is better than plum-cake at Christmas. It is an enduring plum-cake, which you may eat, and which you may slice and deliver to your friends; and to which, having cut it, you may come again and welcome, from year's end to year's end. In the frontispiece you see Mr. Punch examining the pictures in his gallery, — a portly, well-dressed, middle-aged, respectable gentleman, in a white neckcloth, and a polite evening costume, — smiling in a very bland and agreeable manner upon one of his pleasant drawings, taken out of one of his handsome portfolios. Mr. Punch has very good reason to smile at the work and be satisfied with the artist. Mr. Leech, his chief contributor, and some kindred humorists, with pencil and pen have served Mr. Punch admirably. Time was, if we remember Mr. P's history rightly, that he did not wear silk stockings nor well-made clothes (the little dorsal irregularity in his figure is almost an ornament now, so excellent a tailor has he). He was of humble beginnings. It is said he kept a ragged little booth, which he put up at corners of streets; associated with beadles, policemen, his own ugly wife (whom he treated most scandalously), and persons in a low station of life; earning a precarious livelihood by the cracking of wild jokes, the singing of ribald songs, and halfpence extorted from passers by. He is the Satyric genius we spoke of anon: he cracks his jokes still, for satire must live; but he is combed, washed, neatly clothed, and ,perfectly presentable. He goes into the very best company; he keeps a stud at Melton; he has a moor in Scotland; he rides in the Park; has his stall at the opera; is constantly dining out at clubs and in private society; and goes every night in the season to balls and parties, where you see the most beautiful women possible. He is welcomed amongst his new friends, the great; though, like the good old English gentleman of the song, he does not forget the small. He pats the heads of street boys and girls; relishes the jokes of Jack the costermonger and Bob the dustman; good-naturedly spies out Molly the cook, flirting with policeman X, or Mary the nursemaid, as she listens to the fascinating guardsman. He used rather to laugh at guardsmen, "plungers," and other military men; and was until latter days very contemptuous in his behavior towards Frenchmen. He has a natural antipathy to pomp, and swagger, and fierce demeanor. But now that the guardsmen are gone to war, and the dandies of "The Rag" — dandies no more — are battling like heroes at Balaklava and Inkermann, by the side of their heroic allies, Mr. Punch's laughter is changed to hearty respect and enthusiasm. It is not against courage and honor he wars: but this great moralist — must it be owned? — has some popular British prejudices, and these led him in peace-time to laugh at soldiers and Frenchmen. If those hulking footmen who accompanied the carriages to the opening of Parliament the other day, would form a plush brigade, wear only gunpowder in their hair, and strike with their great canes on the enemy, Mr. Punch would leave off laughing at Jeames, who, meanwhile, remains among us, to all outward appearance regardless of satire, and calmly consuming his five meals per diem. Against lawyers, beadles, bishops and clergy, and authorities, Mr. Punch is still rather bitter. At the time of the Papal aggression he was prodigiously angry; and one of the chief misfortunes which happened to him at that period was that, through the violent opinions which he expressed regarding the Roman Catholic hierarchy, he lost the invaluable services, the graceful pencil, the harmless wit, the charming fancy of Mr. Doyle. Another member of Mr. Punch's cabinet, the biographer of Jeames, the author of "The Snob Papers," resigned his functions on account of Mr. Punch's assaults upon the present Emperor of the French nation, whose anger Jeames thought it was unpatriotic to arouse. Mr. Punch parted with these contributors: he filled their places with others as good. The boys at the railroad stations cried Punch just as cheerily, and sold just as many numbers, after these events as before.

There is no blinking the fact that in Mr. Punch's cabinet John Leech is the right-hand man. Fancy a number of Punch without Leech's pictures! What would you give for it? The learned gentlemen who write the work must feel that, without him, it were as well left alone. Look at the rivals whom the popularity of Punch has brought into the field; the direct imitators of Mr. Leech's manner, — the artists with a manner of their own, — how inferior their pencils are to his in humor, in depicting the public manners, in arresting, amusing the nation. The truth, the strength, the free vigor, the kind humor, the John Bull pluck and spirit of that hand are approached by no competitor. With what dexterity he draws a horse, a woman, a child! He feels them all, so to speak, like a man. What plump young beauties those are with which Mr. Punch's chief contributor supplies the old gentleman's pictorial harem! What famous thews and sinews Mr. Punch's horses have, and how Briggs, on the back of them, scampers across country! You see youth, strength, enjoyment, manliness in those drawings, and in none more so, to our thinking, than in the hundred pictures of children which this artist loves to design. Like a brave, hearty, good-natured

Briton, he becomes quite soft and tender with the little creatures, pats gently their little golden heads, and watches with unfailing pleasure their ways, their sports, their jokes, laughter, caresses. *Enfans terribles* come home from Eton; young Miss practising her first flirtation; poor little ragged Polly making dirt pies in the gutter, or staggering under the weight of Jacky, her nurse-child, who is as big as herself, — all these little ones, patrician and plebeian, meet with kindness from this kind heart, and are watched with curious nicety by this amiable observer.

We remember, in one of those ancient Gillray portfolios, a print which used to cause a sort of terror in us youthful spectators, and in which the Prince of Wales (His Royal Highness was a Foxite then) was represented as sitting alone in a magnificent hall after a voluptuous meal, and using a great steel fork in the guise of a toothpick. Fancy the first young gentleman living employing such a weapon in such a way! The most elegant Prince of Europe engaged with a two-pronged iron fork, — the heir of Britannia with a *bident!* The man of genius who drew that picture saw little of the society which he satirized and amused. Gillray watched public characters as they walked by the shop in St. James's Street, or passed through the lobby of the House of Commons. His studio was a garret, or little better; his place of amusement, a tavern-parlor where his club held its nightly sittings over their pipes and sanded floor. You could not have society represented by men to whom it was not familiar. When Gavarni came to England a few years since — one of the wittiest of men, one of the most brilliant and dexterous of draughtsmen — he published a book of *Les Anglais*, and his *Anglais* were all

Frenchmen. The eye, so keen and so long practised to observe Parisian life, could not perceive English character. A social painter must be of the world which he depicts, and native to the manners which he portrays.

Now, any one who looks over Mr. Leech's portfolio must see that the social pictures which he gives us are authentic. What comfortable little drawing-rooms and dining-rooms, what snug libraries we enter; what fine young-gentlemanly wags they are, those beautiful little dandies who wake up gouty old grandpapa to ring the bell; who decline aunt's pudding and custards, saying that they will reserve themselves for an anchovy toast with the claret; who talk together in ball-room doors, where Fred whispers Charley, — pointing to a dear little partner seven years old, — "My dear Charley, she has very much gone off; you should have seen that girl last season!" Look well at everything appertaining to the economy of the famous Mr. Briggs; how snug, quiet, appropriate all the appointments are! What a comfortable, neat, clean, middle-class house Briggs's is (in the Bayswater suburb of London, we should guess, from the sketches of the surrounding scenery)! What a good stable he has, with a loose box for those celebrated hunters which he rides! How pleasant, clean, and warm his breakfast-table looks! What a trim little maid brings in the top-boots which horrify Mrs. B.! What a snug dressing-room he has, complete in all its appointments, and in which he appears trying on the delightful hunting-cap which Mrs. Briggs flings into the fire! How cosey all the Briggs party seem in their dining-room, Briggs reading a Treatise on Dog-breaking by a lamp; Mamma and Grannie with their respective needle-works; the children clustering round a great book of prints, —

a great book of prints such as this before us, which, at this season, must make thousands of children happy by as many firesides! The inner life of all these people is represented: Leech draws them as naturally as Teniers depicts Dutch boors, or Morland pigs and stables. It is your house and mine: we are looking at everybody's family circle. Our boys coming from school give themselves such airs, the young scapegraces! our girls, going to parties, are so tricked out by fond mammas, — a social history of London in the middle of the nineteenth century. As such future students — lucky they to have a book so pleasant — will regard these pages: even the mutations of fashion they may follow here if they be so inclined. Mr. Leech has as fine an eye for tailory and millinery as for horse-flesh. How they change those cloaks and bonnets! How we have to pay milliners' bills from year to year! Where are those prodigious châtelaines of 1850 which no lady could be without? Where those charming waistcoats, those "stunning" waistcoats, which our young girls used to wear a few brief seasons back, and which cause 'Gus, in the sweet little sketch of "La Mode," to ask Ellen for her tailor's address! 'Gus is a young warrior by this time, very likely facing the enemy at Inkermann; and pretty Ellen, and that love of a sister of hers, are married and happy, let us hope, superintending one of those delightful nursery scenes which our artist depicts with such tender humor. Fortunate artist, indeed! You see he must have been bred at a good public school; that he has ridden many a good horse in his day; paid, no doubt, out of his own purse for the originals of some of those lovely caps and bonnets; and watched paternally the ways, smiles, frolics, and slumbers of his favorite little people.

As you look at the drawings, secrets come out of them, — private jokes, as it were, imparted to you by the author for your special delectation. How remarkably, for instance, has Mr. Leech observed the hair-dressers of the present age! Look at "Mr. Tongs," whom that hideous old bald woman, who ties on her bonnet at the glass, informs that "she has used the whole bottle of Balm of California, but her hair comes off yet." You can see the bear's grease not only on Tongs's head but on his hands, which he is clapping clammily together. Remark him who is telling his client "there is cholera in the hair"; and that lucky rogue whom the young lady bids to cut off "a long thick piece" — for somebody, doubtless. All these men are different, and delightfully natural and absurd. Why should hair-dressing be an absurd profession?

The amateur will remark what an excellent part hands play in Mr. Leech's pieces: his admirable actors use them with perfect naturalness. Look at Betty, putting the urn down; at cook, laying her hands on the kitchen table, whilst her policeman grumbles at the cold meat. They are cook's and housemaid's hands without mistake, and not without a certain beauty too. The bald old lady, who is tying her bonnet at Tongs's, has hands which you see are trembling. Watch the fingers of the two old harridans who are talking scandal: for what long years past they have pointed out holes in their neighbors' dresses and mud on their flounces. "Here's a go! I've lost my diamond ring." As the dustman utters this pathetic cry, and looks at his hand, you burst out laughing. These are among the little points of humor. One could indicate hundreds of such as one turns over the pleasant pages.

There is a little snob or gent, whom we all of us know,

who wears little tufts on his little chin, outrageous pins and pantaloons, smokes cigars on tobacconists' counters, sucks his cane in the streets, struts about with Mrs. Snob and the baby (the latter an immense woman, whom Snob nevertheless bullies), who is a favorite abomination of Leech, and pursued by that savage humorist into a thousand of his haunts. There he is, choosing waistcoats at the tailor's, — such waistcoats! Yonder he is giving a shilling to the sweeper who calls him "capting"; now he is offering a paletot to a huge giant who is going out in the rain. They don't know their own pictures, very likely; if they did, they would have a meeting, and thirty or forty of them would be deputed to thrash Mr. Leech. One feels a pity for the poor little bucks. In a minute or two, when we close this discourse and walk the streets, we shall see a dozen such.

Ere we shut the desk up, just one word to point out to the unwary specially to note the backgrounds of landscapes in Leech's drawings, — homely drawings of moor and wood, and sea-shore and London street, — the scenes of his little dramas. They are as excellently true to nature as the actors themselves; our respect for the genius and humor which invented both increases as we look and look again at the designs. May we have more of them; more pleasant Christmas volumes, over which we and our children can laugh together. Can we have too much of truth, and fun, and beauty, and kindness?

LITTLE TRAVELS AND ROAD-SIDE SKETCHES.

No. I.

FROM RICHMOND IN SURREY TO BRUSSELS IN BELGIUM.

QUITTED the Rose Cottage Hotel at Richmond, one of the comfortablest, quietest, cheapest, neatest, little inns in England, and a thousand times preferable, in my opinion, to the Star and Garter, whither, if you go alone, a sneering waiter, with his hair curled, frightens you off the premises; and where, if you are bold enough to brave the sneering waiter, you have to pay ten shillings for a bottle of claret; and whence, if you look out of the window, you gaze on a view which is so rich that it seems to knock you down with its splendor, — a view that has its hair curled like the swaggering waiter: I say, I quitted the Rose Cottage Hotel with deep regret, believing that I should see nothing so pleasant as its gardens, and its veal-cutlets, and its dear little bowling-green, elsewhere. But the time comes when people must go out of town, and so I got on the top of the omnibus, and the carpet-bag was put inside.

If I were a great prince and rode outside of coaches (as I should if I were a great prince), I would, whether I smoked or not, have a case of the best Havanas in my pocket, — not for my own smoking, but to give them to the snobs on the coach, who smoke the vilest cheroots. They poison the air with the odor of their filthy weeds. A man at all easy in his circumstances would spare himself much annoyance by taking the above simple precaution.

A gentleman sitting behind me tapped me on the back and asked for a light. He was a footman, or rather valet. He had no livery, but the three friends who accompanied him were tall men in pepper-and-salt undress jackets, with a duke's coronet on their buttons.

After tapping me on the back, and when he had finished his cheroot, the gentleman produced another wind-instrument, which he called a "kinopium," — a sort of trumpet, on which he showed a great inclination to play. He began puffing out of the "kinopium" a most abominable air, which he said was the "Duke's March." It was played by particular request of one of the pepper-and-salt gentry.

The noise was so abominable that even the coachman objected (although my friend's brother footmen were ravished with it), and said that it was not allowed to play toons on *his* bus. "Very well," said the valet, "*we 're only of the Duke of B——'s establishment,* THAT 'S ALL." The coachman could not resist that appeal to his fashionable feelings. The valet was allowed to play his infernal kinopium, and the poor fellow (the coachman), who had lived in some private families, was quite anxious to conciliate the footmen of the Duke of Buccleuch's establishment, that 's all, and told several stories of his having been groom in Captain Hoskins's family, *nephew of Governor Hoskins,* which stories the footmen received with great contempt.

The footmen were like the rest of the fashionable world in this respect. I felt for my part that I respected them. They were in daily communication with a duke! They were not the rose, but they had lived beside it. There is an odor in the English aristocracy which intoxicates plebeians. I am sure that any commoner in England, though he would die rather than confess it, would have a respect for those great, big, hulking duke's footmen.

The day before, her Grace, the Duchess, had passed us alone in a chariot-and-four with two outriders. What better mark of innate superiority could man want? Here was a slim lady who required four — six horses to herself, and four servants (kinopium was, no doubt, one of the number) to guard her.

We were sixteen inside and out, and had consequently an eighth of a horse a-piece.

A duchess $= 6$, a commoner $= \frac{1}{8}$, that is to say,

$$1 \text{ duchess} = 48 \text{ commoners.}$$

If I were a duchess of the present day, I would say to the duke, my noble husband, "My dearest Grace, I think, when I travel alone in my chariot from Hammersmith to London, I will not care for the outriders. In these days, when there is so much poverty and so much disaffection in the country, we should not *éclabousser* the *canaille* with the sight of our preposterous prosperity."

But this is, very likely, only plebeian envy, and, I dare say, if I were a lovely duchess of the realm, I would ride in a coach-and-six, with a coronet on the top of my bonnet, and a robe of velvet and ermine, even in the dog-days.

Alas! these are the dog-days. Many dogs are abroad, — snarling dogs, biting dogs, envious dogs, mad dogs;

beware of exciting the fury of such with your flaming red velvet and dazzling ermine. It makes ragged Lazarus doubly hungry to see Dives feasting in cloth of gold; and so if I were a beauteous duchess * * * Silence, vain man, can the queen herself make you a duchess? Be content, then, nor jibe at thy betters of "the Duke of B———'s establishment, — that 's all."

On board the Antwerpen, off everywhere.

We have bidden adieu to Billingsgate, we have passed the Thames Tunnel; it is one o'clock, and, of course, people are thinking of being hungry. What a merry place a steamer is on a calm sunny summer forenoon, and what an appetite every one seems to have! We are, I assure you, no less than one hundred and seventy noblemen and gentlemen together, pacing up and down under the awning, or lolling on the sofas in the cabin, and hardly have we passed Greenwich when the feeding begins. The company was at the brandy and soda-water in an instant (there is a sort of legend that the beverage is a preservative against sea-sickness), and I admired the penetration of gentlemen who partook of the drink. In the first place, the steward *will* put so much brandy into the tumbler that it is fit to choke you; and, secondly, the soda-water, being kept as near as possible to the boiler of the engine, is of a fine wholesome heat when presented to the hot and thirsty traveller. Thus he is prevented from catching any sudden cold which might be dangerous to him.

The forepart of the vessel is crowded to the full as much as the genteeler quarter. There are four carriages, each with piles of imperials and aristocratic gimcracks of travel, under the wheels of which those personages have to clamber who have a mind to look at the bowsprit, and perhaps to smoke a cigar at ease. The carriages overcome, you find yourself confronted by a huge penful of Durham oxen, lying on hay and surrounded by a barricade of oars. Fifteen of these horned monsters maintain an incessant mooing and bellowing. Beyond the cows come a heap of cotton-bags, beyond the cotton-bags more carriages, more pyramids of travelling trunks, and valets and couriers bustling and swearing round about them. And already, and in various corners and niches, lying on coils of rope, black tar cloths, ragged cloaks, or hay, you see a score of those dubious fore-cabin passengers, who are never shaved, who always look unhappy, and appear getting ready to be sick.

At one, dinner begins in the after-cabin, — boiled salmon, boiled beef, boiled mutton, boiled cabbage, boiled potatoes, and parboiled wine for any gentlemen who like it, and two roast ducks between seventy. After this, knobs of cheese are handed round on a plate, and there is a talk of a tart somewhere at some end of the table. All this I saw peeping through a sort of meat-safe which ventilates the top of the cabin, and very happy and hot did the people seem below.

"How the deuce *can* people dine at such an hour?" say several genteel fellows who are watching the manœuvres. "I can't touch a morsel before seven."

But somehow at half past three o'clock we had dropped a long way down the river. The air was delightfully fresh, the sky of a faultless cobalt, the river shining and flashing like quicksilver, — and at this period steward runs against me, bearing two great smoking dishes covered by two great glistening hemispheres of tin. "Fellow," says I, "what's that?"

He lifted up the cover, it was ducks and green peas, by jingo!

"What, have n't they done *yet*, the greedy creatures?" I asked. "Have the people been feeding for three hours?"

"Law bless you, sir, it 's the second dinner. Make haste, or you won't get a place"; at which words a genteel party, with whom I had been conversing, instantly tumbled down the hatchway, and I find myself one of the second relay of seventy who are attacking the boiled salmon, boiled beef, boiled cabbage, &c. As for the ducks, I certainly had some peas, very fine yellow stiff peas, that ought to have been split before they were boiled; but, with regard to the ducks, I saw the animals gobbled up before my eyes by an old widow lady and her party just as I was shrieking to the steward to bring a knife and fork to carve them. The fellow (I mean the widow lady's whiskered companion)! I saw him eat peas with the very knife with which he had dissected the duck!

After dinner (as I need not tell the keen observer of human nature who peruses this) the human mind, if the body be in a decent state, expands into gayety and benevolence, and the intellect longs to measure itself in friendly converse with the divers intelligences around it. We ascend upon deck, and after eying each other for a brief space, and with a friendly modest hesitation, we begin anon to converse about the weather, and other profound and delightful themes of English discourse. We confide to each other our respective opinions of the ladies round about us. Look at that charming creature in a pink bonnet, and a dress of the pattern of a Kilmarnock snuff-box; a stalwart Irish gentleman in a green coat and bushy red whiskers is whispering something very agreeable into her ear, as is the wont of gentlemen of his nation; for her dark eyes kindle, her red lips open, and give an opportunity to a dozen beautiful pearly teeth to display themselves, and glance brightly in the sun, while round the teeth and the lips a number of lovely dimples make their appearance, and her whole countenance assumes a look of perfect health and happiness. See her companion in shot silk and a dove-colored parasol; in what a graceful Watteau-like attitude she reclines. The tall courier, who has been bouncing about the deck in attendance upon these ladies (it is his first day of service, and he is eager to make a favorable impression on them and the lady's-maids too), has just brought them from the carriage a small paper of sweet cakes (nothing is prettier than to see a pretty woman eating sweet biscuits), and a bottle that evidently contains Malmsey madeira. How daintily they sip it; how happy they seem; how that lucky rogue of an Irishman prattles away! Yonder is a noble group indeed; an English gentleman and his family. Children, mother, grandmother, grown-up daughters, father, and domestics, twenty-two in all. They have a table to themselves on the deck, and the consumption of eatables among them is really endless. The nurses have been bustling to and fro, and bringing first, slices of cake; then dinner; then tea, with huge family jugs of milk; and the little people have been playing hide-and-seek round the deck, — coquetting with the other children, and making friends of every soul on board. I love to see the kind eyes of women fondly watching them as they gambol about; a female face, be it ever so plain, when occupied in regarding children, becomes celestial almost, and a man can hardly fail to be good and happy while he is looking on at such sights. "Ah, sir," says a great big man, whom you would not accuse of sentiment, "I have a couple of those little things at home"; and he stops and heaves a great big sigh and swallows down a half tumbler of cold something and water. We know what the honest fellow means well enough. He is saying to himself, "God bless my girls and their mother!" but, being a Briton, is too manly to speak out in a more intelligible way. Perhaps it is as well for him to be quiet, and not chatter and gesticulate like those Frenchmen a few yards from him, who are chirping over a bottle of champagne.

There is, as you may fancy, a number of such groups on the deck, and a pleasant occupation it is for a lonely man to watch them and build theories upon them, and examine those two personages seated cheek by jowl. One is an English youth, travelling for the first time, who has been hard at his guide-book during the whole journey. He has a *Manuel du Voyageur* in his pocket; a very pretty, amusing little oblong work it is too, and might be very useful, if the foreign people in three languages, among whom you travel, would but give the answers set down in the book, or understand the questions you put to them out of it. The other honest gentleman in the fur cap, what can his occupation be? We know him at once for what he is. "Sir," says he, in a fine German accent, "I am a brofessor of languages, and will gif you lessons in Danish, Swedish, English, Bortuguese, Spanish, and Bersian." Thus occupied in meditations, the rapid hours and the rapid steamer pass quickly on. The sun is sinking, and, as he drops, the ingenious luminary sets the Thames on fire: several worthy gentlemen, watch in hand, are eagerly examining the phenomena attending his disappearance, — rich clouds of purple and gold, that form the curtains of his bed, — little barks that pass black across his disk, his disk every instant dropping nearer and nearer into the water. "There he goes!" says one sagacious observer. "No he does n't," cries another. Now he is gone, and the steward is already threading the deck, asking the passengers, right and left, if they will take a little supper. What a grand object is a sunset, and what a wonder is an appetite at sea! Lo! the horned moon shines pale over Margate, and the red beacon is gleaming from distant Ramsgate pier.

* * * * *

A great rush is speedily made for the mattresses that lie in the boat at the ship's side; and, as the night is delightfully calm, many fair ladies and worthy men determine to couch on deck for the night. The proceedings of the former, especially if they be young and pretty, the philosopher watches with indescribable emotion and interest. What a number of pretty coquetries do the ladies perform, and into what pretty attitudes do they take care to fall! All the little children have been gathered up by the nursery-maids, and are taken down to roost below. Balmy sleep seals the eyes of many tired wayfarers, as you see in the case of the Russian nobleman asleep among the portmanteaus; and Titmarsh, who has been walking the deck for some time with a great mattress on his shoulders, knowing full well, that were he to relinquish it for an instant, some other person would seize on it, now stretches his bed upon the deck, wraps his cloak about his knees, draws his white cotton nightcap tight over his head and ears, and, as the smoke of his cigar rises calmly upwards to the deep sky and the cheerful twinkling stars, he feels himself exquisitely happy, and thinks of thee, my Juliana!

* * * * *

Why people, because they are in a steamboat, should get up so deucedly early I cannot understand. Gentlemen have been walking over my legs ever since three o'clock this morning, and, no doubt, have been indulging in personalities (which I hate) regarding my appearance and manner of sleeping, lying, snoring. Let the wags laugh on; but a far pleasanter occupation is to sleep until breakfast-time, or near it.

The tea and ham and eggs, which, with a beef-steak or two, and three or four rounds of toast, form the component parts of the above-named elegant meal, are taken in the river Scheldt. Little, neat, plump-looking churches and villages are rising here and there among tufts of trees and pastures that are wonderfully green. To the right, as the Guide-book says, is Walcheren; and on the left, Cadsand, memorable for the English expedition, of 1809, when Lord Chatham, Sir Walter Manny, and Henry, Earl of Derby, at the head of the English, gained a great victory over the Flemish mercenaries in the pay of Philippe of Valois. The cloth-yard shafts of the English archers did great execution. Flushing was taken, and Lord Chatham returned to England, where he distinguished himself greatly in the debates on the American war, which he called the brightest jewel of the British crown. You see, my love, that, though an artist by profession, my education has by no means been neglected; and what, indeed, would be the pleasure of travel, unless these charming historical recollections were brought to bear upon it?

Antwerp.

As many hundreds of thousands of English visit this city (I have met at least a hundred of them in this half-hour walking the streets, Guide-book in hand), and as the ubiquitous Murray has already depicted the place, there is no need to enter into a long description of it,— its neatness, its beauty, and its stiff antique splendor. The tall, pale houses have many of them crimped gables, that look like Queen Elizabeth's ruffs. There are as many people in the streets as in London at three o'clock in the morning. The market-women wear bonnets of a flower-pot shape, and have shining brazen milk-pots, which are delightful to the eyes of a painter. Along the quays of the lazy Scheldt are innumerable good-natured groups of beer-drinkers (small-beer is the most good-natured drink in the world); along the barriers outside of the town, and by the glistening canals, are more beer-shops, and more beer-drinkers. The city is defended by the queerest fat military. The chief traffic is between the hotels and the railroad. The hotels give wonderful good dinners; and especially at the Grand Laboureur may be mentioned a peculiar tart, which is the best of all tarts that ever a man ate since he was ten years old. A moonlight walk is delightful. At ten o'clock the whole city is quiet; and so little changed does it seem to be, that you may walk back three hundred years into time, and fancy yourself a majestical Spaniard, or an oppressed and patriotic Dutchman, at your leisure. You enter the inn, and the old Quentin Durward courtyard, in which the old towers look down. There is a sound of singing, — singing at midnight. Is it Don Sombrero, who is singing an Andalusian seguidilla under the window of the Flemish burgomaster's daughter? Ah, no! it is a fat Englishman in a zephyr coat; he is drinking cold gin-and-water in the moonlight, and warbling softly: —

"Nix my dolly, pals, fake away,
N—ix my dolly, pals, fake a—a—way."

I wish the good people would knock off the top part of Antwerp Cathedral spire. Nothing can be more gracious and elegant than the lines of the first two compartments; but near the top there bulges out a little round, ugly, vulgar, Dutch monstrosity (for which the architects have, no doubt, a name) which offends the eye cruelly. Take the Apollo, and set upon him a bob-wig and a little cocked hat; imagine God save the King ending with a jig; fancy a polonaise, or procession of slim, stately, elegant court beauties, headed by a buffoon dancing a hornpipe. Marshal Gérard should have discharged a bomb-shell at that abomination, and have given the noble steeple a chance to be finished in the grand style of the early fifteenth century, in which it was begun.

This style of criticism is base and mean, and quite contrary to the orders of the immortal Goethe, who w[illegible] only for allowing the eye to recognize the beauties of a great work, but would have its defects passed over. It is an unhappy, luckless organization which will be perpetually fault-finding, and in the midst of a grand concert of music will persist only in hearing that unfortunate fiddle out of tune.

Within — except where the rococo architects have introduced their ornaments (here is the fiddle out of tune again) — the cathedral is noble. A rich, tender sunshine is streaming in through the windows, and gilding the stately edifice with the purest light. The admirable stained glass windows are not too brilliant in their colors. The organ is playing a rich, solemn music; some two hundred of people are listening to the service; and there is scarce one of the women kneeling on her chair, enveloped in her full, majestic black drapery, but is not a fine study for a painter. These large black mantles of heavy silk brought over the heads of the women, and covering their persons, fall into such fine folds of drapery, that they cannot help being picturesque and noble. See, kneeling by the side of two of those fine devout-looking figures, is a lady in a little twiddling Parisian hat and feather, in a little lace mantelet, in a tight gown and a bustle. She is almost as monstrous as yonder figure of the Virgin, in a hoop, and with a huge crown and a ball and a sceptre; and a bambino dressed in a little hoop, and in a little crown, round which are clustered flowers and pots of orange-trees, and before which many of the faithful are at prayer. Gentle clouds of incense come wafting through the vast edifice; and in the lulls of the music you hear the faint chant of the priest, and the silver tinkle of the bell.

Six Englishmen, with the Commissionaires and the Murray's Guide-books in their hands, are looking at the "Descent from the Cross." Of this picture the Guide-book gives you orders how to judge. If it is the end of religious painting to express the religious sentiment, a hundred of inferior pictures must rank before Rubens. Who was ever piously affected by any picture of the master? He can depict a livid thief writhing upon the cross, sometimes a blonde Magdalen weeping below it; but it is a Magdalen a very short time indeed after her repentance; her yellow brocades and flaring satins are still those which she wore when she was of the world; her body has not yet lost the marks of the feasting and voluptuousness in which she used to indulge, according to the legend. Not one of Rubens's pictures, among all the scores that decorate chapels and churches here, has the least tendency to purify, to touch the affections, or to awaken the feelings of religious respect and wonder. The "Descent from the Cross" is vast, gloomy, and awful; but the awe inspired by it is, as I take it, altogether material. He might have painted a picture of any criminal broken on the wheel, and the sensation inspired by it would have been precisely similar. Nor in a religious picture do you want the *savoir-faire* of the master to be always protruding itself; it detracts from the feeling of reverence, just as the thumping of cushion and the spouting of tawdry oratory does from a sermon. Meek religion disappears, shouldered out of the desk by the pompous, stalwart, big-chested, fresh-colored, bushy-whiskered pulpiteer. Rubens's piety has always struck us as of this sort. If he takes a pious subject, it is to show you in what a fine way he, Peter Paul Rubens, can treat it. He never seems to doubt but that he is doing it a great honor. His "Descent from the Cross," and its accompanying wings and cover, are a set of puns upon the word Christopher, of which the taste is more odious than that of the hooped-petticoated Virgin yonder, with her artificial flowers, and her rings and brooches. The people who made an offering of that hooped-petticoat did their best, at any rate; they knew no better. There is humility in that simple, quaint present; trustfulness and kind intention. Looking about at other altars, you see (much to the horror of our pious) all sorts of queer little emblems hanging up under little pyramids of penny candles that are sputtering and flaring there. Here you have a silver arm, or a little gold toe, or a wax leg, or a gilt eye, signifying and commemorating cures that have been performed by the supposed intercession of the saint over whose chapel they hang. Well, although they are abominable superstitions, yet these queer little offerings seem to me to be a great deal more pious than Rubens's big pictures; just as is the widow with her poor little mite compared to the swelling Pharisee, who flings his purse of gold into the plate.

A couple of days of Rubens and his church pictures makes one thoroughly and entirely sick of him. His very genius and splendor palls upon one, even taking the pictures as worldly pictures. One grows weary of being perpetually feasted with this rich, coarse, steaming food. Considering them as church pictures, I don't want to go to church to hear, however splendid, an organ play the "British Grenadiers."

The Antwerpians have set up a clumsy bronze statue of their divinity in a square of the town; and those who have not enough of Rubens in the churches may study him, and, indeed, to much greater advantage, in a good, well-lighted museum. Here there is one picture, a dying saint taking the communion, a large piece, ten or eleven feet high, and painted in an incredibly short space of time, which is extremely curious, indeed, for the painter's study. The picture is scarcely more than an immense magnificent sketch; but it tells the secret of the artist's manner, which, in the midst of its dash and splendor, is curiously methodical. Where the shadows are warm the lights are cold, and *vice versâ;* and the picture has been so rapidly painted, that the tints lie raw by the side of one another, the artist not having taken the trouble to blend them.

There are two exquisite Vandykes (whatever Sir Joshua may say of them), and in which the very management of the gray tones which the president abuses forms the principal excellence and charm. Why, after all, are we not to have our opinion? Sir Joshua is not the Pope. The color of one of those Vandykes is as fine as *fine*

Paul Veronese, and the sentiment beautifully tender and graceful.

I saw, too, an exhibition of the modern Belgian artists (1843), the remembrance of whose pictures after a month's absence has almost entirely vanished. Wapper's hand, as I thought, seemed to have grown old and feeble, Verboeckhoven's cattle-pieces are almost as good as Paul Potter's, and Keyser has dwindled down into namby-pamby prettiness, pitiful to see in the gallant young painter who astonished the Louvre artists ten years ago by a hand almost as dashing and ready as that of Rubens himself. There were besides many caricatures of the new German school, which are in themselves caricatures of the masters before Raphael.

An instance of honesty may be mentioned here with applause. The writer lost a pocket-book, containing a passport and a couple of modest ten-pound notes. The person who found the portfolio ingeniously put it into the box of the post-office, and it was faithfully restored to the owner; but somehow the two ten-pound notes were absent. It was, however, a great comfort to get the passport, and the pocket-book, which must be worth about ninepence.

BRUSSELS.

It was night when we arrived by the railroad from Antwerp at Brussels; the route is very pretty and interesting, and the flat countries through which the road passes in the highest state of peaceful, smiling cultivation. The fields by the roadside are enclosed by hedges as in England, the harvest was in part down, and an English country gentleman who was of our party pronounced the crops to be as fine as any he had ever seen. Of this matter a Cockney cannot judge accurately, but any man can see with what extraordinary neatness and care all these little plots of ground are tilled, and admire the richness and brilliancy of the vegetation. Outside of the moat of Antwerp, and at every village by which we passed, it was pleasant to see the happy congregations of well-clad people that basked in the evening sunshine, and soberly smoked their pipes and drank their Flemish beer. Men who love this drink must, as I fancy, have something essentially peaceful in their composition, and must be more easily satisfied than folks on our side of the water. The excitement of Flemish beer is, indeed, not great. I have tried both the white beer and the brown; they are both of the kind which schoolboys denominate "swipes," very sour and thin to the taste, but served, to be sure, in quaint Flemish jugs that do not seem to have changed their form since the days of Rubens, and must please the lovers of antiquarian knick-knacks. Numbers of comfortable-looking women and children sat beside the head of the family upon the tavern-benches, and it was amusing to see one little fellow of eight years old smoking, with much gravity, his father's cigar. How the worship of the sacred plant of tobacco has spread through all Europe! I am sure that the persons who cry out against the use of it are guilty of superstition and unreason, and that it would be a proper and easy task for scientific persons to write an encomium upon the weed. In solitude it is the pleasantest companion possible, and in company never *de trop*. To a student it suggests all sorts of agreeable thoughts, it refreshes the brain when weary, and every sedentary cigar-smoker will tell you how much good he has had from it, and how he has been able to return to his labor, after a quarter of an hour's mild interval of the delightful leaf of Havannah. Drinking has gone from among us since smoking came in. It is a wicked error to say that smokers are drunkards; drink they do, but of gentle diluents mostly, for fierce stimulants of wine or strong liquors are abhorrent to the real lover of the Indian weed. Ah! my Juliana, join not in the vulgar cry that is raised against us. Cigars and cool drinks beget quiet conversations, good-humor, meditation; not hot blood such as mounts into the head of drinkers of apoplectic port or dangerous claret. Are we not more moral and reasonable than our forefathers? Indeed, I think so, somewhat; and many improvements of social life and converse must date with the introduction of the pipe.

We were a dozen tobacco-consumers in the wagon of the train that brought us from Antwerp; nor did the women of the party (sensible women!) make a single objection to the fumigation. But enough of this; only let me add, in conclusion, that an excellent Israelitish gentleman, Mr. Hartog of Antwerp, supplies cigars for a penny a-piece, such as are not to be procured in London for four times the sum.

Through smiling cornfields, then, and by little woods, from which rose here and there the quaint peaked towers of some old-fashioned *châteaux*, our train went smoking along at thirty miles an hour. We caught a glimpse of Mechlin steeple, at first dark against the sunset, and afterwards bright as we came to the other side of it, and admired long glistening canals or moats that surrounded the queer old town, and were lighted up in that wonderful way which the sun only understands, and not even Mr. Turner, with all his vermilion and gamboge, can put down on canvas. The verdure was everywhere astonishing, and we fancied we saw many golden Cuyps as we passed by these quiet pastures.

Steam-engines and their accompaniments, blazing forges, gaunt manufactories, with numberless windows and long black chimneys, of course take away from the romance of the place; but, as we whirled into Brussels, even these engines had a fine appearance. Three or four of the snorting, galloping monsters had just finished their journey, and there was a quantity of flaming ashes lying under the brazen bellies of each that looked properly lurid and demoniacal. The men at the station came out with flaming torches, — awful-looking fellows, indeed! Presently the different baggage was handed out, and, in the very worst vehicle I ever entered, and at the very slowest pace, we were borne to the Hôtel de Suède, from which house of entertainment this letter is written.

We strolled into the town, but, though the night was excessively fine and it was not yet eleven o'clock, the streets of the little capital were deserted, and the handsome blazing *cafés* round about the theatres contained no inmates. Ah, what a pretty sight is the Parisian Boulevard on a night like this! how many pleasant hours has one passed in watching the lights, and the hum, and the stir, and the laughter of those happy, idle people! There was none of this gayety here; nor was there a person to be found, except a skulking commissioner or two (whose real name in French is that of a fish that is eaten with fennel-sauce), and who offered to conduct us to certain curiosities in the town. What must we English not have done, that in every town in Europe we are to be fixed upon by scoundrels of this sort; and what a pretty reflection it is on our country that such rascals find the means of living on us!

Early the next morning we walked through a number of streets in the place, and saw certain sights. The Park is very pretty, and all the buildings round about it have an air of neatness,—almost of stateliness. The houses are tall, the streets spacious, and the roads extremely clean. In the Park is a little theatre, a *café* somewhat ruinous, a little palace for the king of this little kingdom, some smart public buildings (with S. P. Q. B. emblazoned on them, at which pompous inscription one cannot help laughing), and other rows of houses somewhat resembling a little Rue de Rivoli. Whether from my own natural greatness and magnanimity, or from that handsome share of national conceit that every Englishman possesses, my impressions of this city are certainly anything but respectful. It has an absurd kind of Lilliput look with it. There are soldiers, just as in Paris, better dressed, and doing a vast deal of drumming and bustle; and yet, somehow, far from being frightened at them, I feel inclined to laugh in their faces. There are little ministers, who work at their little bureaux, and to read the journals, how fierce they are! A great thundering *Times* could hardly talk more big. One reads about the rascally ministers, the miserable opposition, the designs of tyrants, the eyes of Europe, &c., just as one would in real journals. The *Moniteur* of Ghent belabors the *Independent* of Brussels; the *Independent* falls foul of the *Lynx;* and really it is difficult not to suppose sometimes that these working people are in earnest. And yet how happy were they *sua si bona norint!* Think what a comfort it would be to belong to a little state like this; not to abuse their privilege, but philosophically to use it. If I were a Belgian, I would not care one single fig about politics. I would not read thundering leading articles.

I would not have an opinion. What 's the use of an opinion here? Happy fellows! do not the French, the English, and the Prussians, spare them the trouble of thinking, and make all their opinions for them? Think of living in a country free, easy, respectable, wealthy, and with the nuisance of talking politics removed from out of it. All this might the Belgians have, and a part do they enjoy, but not the best part; no, these people will be brawling and by the ears, and parties run as high here as at Stoke Pogis or little Pedlington.

These sentiments were elicited by the reading of a paper at the *café* in the Park, where we sat under the trees for a while and sipped our cool lemonade. Numbers of statues decorate the place, the very worst I ever saw. These Cupids must have been erected in the time of the Dutch dynasty, as I judge from the immense posterior developments. Indeed the arts of the country are very low. The statues here, and the lions before the Prince of Orange's palace, would disgrace almost the figure-head of a ship.

Of course we paid our visit to this little lion of Brussels (the prince's palace, I mean). The architecture of the building is admirably simple and firm; and you remark about it, and all other works here, a high finish in doors, wood-works, paintings, &c., that one does not see in France, where the buildings are often rather sketched than completed, and the artist seems to neglect the limbs, as it were, and extremities of his figures.

The finish of this little place is exquisite. We went through some dozen of state rooms, paddling along over the slippery floors of inlaid woods in great slippers, without which we must have come to the ground. How did his Royal Highness the Prince of Orange manage when he lived here, and her Imperial Highness the Princess, and their excellencies the chamberlains, and the footmen? They must have been on their tails many times a day, that 's certain, and must have cut queer figures.

The ball-room is beautiful, — all marble, and yet with a comfortable, cheerful look. The other apartments are not less agreeable, and the people looked with intense satisfaction at some great lapis-lazuli tables, which the guide informed us were worth four millions, more or less; adding, with a very knowing look, that they were *un peu plus cher que l'or*. This speech has a tremendous effect on visitors, and when we met some of our steamboat companions in the Park or elsewhere, — in so small a place as this one falls in with them a dozen times a day, — "Have you seen the tables?" was the general question. Prodigious tables are they, indeed! Fancy a table, my dear, — a table four feet wide, — a table with legs. Ye Heavens! the mind can hardly picture to itself anything so beautiful and so tremendous!

There are some good pictures in the palace, too, but not so extraordinarily good as the guide-books and the guide would have us to think. The latter, like most men of his class, is an ignoramus, who showed us an Andrea del Sarto (copy or original), and called it a Correggio, and made other blunders of a like nature. As is the case in England, you are hurried through the rooms without being allowed time to look at the pictures, and, consequently, to pronounce a satisfactory judgment on them.

In the museum more time was granted me, and I spent some hours with pleasure there. It is an absurd little gallery, absurdly imitating the Louvre, with just such compartments and pillars as you see in the noble Paris gallery; only here the pillars and capitals are stucco and white in place of marble and gold, and plaster of Paris busts of great Belgians are placed between the pillars. An artist of the country has made a portrait containing them, and you will be ashamed of your ignorance when you hear many of their names. Old Tilly of Magdeburg figures in one corner; Rubens, the endless Rubens, stands in the midst. What a noble countenance it is, and what a manly, swaggering consciousness of power!

The picture to see here is a portrait, by the great Peter Paul, of one of the governesses of the Netherlands. It is just the finest portrait that ever was seen. Only a half-length, but such a majesty, such a force, such a splendor, such a simplicity about it! The woman is in a stiff, black dress, with a ruff, and a few pearls; a yellow curtain is behind her, — the simplest arrangement that can be conceived. But this great man knew how to rise to his occasion; and no better proof can be shown of what a fine gentleman he was than this his homage to the vice-queen. A common bungler would have painted her in her best clothes, with crown and sceptre, just as our queen has been painted by — but comparisons are odious. Here stands this majestic woman in her everyday working-dress of black satin, *looking your hat off*, as it were. Another portrait of the same personage hangs elsewhere in the gallery, and it is curious to observe the difference between the two, and see how a man of genius paints a portrait, and how a common limner executes it.

Many more pictures are there here by Rubens, or rather from Rubens's manufactory, — odious and vulgar most of them are, — fat Magdalens, coarse Saints, vulgar Virgins, with the scene-painter's tricks far too evident upon the canvas. By the side of one of the most astonishing color-pieces in the world, the "Worshipping of the Magi," is a famous picture of Paul Veronese, that cannot be too much admired. As Rubens sought in the first picture to dazzle and astonish by gorgeous variety, Paul in his seems to wish to get his effect by simplicity, and has produced the most noble harmony that can be conceived. Many more works are there that merit notice,— a singularly clever, brilliant, and odious Jordeans, for example; some curious costume-pieces; one or two works by the Belgian Raphael, who was a very Belgian Raphael, indeed; and a long gallery of pictures of the very oldest school, that, doubtless, afford much pleasure to the amateurs of ancient art. I confess that I am inclined to believe in very little that existed before the time of Raphael. There is, for instance, the Prince of Orange's picture by Perrugino, very pretty, indeed, up to a certain point, but all the heads are repeated, all the drawing is bad and affected; and this very badness and affectation is what the so-called Catholic school is always anxious to imitate. Nothing can be more juvenile or paltry than the works of the native Belgians here exhibited. Tin crowns are suspended over many of them, showing that the pictures are prize compositions, and pretty things, indeed, they are! Have you ever read an Oxford prize-poem? Well, these pictures are worse even than the Oxford poems,— an awful assertion to make.

In the matter of eating, dear sir, which is the next subject of the fine arts,— a subject that, after many hours' walking, attracts a gentleman very much, let me attempt to recall the transactions of this very day at the *table-d'hôte*. 1. green pea-soup; 2. boiled salmon; 3. muscles; 4. crimped skate; 5. roast meat; 6. patties; 7. melon; 8. carp, stewed with mushrooms and onions;

9. roast turkey; 10. cauliflower and butter; 11. fillets of venison *piqués,* with assafœtida sauce; 12. stewed calf's ear; 13. roast veal; 14. roast lamb; 15. stewed cherries; 16. rice pudding; 17. Gruyère cheese, and about twenty-four cakes of different kinds. Except 5, 13, and 14, I give you my word I ate of all written down here, with three rolls of bread and a score of potatoes. What is the meaning of it? How is the stomach of man brought to desire and to receive all this quantity? Do not gastronomists complain of heaviness in London after eating a couple of mutton-chops? Do not respectable gentlemen fall asleep in their arm-chairs? Are they fit for mental labor? Far from it. But look at the difference here; after dinner here one is as light as a gossamer. One walks with pleasure, reads with pleasure, writes with pleasure, — nay, there is the supper-bell going at ten o'clock, and plenty of eaters, too. Let lord-mayors and aldermen look to it, this fact of the extraordinary increase of appetite in Belgium, and, instead of steaming to Blackwall, come a little farther to Antwerp.

Of ancient architectures in the place, there is a fine old Port de Halle, which has a tall, gloomy, bastile look; a most magnificent town-hall, that has been sketched a thousand of times, and, opposite it, a building that I think would be the very model for a Conservative club-house in London. O how charming it would be to be a great painter, and give the character of the building, and the numberless groups round about it. The booths lighted up by the sun, the market-women in their gowns of brilliant hue, each group having a character, and telling its little story, the troops of men lolling in all sorts of admirable attitudes of ease round the great lamp.

Half a dozen light blue dragoons are lounging about, and peeping over the artist as the drawing is made, and the sky is more bright and blue than one sees it in an hundred years in London.

The priests of the country are a remarkably well-fed and respectable race, without that scowling, hang-dog look which one has remarked among reverend gentlemen in the neighboring country of France. Their reverences wear buckles to their shoes, light-blue neckcloths, and huge three-cornered hats in good condition. To-day, strolling by the cathedral, I heard the tinkling of a bell in the street, and beheld certain persons, male and female, suddenly plump down on their knees before a little procession that was passing. Two men in black held a tawdry red canopy, a priest walked beneath it holding the sacrament covered with a cloth, and before him marched a couple of little altar-boys in short white surplices, such as you see in Rubens, and holding lacquered lamps. A small train of street-boys followed the procession, cap in hand, and the clergyman finally entered a hospital for old women, near the church, the canopy and the lamp-bearers remaining without.

It was a touching scene, and, as I stayed to watch it, I could not but think of the poor old soul who was dying within, listening to the last words of prayer, led by the hand of the priest to the brink of the black, fathomless grave. How bright the sun was shining without all the time, and how happy and careless everything around us looked!

The Duke d'Arenberg has a picture-gallery worthy of his princely house. It does not contain great pieces, but titbits of pictures, such as suit an aristocratic epicure.

For such persons a great huge canvas is too much, it is like sitting down alone to a roasted ox; and they do wisely, I think, to patronize small, high-flavored, delicate *morceaux*, such as the duke has here.

Among them may be mentioned, with special praise, a magnificent small Rembrandt, a Paul Potter of exceeding minuteness and beauty, an Ostade, which reminds one of Wilkie's early performances, and a Dusart quite as good as Ostade. There is a Bergham, much more unaffected than that artist's works generally are; and, what is more precious in the eyes of many ladies as an object of art, there is, in one of the grand saloons, some needle-work done by the duke's own grandmother, which is looked at with awe by those admitted to see the palace.

The chief curiosity, if not the chief ornament of a very elegant library, filled with vases and bronzes, is a marble head, supposed to be the original head of the Laocoon. It is, unquestionably, a finer head than that which at present figures upon the shoulders of the famous statue. The expression of woe is more manly and intense; in the group, as we know it, the head of the principal figure has always seemed to me to be a grimace of grief, as are the two accompanying young gentlemen, with their pretty attitudes, and their little, silly, open-mouthed despondency. It has always had upon me the effect of a trick, that statue, and not of a piece of true art. It would look well in the vista of a garden; it is not august enough for a temple, with all its jerks, and twirls, and polite convulsions. But who knows what susceptibilities such a confession may offend? Let us say no more about the Laocoon, nor its head, nor its tail. The duke was offered its weight in gold, they say, for this head, and refused. It would be a shame to speak ill of such a treasure, but I have my opinion of the man who made the offer.

In the matter of sculpture almost all the Brussels churches are decorated with the most laborious wooden pulpits, which may be worth their weight in gold, too, for what I know, including his reverence preaching inside. At St. Gudule the preacher mounts into no less a place than the garden of Eden, being supported by Adam and Eve, by Sin and Death, and numberless other animals; he walks up to his desk by a rustic railing of flowers, fruits, and vegetables, with wooden peacocks, parroquets, monkeys biting apples, and many more of the birds and beasts of the field. In another church the clergyman speaks from out a hermitage; in a third from a carved palm-tree, which supports a set of oak clouds that form the canopy of the pulpit, and are, indeed, not much heavier in appearance than so many huge sponges. A priest, however tall or stout, must be lost in the midst of all these queer gimcracks; in order to be consistent, they ought to dress him up, too, in some odd, fantastical suit. I can fancy the curé of Meudon preaching out of such a place, or the Rev. Sydney Smith, or that famous clergyman of the time of the League, who brought all Paris to laugh and listen to him.

But let us not be too supercilious and ready to sneer. It is only bad taste. It may have been very true devotion which erected these strange edifices.

No. II.

GHENT. — BRUGES.

GHENT (1840).

THE Béguine College or Village is one of the most extraordinary sights that all Europe can show. On the confines of the town of Ghent you come upon an old-fashioned brick gate, that seems as if it were one of the city barriers; but, on passing it, one of the prettiest sights possible meets the eye: at the porter's lodge you see an old lady, in black and a white hood, occupied over her book; before you is a red church with a tall roof and fantastical Dutch pinnacles, and all around it rows upon rows of small houses, the queerest, neatest, nicest that ever were seen (a doll's house is hardly smaller or prettier); right and left, on each side of little alleys, these little mansions rise; they have a courtlet before them, in which some green plants or hollyhocks are growing; and to each house is a gate, that has mostly a picture or queer-carved ornament upon or about it, and bears the name, not of the Béguine who inhabits it, but of the saint to whom she may have devoted it, — the house of St. Stephen, the house of St. Donatus, the English or Angel Convent, and so on. Old ladies in black are pacing in the quiet alleys here and there, and drop the stranger a courtesy as he passes them and takes off his hat. Never were such patterns of neatness seen as these old ladies and their houses. I peeped into one or two of the chambers, of which the windows were open to the pleasant evening sun, and saw beds scrupulously plain, a quaint old chair or two, and little pictures of favorite saints decorating the spotless white walls. The old ladies kept up a quick, cheerful clatter, as they paused to gossip at the gates of their little domiciles; and with a great deal of artifice, and lurking behind walls, and looking at the church as if I intended to design that, I managed to get a sketch of a couple of them.

But what white paper can render the whiteness of their linen? what black ink can do justice to the lustre of their gowns and shoes? Both of the ladies had a neat ankle and a tight stocking; and I fancy that Heaven is quite as well served in this costume as in the dress of a scowling, stockingless friar, whom I had seen passing just before. The look and dress of the man made me shudder. His great red feet were bound up in a shoe open at the toes, a kind of compromise for a sandal. I had just seen him and his brethren at the Dominican Church, where a mass of music was sung, and orange-trees, flags, and banners, decked the aisle of the church.

One begins to grow sick of these churches, and the hideous exhibitions of bodily agonies that are depicted on the sides of all the chapels. Into one wherein we went this morning was what they call a Calvary, a horrible, ghastly image of a Christ in a tomb, the figure of the natural size, and of the livid color of death; gaping red wounds on the body and round the brows: the whole piece enough to turn one sick, and fit only to brutalize the beholder of it. The Virgin is commonly represented with a dozen swords stuck in her heart; bleeding throats of headless John-Baptists are perpetually thrust before your eyes. At the cathedral-gate was a papier-mâché church-ornament shop, — most of the carvings and reliefs of the same dismal character; one, for instance, represented a heart with a great gash in it, and a double row of large blood-drops dribbling from it; nails and a knife were thrust into the heart; round the whole was a crown of thorns. Such things are dreadful to think of. The same gloomy spirit which made a religion of them, and worked upon the people by the grossest of all means, terror, distracted the natural feelings of man to maintain its power, — shut gentle women into lonely, pitiless convents, — frightened poor peasants with tales of torment, — taught that the end and labor of life was silence, wretchedness, and the scourge, — murdered those by fagot and prison who thought otherwise. How has the blind and furious bigotry of man perverted that which God gave us as our greatest boon, and bid us hate where God bade us love! Thank Heaven that monk has gone out of sight! It is pleasant to look at the smiling, cheerful old Béguine, and think no more of yonder livid face.

One of the many convents in this little religious city seems to be the specimen-house which is shown to strangers, for all the guides conduct you thither, and I saw in a book kept for the purpose the names of innumerable Smiths and Joneses registered.

A very kind, sweet-voiced, smiling nun (I wonder, do they always choose the most agreeable and best-humored sister of the house to show it to strangers?) came tripping down the steps and across the flags of the little garden court, and welcomed us with much courtesy into the neat little old-fashioned, red-bricked, gable-ended, shining-windowed Convent of the Angels. First, she showed us a whitewashed parlor, decorated with a grim picture or two and some crucifixes and other religious emblems, where, upon stiff old chairs, the sisters sit and work. Three or four of them were still there, pattering over their laces and bobbins; but the chief part of the sisterhood were engaged in an apartment hard by, from which issued a certain odor which I must say resembled onions, and which was in fact the kitchen of the establishment.

Every Béguine cooks her own little dinner in her own little pipkin; and there was half a score of them, sure enough, busy over their pots and crockery, cooking a repast which, when ready, was carried off to a neighboring room, the refectory, where, at a ledge-table which is drawn out from under her own particular cupboard, each nun sits down and eats her meal in silence. More religious emblems ornamented the carved cupboard-doors, and within, everything was as neat as neat could be: shining pewter ewers and glasses, snug baskets of eggs and pats of butter, and little bowls with about a farthing's worth of green tea in them, — for some great day of fête, doubtless. The old ladies sat round as we examined these things, each eating soberly at her ledge and never looking round. There was a bell ringing in the chapel hard by. "Hark!" said our guide, "that is one of the sisters dying. Will you come up and see the cells?"

The cells, it need not be said, are the snuggest little nests in the world, with serge-curtained beds and snowy linen, and saints and martyrs pinned against the wall. "We may sit up till twelve o'clock if we like," said the nun; "but we have no fire and candle, and so what 's the use of sitting up? When we have said our prayers we are glad enough to go to sleep."

I forget, although the good soul told us, how many times in the day, in public and in private, these devotions are made, but fancy that the morning service in the chapel takes place at too early an hour for most easy travellers. We did not fail to attend in the evening, when likewise is a general muster of the seven hundred, minus the absent and sick, and the sight is not a little curious and striking to a stranger.

The chapel is a very big whitewashed place of worship, supported by half a dozen columns on either side, over each of which stands the statue of an Apostle, with his emblem of martyrdom. Nobody was as yet at the distant altar, which was too far off to see very distinctly; but I could perceive two statues over it, one of which (St. Lawrence, no doubt) was leaning upon a huge gilt gridiron that the sun lighted up in a blaze, — a painful but not a romantic instrument of death. A couple of old ladies in white hoods were tugging and swaying about at two bell-ropes that came down into the middle of the church, and at least five hundred others in white veils were seated all round about us in mute contemplation until the service began, looking very solemn, and white, and ghastly, like an army of tombstones by moonlight.

The service commenced as the clock finished striking seven; the organ pealed out, a very cracked and old one, and presently some weak old voice from the choir overhead quavered out a canticle; which done, a thin old voice of a priest at the altar far off (and which had now become quite gloomy in the sunset) chanted feebly another part of the service; then the nuns warbled once more overhead; and it was curious to hear, in the intervals of the most lugubrious chants, how the organ went off with some extremely cheerful military or profane air. At one time was a march, at another a quick tune; which ceasing, the old nuns began again, and so sung until the service was ended.

In the midst of it one of the white-veiled sisters approached us with a very mysterious air, and put down her white veil close to our ears, and whispered. Were we doing anything wrong, I wondered? Were they come to that part of the service where heretics and infidels ought to quit the church? What have you to ask, O sacred, white-veiled maid?

All she said was, "*Deux centièmes pour les suisses,*" which sum was paid; and presently the old ladies, rising from their chairs one by one, came in face of the altar, where they knelt down, and said a short prayer; then, rising, unpinned their veils, and folded them up all exactly in the same folds and fashion, and laid them square like napkins on their heads, and tucked up their long black outer dresses, and trudged off to their convents.

The novices wear black veils, under one of which I saw a young, sad, handsome face. It was the only thing in the establishment that was the least romantic or gloomy; and, for the sake of any reader of a sentimental turn, let us hope that the poor soul has been crossed in love, and that over some soul-stirring tragedy that black curtain has fallen.

Ghent has, I believe, been called a vulgar Venice. It contains dirty canals and old houses that must satisfy the most eager antiquary, though the buildings are not quite in so good preservation as others that may be seen in the Netherlands. The commercial bustle of the place seems considerable, and it contains more beer-shops than any city I ever saw.

These beer-shops seem the only amusement of the inhabitants, until, at least, the theatre shall be built, of which the elevation is now complete, — a very handsome and extensive pile. There are beer-shops in the cellars of the houses, which are frequented, it is to be presumed, by the lower sort; there are beer-shops at the barriers, where the citizens and their families repair; and beer-shops in the town, glaring with gas; with long gauze blinds, however, to hide what I hear is a rather questionable reputation.

Our inn, the Hôtel of the Post, a spacious and comfortable residence, is on a little place planted round with trees, and that seems to be the Palais Royal of the town. Three clubs, which look from without to be very comfortable, ornament this square with their gas-lamps. Here stands, too, the theatre that is to be; there is a café, and on evenings a military band plays the very worst music I ever remember to have heard. I went out to-night to take a quiet walk upon this place, and the horrid brazen discord of these trumpeters set me half mad.

I went to the café for refuge, passing on the way a subterraneous beer-shop, where men and women were drinking to the sweet music of a cracked barrel-organ. They take in a couple of French papers at this café, and the same number of Belgian journals. You may imagine how well the latter are informed, when you hear that the battle of Boulogne, fought by the immortal Louis Napoleon, was not known here until some gentlemen out of Norfolk brought the News from London, and until it had travelled to Paris, and from Paris to Brussels. For a whole hour I could not get a newspaper at the café; the horrible brass band in the mean time had quitted the place, and now, to amuse the Ghent citizens, a couple of little boys came to the café, and set up a small concert. One played ill on the guitar, but sang, very sweetly, plaintive French ballads. The other was the comic singer. He carried about with him a queer, long, damp-looking, mouldy white hat, with no brim. "*Ecoutez,*" said the waiter to me, "*il va faire l'Anglais, c'est très drôle!*" The little rogue mounted his immense brimless hat, and, thrusting his thumbs into the arm-holes of his waistcoat, began to *faire l'Anglais*, with a song in which swearing was the principal joke. We all laughed at this, and, indeed, the little rascal seemed to have a good deal of humor.

How they hate us, these foreigners, in Belgium as much as in France! What lies they tell of us, how gladly they would see us humiliated! Honest folks at home over their port wine say, "Ay, ay (and very good reason they have too), national vanity, sir, wounded,— we have beaten them so often." My dear sir, there is not a greater error in the world than this. They hate you because you are stupid, hard to please, and intolerably insolent and air-giving. I walked with an Englishman yesterday, who asked the way to a street of which he pronounced the name very badly to a little Flemish boy; the Flemish boy did not answer, and there was my Englishman quite in a rage, shrieking in the child's ear as if he must answer. He seemed to think that it was the duty of "the snob," as he called him, to obey the gentleman. This is why we are hated—for pride. In our free country a tradesman, a lacquey, or a waiter, will submit to almost any given insult from a gentleman: in these benighted lands one man is as good as another; and pray God it may soon be so with us! Of all European people, which is the nation that has the most haughtiness, the strongest prejudices, the greatest reserve, the greatest dulness? I say an Englishman of the genteel classes. An honest groom jokes and hobs-and-nobs and makes his way with the kitchen-maids, for there is good social nature in the man; his master dare not unbend. Look at him, how he scowls at you on your entering an inn-room; think how you scowl yourself to meet his scowl. To-day, as we were walking and staring about the place, a worthy old gentleman in a carriage, seeing a pair of strangers, took off his hat and bowed very gravely with his old powdered head out of the window: I am sorry to say that our first impulse was to burst out laughing, — it seemed so supremely ridiculous that a stranger should notice and welcome another.

As for the notion that foreigners hate us because we have beaten them so often, my dear sir, this is the greatest error in the world: well-educated Frenchmen *do not believe that we have beaten them.* A man was once ready to call me out in Paris because I said that we had beaten the French in Spain; and here before me is a French paper, with a London correspondent discoursing about Louis Bonaparte and his jackass expedition to Boulogne. "He was received at Eglintoun, it is true," says the correspondent, "but what do you think was the reason? Because the English nobility were anxious *to revenge upon his person* (with some *coups de lance*) *the checks which the 'grand homme' his uncle had inflicted on us in Spain.*"

This opinion is so general among the French, that they would laugh at you with scornful incredulity if you ventured to assert any other. Foy's history of the Spanish War, does not, unluckily, go far enough. I have read a French history which hardly mentions the war in Spain, and calls the battle of Salamanca a French victory. You know how the other day, and in the teeth of all evidence, the French swore to their victory of Toulouse: and so it is with the rest; and you may set it down as pretty certain, 1st, That only a few people know the real state of things in France, as to the matter in dispute between us; 2d, That those who do, keep the truth to themselves, and so it is as if it had never been.

These Belgians have caught up, and quite naturally, the French tone. We are *perfide Albion* with them still. Here is the Ghent paper, which declares that it is beyond a doubt that Louis Napoleon was sent by the English and Lord Palmerston; and though it states in another part of the journal (from English authority) that the prince had never seen Lord Palmerston, yet the lie will remain uppermost, — the people and the editor will believe it to the end of time. * * See to what a digression yonder little fellow in the tall hat has given rise! Let us make his picture, and have done with him.

I could not understand, in my walks about this place, which is certainly picturesque enough, and contains extraordinary charms in the shapes of old gables, quaint spires, and broad shining canals, — I could not at first comprehend why, for all this, the town was especially disagreeable to me, and have only just hit on the reason why. Sweetest Juliana, you will never guess it: it is simply this, that I have not seen a single decent-looking woman in the whole place; they look all ugly, with coarse mouths, vulgar figures, mean mercantile faces; and so the traveller walking among them finds the pleasure of his walk excessively damped, and the impressions made upon him disagreeable.

In the Academy there are no pictures of merit; but sometimes a second-rate picture is as pleasing as the best, and one may pass an hour here very pleasantly. There is a room appropriated to Belgian artists, of which I never saw the like; they are, like all the rest of the things in this country, miserable imitations of the French school, — great nude Venuses, and Junos *à la* David, with the drawing left out.

BRUGES.

The change from vulgar Ghent, with its ugly women and coarse bustle, to this quiet, old, half-deserted, cleanly Bruges, was very pleasant. I have seen old men at Versailles, with shabby coats and pigtails, sunning themselves on the benches in the walls. They had seen better days, to be sure, but they were gentlemen still. And so we found, this morning, old dowager Bruges basking in the pleasant August sun, and looking, if not prosperous, at least cheerful and well-bred. It is the quaintest and prettiest of all the quaint and pretty towns I have seen. A painter might spend months here, and wander from church to church, and admire old towers and pinnacles, tall gables, bright canals, and pretty little patches of green garden and moss-grown wall, that reflect in the clear quiet water. Before the inn-window is a garden, from which in the early morning issues a most wonderful odor of stocks and wall-flowers. Next comes a road with trees of admirable green. Numbers of little children are playing in this road (the place is so clean that they may roll in it all day without soiling their pinafores), and on the other side of the trees are little old-fashioned, dumpy, whitewashed, red-tiled houses. A poorer landscape to draw never was known, nor a pleasanter to see, — the children, especially, who are inordinately fat and rosy. Let it be remembered, too, that here we are out of the country of ugly women. The expression of the face is almost uniformly gentle and pleasing, and the figures of the women, wrapped in long black monk-like cloaks and hoods, very picturesque. No wonder there are so many children. The Guide-book (omniscient Mr. Murray!) says there are fifteen thousand paupers in the town, and we know how such multiply. How the deuce do their children look so fat and rosy? By eating dirt pies, I suppose. I saw a couple making a very nice savory one, and another employed in gravely sticking strips of stick betwixt the pebbles at the house-door, and so making for herself a stately garden. The men and women don't seem to have much more to do. There are a couple of tall chimneys at either suburb of the town, where no doubt manufactories are at work, but within the walls everybody seems decently idle.

We have been, of course, abroad to visit the lions. The tower in the Grand Place is very fine, and the bricks of which it is built do not yield a whit in color to the best stone. The great building round this tower is very like the pictures of the Ducal Palace at Venice, and there is a long market area, with columns down the middle, from which hung shreds of rather lean-looking meat, that would do wonders under the hands of Cattermole or Haghe. In the tower there is a chime of bells that keep ringing perpetually. They not only play tunes of themselves, and every quarter of an hour, but an individual performs selections from popular operas on them at certain periods of the morning, afternoon, and evening. I have heard to-day "Suoni la Tromba," "Son Vergin Vezzosa," from the *Puritani*, and other airs, and very badly they were played, too; for such a great monster as a tower-bell cannot be expected to imitate Madame Grisi, or even Signor Lablache. Other churches indulge in the same amusement; so that one may come here, and live in melody all day or night, like the young woman in Moore's *Lalla Rookh.*

In the matter of art, the chief attractions of Bruges are the pictures of Hemling, that are to be seen in the churches, the hospital, and the picture-gallery of the place. There are no more pictures of Rubens to be seen; and, indeed, in the course of a fortnight one has had quite enough of the great man and his magnificent, swaggering canvases. What a difference is here with simple Hemling, and the extraordinary creations of his pencil! The hospital is particularly rich in them; and the legend there is that the painter, who had served Charles the Bold in his war against the Swiss, and his last battle and defeat, wandered back wounded and penniless to Bruges, and here found cure and shelter.

This hospital is a noble and curious sight. The great hall is almost as it was in the twelfth century. It is spanned by Saxon arches, and lighted by a multiplicity of Gothic windows of all sizes. It is very lofty, clean, and perfectly well ventilated. A screen runs across the middle of the room, to divide the male from the female patients, and we were taken to examine each ward, where the poor people seemed happier than possibly they would have been in health and starvation without it. Great yellow blankets were on the iron beds, the linen was scrupulously clean, glittering pewter jugs and goblets stood by the side of each patient, and they were provided with godly books (to judge from the binding), in which several were reading at leisure. Honest old comfortable nuns, in queer dresses of blue, black, white, and flannel, were bustling through the room, attending to the wants of the sick. I saw about a dozen of these kind women's faces; one was young, — all were healthy and cheerful. One came with bare blue arms and a great pile of linen from an outhouse, — such a grange as Cedric the Saxon might have given to a guest for the night. A couple were in a laboratory, a tall, bright, clean room, five hundred years old at least. "We saw you were not very religious," said one of the old ladies, with a red, wrinkled, good-humored face, "by your behavior yesterday in chapel." And yet, we did not laugh and talk as we used at college, but were profoundly affected by the scene that we saw there. It was a fête-day; a mass of Mozart was sung in the evening, — not well sung, and yet so exquisitely tender and melodious, that it brought tears into our eyes. There were not above twenty people in the church, all, save three or four, were women in long black cloaks. I took them for nuns at first. They were, however, the common people of the town, very poor indeed, doubtless, for the priest's box that was brought round was not added to by most of them, and their contributions were but two-cent pieces, — five of these go to a penny; but we know the value of such, and can tell the exact worth of a poor woman's mite! The box-bearer did not seem at first willing to accept our donation, — we were strangers and heretics; however, I held out my hand, and he came perforce, as it were. Indeed, it had only a franc in it: but *que voulez-vous?* I had been drinking a bottle of Rhine wine that day, and how was I to afford more? The Rhine wine is dear in this country, and costs four francs a bottle.

Well, the service proceeded. Twenty poor women, two Englishmen, four ragged beggars, cowering on the steps; and there was the priest at the altar, in a great robe of gold and damask, two little boys in white surplices serving him, holding his robe as he rose and bowed, and the money-gatherer swinging his censer, and filling the little chapel with smoke. The music pealed with wonderful sweetness: you could see the prim white heads of the nuns in their gallery. The evening light streamed down upon old statues of saints and carved brown stalls, and lighted up the head of the golden-haired Magdalen in a picture of the entombment of Christ. Over the gallery, and, as it were, a kind protectress to the poor below, stood the statue of the Virgin.

No. III.

WATERLOO.

It is, my dear, the happy privilege of your sex in England to quit the dinner-table after the wine-bottles have once or twice gone round it, and you are thereby saved (though, to be sure, I can't tell what the ladies do up stairs) — you are saved two or three hours' excessive dulness, which the men are obliged to go through.

I ask any gentleman who reads this — the letters to my Juliana being written with an eye to publication — to remember especially how many times, how many hundred times, how many thousand times, in his hearing, the battle of Waterloo has been discussed after dinner, and to call to mind how cruelly he has been bored by the discussion. "Ah, it was lucky for us that the Prussians came up!" says one little gentleman, looking particularly wise and ominous. "Hang the Prussians!" (or, perhaps, something stronger) — "the Prussians!" says a stout old major on half pay; "we beat the French without them, sir, as beaten them we always have! We were thundering down the hill of Belle Alliance, sir, at the backs of them, and the French were crying '*Sauve qui peut*' long before the Prussians ever touched them!" And so the battle opens, and for many mortal hours, amid rounds of claret, rages over and over again.

I thought to myself, considering the above things, what a fine thing it will be in after-days to say that I have been to Brussels and never seen the field of Waterloo; indeed, that I am such a philosopher as not to care a fig about the battle, — nay, to regret, rather, that when Napoleon came back, the British government had not spared their men and left him alone.

But this pitch of philosophy was unattainable. This morning, after having seen the park, the fashionable boulevard, the pictures, the cafés, — having sipped, I say, the sweets of every flower that grows in this paradise of Brussels, quite weary of the place, we mounted on a Namur diligence, and jingled off at four miles an hour for Waterloo.

The road is very neat and agreeable, the forest of Soignies here and there interposes pleasantly, to give your vehicle a shade; the country, as usual, is vastly fertile and well cultivated. A farmer and the conductor were my companions in the Imperial, and, could I have understood their conversation, my dear, you should have had certainly a report of it. The jargon which they talked was, indeed, most queer and puzzling, — French, I believe, strangely hushed up and pronounced, for here and there one could catch a few words of it. Now and anon, however, they condescended to speak in the purest French they could muster, and, indeed, nothing is more curious than to hear the French of the country. You can't understand why all the people insist upon speaking it so badly. I asked the conductor if he had been at the battle; he burst out laughing like a philosopher, as he was, and said, "*Pas si bête.*" I asked the farmer whether his contributions were lighter now than in King William's time, and lighter than those in the time of the emperor?

He vowed that in war-time he had not more to pay than in time of peace (and this strange fact is vouched for by every person of every nation), and, being asked wherefore the King of Holland had been ousted from his throne, replied at once, "*Parce que c'étoit un voleur,*" for which accusation I believe there is some show of reason, his majesty having laid hands on much Belgian property before the lamented outbreak which cost him his crown. A vast deal of laughing and roaring passed between these two worldly people and the postilion, whom they called "baron," and I thought no doubt that this talk was one of the many jokes that my companions were in the habit of making. But not so; the postilion was an actual baron, the bearer of an ancient name, the descendant of gallant gentlemen. Good heavens! what would Mrs. Trollope say to see his lordship here? His father, the old baron, had dissipated the family fortune, and here was this young nobleman, at about five-and-forty, compelled to bestride a clattering Flemish stallion, and bump over dusty pavements at the rate of five miles an hour. But see the beauty of high blood, — with what a calm grace the man of family accommodates himself to fortune. Far from being cast down, his lordship met his fate like a man; he swore, and laughed, the whole of the journey, and, as we changed horses, condescended to partake of half a pint of Louvain beer, to which the farmer treated him, — indeed the worthy rustic treated me to a glass too.

Much delight and instruction have I had in the course of the journey from my guide, philosopher, and friend, the author of "Murray's Hand-book." He has gathered together, indeed, a store of information, and must, to make his single volume, have gutted many hundreds of guide-books. How the Continental ciceroni must hate him, whoever he is! Every English party I saw had this infallible red book in their hands, and gained a vast deal of historical and general information from it. Thus I heard, in confidence, many remarkable anecdotes of Charles V., the Duke of Alva, Count Egmont, all of which I had before perceived, with much satisfaction, not only in the Hand-book, but even in other works.

The laureate is, among the English poets, evidently the great favorite of our guide. The choice does honor to his head and heart. A man must have a very strong bent for poetry, indeed, who carries Southey's works in his portmanteau, and quotes them in proper time and occasion. Of course, at Waterloo a spirit like our guide's cannot fail to be deeply moved, and to turn to his favorite poet for sympathy. Hark how the laureated bard sings about the tombstones at Waterloo:—

"That temple to our hearts was hallowed now,
  For many a wounded Briton there was laid,
With such for help as time might then allow
  From the fresh carnage of the field conveyed.
And they whom human succor could not save,
  Here, in its precincts, found a hasty grave.
And here, on marble tablets set on high,
  In English lines by foreign workmen traced,
The names familiar to an English eye
  Their brethren here the fit memorial placed,
Whose unadorned inscriptions briefly tell
  Their gallant comrades' rank, and where they fell.
The stateliest monument of human pride,
  Enriched with all magnificence of art,
To honor chieftains who in victory died,
  Would wake no stronger feeling in the heart
Than these plain tablets, by the soldier's hand
  Raised to his comrades in a foreign land."

There are lines for you! wonderful for justice, rich in thought and novel ideas. The passage concerning their gallant comrades' rank should be specially remarked.

There, indeed, they lie, sure enough, — the Honorable Colonel This, of the Guards, Captain That, of the Hussars, Major So-and-So, of the Dragoons, — brave men and good, who did their duty by their country on that day, and died in the performance of it.

Amen: but I confess fairly, that in looking at these tablets I felt very much disappointed at not seeing the names of the *men* as well as the officers. Are they to be counted for naught? A few more inches of marble to each monument would have given space for all the names of the men; and the men of that day were the winners of the battle. We have a right to be as grateful individually to any given private as to any given officer; their duties were very much the same. Why should the country reserve its gratitude for the genteel occupiers of the army-list, and forget the gallant fellows whose humble names were written in the regimental books? In reading of the Wellington wars, and the conduct of the men engaged in them, I don't know whether to respect them or to wonder at them most. They have death, wounds, and poverty in contemplation; in possession, poverty, hard labor, hard fare, and small thanks. If they do wrong, they are handed over to the inevitable provost-marshal; if they are heroes, heroes they may be, but they remain privates still, handling the old brown Bess, starving on the old twopence a day. They grow gray in battle and victory, and, after thirty years of bloody service, a young gentleman of fifteen, fresh from a preparatory school, who can scarcely read, and came but yesterday with a pinafore on to papa's dessert, — such a young gentleman, I say, arrives in a spick and span red coat, and calmly takes the command over our veteran, who obeys him as if God and nature had ordained that so throughout time it should be.

That privates should obey, and that they should be smartly punished if they disobey, this one can understand very well. But to say obey forever and ever, — to say that Private John Styles is, by some physical disproportion, hopelessly inferior to Cornet Snooks, — to say that Snooks shall have honors, epaulets, and a marble tablet if he dies, and that Styles shall fight his fight, and have his twopence a day, and when shot down shall be shovelled into a hole with other Styleses, and so forgotten; and to think that we had in the course of the last war some 400,000 of these Styleses, and some 10,000, say, of the Snooks sort, — Styles being by nature exactly as honest, clever, and brave as Snooks, — and to think that the 400,000 should bear this, is the wonder!

Suppose Snooks makes a speech. Look at these Frenchmen, British soldiers, says he, and remember who they are. Two-and-twenty years since they hurled their king from his throne and murdered him (groans). They flung out of their country their ancient and famous nobility, — they published the audacious doctrine of equality, — they make a cadet of artillery, a beggarly lawyer's son, into an emperor, and took ignoramuses from the ranks, — drummers and privates, by Jove! — of whom they made kings, generals, and marshals! Is this to be borne? (cries of No! no!) Upon them, my boys! down with these godless revolutionists, and rally round the British lion!

So saying, Ensign Snooks (whose flag, which he can't carry, is held by a huge grizzly color-sergeant) draws a little sword, and pipes out a feeble huzza. The men of his company, roaring curses at the Frenchmen, prepare to receive and repel a thundering charge of French cuirassiers. The men fight, and Snooks is knighted because the men fought so well.

But live or die, win or lose, what do *they* get? English glory is too genteel to meddle with those humble fellows. She does not condescend to ask the names of the poor devils whom she kills in her service. Why was not every private man's name written upon the stones in Waterloo Church as well as every officer's? Five hundred pounds to the stone-cutters would have served to carve the whole catalogue, and paid the poor compliment of recognition to men who died in doing their duty. If the officers deserved a stone, the men did. But come, let us away, and drop a tear over the Marquis of Anglesea's leg!

As for Waterloo, has it not been talked of enough after dinner? Here are some oats that were plucked before Hougomont, where grow not only oats but flourishing crops of grape-shot, bayonets, and legion-of-honor crosses, in amazing profusion.

Well, though I made a vow not to talk about Waterloo either here or after dinner, there is one little secret admission that one must make after seeing it. Let an Englishman go and see that field, and he *never forgets it.* The sight is an event in his life; and, though it has been seen by millions of peaceable *gents,* — grocers from Bond Street, meek attorneys from Chancery Lane, and timid tailors from Piccadilly, — I will wager that there is not one of them but feels a glow as he looks at the place, and remembers that he, too, is an Englishman.

It is a wrong, egotistical, savage, unchristian feeling, and that 's the truth of it. A man of peace has no right to be dazzled by that red-coated glory, and to intoxicate his vanity with those remembrances of carnage and triumph. The same sentence which tells us that on earth there ought to be peace and good-will amongst men, tells us to whom GLORY belongs.

ON MEN AND PICTURES.

À PROPOS OF A WALK IN THE LOUVRE.

PARIS, June, 1841.

N the days of my youth I knew a young fellow that I shall here call Tidbody, and who, born in a provincial town of respectable parents, had been considered by the drawing-master of the place, and, indeed, by the principal tea-parties there, as a great genius in the painting line, and one that was sure to make his fortune.

When he had made portraits of his grandmother, of the house-dog, of the door-knocker, of the church and parson of the place, and had copied, *tant bien que mal*, the most of the prints that were to be found in the various houses of the village, Harry Tidbody was voted to be very nearly perfect; and his honest parents laid out their little savings in sending the lad to Rome and Paris.

I saw him in the latter town in the year '32, before an immense easel, perched upon a high stool, and copying with perfect complacency a Correggio in the gallery, which he thought he had imitated to a nicety. No misgivings ever entered into the man's mind that he was making an ass of himself; he never once paused to consider that his copy was as much like the Correggio as my nose is like the Apollo's. But he rose early of mornings, and scrubbed away all day with his macgilps and varnishes; he worked away through cold and through sunshine; when other men were warming their fingers at the stoves, or wisely lounging on the Boulevard, he worked away, and thought he was cultivating art in the purest fashion, and smiled with easy scorn upon those who took the world more easily than he. Tidbody drank water with his meals, — if meals those miserable scraps of bread and cheese, or bread and sausage, could be called, which he lined his lean stomach with; and voted those persons godless gluttons who recreated themselves with brandy and beef. He rose up at daybreak, and worked away with bladder and brush; he passed all night at life-academies, designing life-guardsmen with chalk and stump; he never was known to take any other recreation; and in ten years he had spent as much time over his drawing as another man spends in thirty. At the end of his second year of academical studies, Harry Tidbody could draw exactly as well as he could eight years after. He had visited Florence, and Rome, and Venice, in the interval; but there he was as he had begun, without one single farther idea, and not an inch nearer the goal at which he aimed.

One day, at the Life-academy in St. Martin's Lane, I saw before me the back of a shock head of hair and a pair of ragged elbows, belonging to a man in a certain pompous attitude which I thought I recognized; and when the model retired behind his curtain to take his ten minutes' repose, the man belonging to the back in question turned round a little, and took out an old snuffy cotton handkerchief and wiped his forehead and lank cheekbones, that were moist with the vast mental and bodily exertions of the night. Harry Tidbody was the man in question. In ten years he had spent at least three thousand nights in copying the model. When abroad, perhaps, he had passed the Sunday evenings too in the same rigorous and dismal pastime. He had piles upon piles of gray paper at his lodgings, covered with worthless nudities in black and white chalk.

At the end of the evening we shook hands, and I asked him how the arts flourished. The poor fellow, with a kind of dismal humor that formed a part of his character, twirled round upon the iron heels of his old patched Blucher boots, and showed me his figure for answer. Such a lean, long, ragged, fantastical-looking personage, it would be hard to match out of the drawing-schools.

"Tit, my boy," said he, when he had finished his pirouette, "you may see that the arts have not fattened me as yet; and, between ourselves, I make by my profession something considerably less than a thousand a year. But, mind you, I am not discouraged; my whole soul is in my calling; I can't do anything else if I would; and I will be a painter, or die in the attempt."

Tidbody is not dead, I am happy to say, but has a snug place in the Excise of eighty pounds a year, and now only exercises the pencil as an amateur. If his story has been told here at some length, the ingenious reader may fancy that there is some reason for it. In the first place, there is so little to say about the present exhibition at Paris, that your humble servant does not know how to fill his pages without some digressions; and, secondly, the Tidbodian episode has a certain moral in it, without which it never would have been related, and which is good for all artists to read.

It came to my mind upon examining a picture of sixty feet by forty (indeed, it cannot be much smaller), which takes up a good deal of room in the large room of the

Louvre. But of this picture anon. Let us come to the general considerations.

Why the deuce will men make light of that golden gift of mediocrity which for the most part they possess, and strive so absurdly at the sublime? What is it that makes a fortune in this world but energetic mediocrity? What is it that is so respected and prosperous as good, honest, emphatic, blundering dulness, bellowing common-places with its great healthy lungs, kicking and struggling with its big feet and fists, and bringing an awe-stricken public down on its knees before it? Think, my good sir, of the people who occupy your attention and the world's. Who are they? Upon your honor and conscience now, are they not persons with thews and sinews like your own, only they use them with somewhat more activity, — with a voice like yours, only they shout a little louder, — with the average portion of brains, in fact, but working them more? But this kind of disbelief in heroes is very offensive to the world, it must be confessed. There, now, is The Times newspaper, which the other day rated your humble servant for publishing an account of one of the great humbugs of modern days, viz. the late funeral of Napoleon, — which rated me, I say, and talked in its own grave, roaring way, about the flippancy and conceit of Titmarsh.

O you thundering old Times! Napoleon's funeral was a humbug, and your constant reader said so. The people engaged in it were humbugs, and this your Michael Angelo hinted at. There may be irreverence in this, and the process of humbug-hunting may end rather awk-wardly for some people. But, surely, there is no conceit. The shamming of modesty is the most pert conceit of all, the *précieuse* affectation of deference where you don't feel it, the sneaking acquiescence in lies. It is very hard that a man may not tell the truth as he fancies it, without being accused of conceit: but so the world wags. As has already been prettily shown in that before-mentioned little book about Napoleon, that is still to be had of the publishers, there is a ballad in the volume, which, if properly studied, will be alone worth two-and-sixpence to any man.

Well, the funeral of Napoleon *was* a humbug; and, being so, what was a man to call it? What do we call a rose? Is it disrespectful to the pretty flower to call it by its own innocent name? And, in like manner, are we bound, out of respect for society, to speak of humbug only in a circumlocutory way, — to call it something else, as they say some Indian people do their devil, — to wrap it up in riddles and charades? Nothing is easier. Take, for instance, the following couple of sonnets on the subject: —

The glad spring sun shone yesterday, as Mr.
  M. Titmarsh wandered with his favorite lassie
  By silver Seine, among the meadows grassy,
— Meadows, like mail-coach guards new clad at Easter
  Fair was the sight 'twixt Neuilly and Passy;
And green the field, and bright the river's glister.

The birds sang salutations to the spring;
  Already buds and leaves from branches burst:
  "The surly winter time hath done its worst,"
Said Michael; "Lo, the bees are on the wing!"
Then on the ground his lazy limbs did fling.
  Meanwhile the bees pass'd by him with my *first*.
My *second* dare I to your notice bring,
  Or name to delicate ears that animal accurst?

To all our earthly family of fools
  My whole, resistless despot, gives the law, —

Humble and great, we kneel to it with awe:
O'er camp and court, the senate and the schools,
Our grand invisible Lama sits and rules,
By ministers that are its men of straw.

Sir Robert utters it in place of wit,
And straight the Opposition shouts "Hear, hear!"
And, oh! but all the Whiggish benches cheer
When great Lord John retorts it, as is fit.
In you, my *Press*,* each day throughout the year,
On vast broad sheets we find its praises writ.
O wondrous are the columns that you rear,
And sweet the morning hymns you roar in praise of it!

Sacred word! It is kept out of the dictionaries, as if the great compilers of those publications were afraid to utter it. Well, then, the funeral of Napoleon was a humbug, as Titmarsh wrote; and a still better proof that it was a humbug was this, that nobody bought Titmarsh's book, and of the ten thousand copies made ready by the publisher, not above three thousand went off. It was a humbug, and an exploded humbug. Peace be to it! *Parlons d'autres choses;* and let us begin to discourse about the pictures without further shilly-shally.

I must confess, with a great deal of shame, that I love to go to the picture gallery of a Sunday after church, on purpose to see the thousand happy people of the working

* The reader can easily accommodate this line to the name of his favorite paper. Thus:—

"In you, my { *Times,* / *Post,* } each day throughout the year."

Or:—

"In you, my { *Herald,* / '*Tiser,* } daily through the year."

Or, in France:—

"In you, my *Galignani's Messengere*";

a capital paper, because you have there the very cream of all the others. In the last line, for "morning" you can read "evening," or "weekly," as circumstances prompt.

sort amusing themselves — not very wickedly, as I fancy — in the only day in the week on which they have their freedom. Genteel people, who can amuse themselves every day throughout the year, do not frequent the Louvre on a Sunday. You can't see the pictures well, and are pushed and elbowed by all sorts of low-bred creatures. Yesterday, there were at the very least two hundred common soldiers in the place, — little vulgar ruffians, with red breeches and three halfpence a-day, examining the pictures in company with fifteen hundred grisettes, two thousand liberated shop-boys, eighteen hundred and forty-one artist-apprentices, half a dozen of livery servants, and many scores of fellows with caps, and jackets, and copper-colored countenances, and gold earrings, and large ugly hands, that are hammering, or weaving, or filing, all the week. *Fi donc!* what a thing it is to have a taste for low company! Every man of decent breeding ought to have been in the Bois de Boulogne, in white kid gloves and on horseback, or on hack-back at least. How the dandies just now went prancing and curvetting down the Champs Elysées, making their horses jump as they passed the carriages, with their japanned boots glittering in the sunshine!

The fountains were flashing and foaming, as if they too were in their best for Sunday; the trees are covered all over with little, twinkling, bright green sprouts; numberless exhibitions of Punch and the Fantoccini are going on beneath them; and jugglers and balancers are entertaining the people with their pranks. I met two fellows the other day, one with a barrel-organ, and the other with a beard, a turban, a red jacket, and a pair of dirty, short, spangled, white trousers, who were cursing each other in the purest St. Giles's English; and if I had had impudence or generosity enough, I should have liked to make up their quarrel over a chopine of Strasbourg beer, and hear the histories of either. Think of these fellows quitting our beloved country, and their homes in some calm nook of Field Lane or Seven Dials, and toiling over to France with their music and their juggling-traps, to balance cart-wheels and swallow knives for the amusement of our natural enemies! They are very likely at work at this minute, with grinning *bonnes* and conscripts staring at their skill. It is pleasant to walk by and see the nurses and the children so uproariously happy. Yonder is one who has got a halfpenny to give to the beggar at the crossing; several are riding gravely in little carriages drawn by goats. Ah, truly, the sunshine is a fine thing; and one loves to see the little people and the poor basking in it, as well as the great in their fine carriages, or their prancing cock-tailed horses.

In the midst of sights of this kind, you pass on a fine Sunday afternoon down the Elysian Fields and the Tuileries, until you reach the before-mentioned low-bred crowd rushing into the Louvre.

Well, then, the pictures of this exhibition are to be numbered by thousands, and these thousands contain the ordinary number of *chefs-d'œuvre;* that is to say, there may be a couple of works of genius, half a dozen very clever performances, a hundred or so of good ones, fifteen hundred very decent good or bad pictures, and the remainder atrocious. What a comfort it is, as I have often thought, that they are not all masterpieces, and that there is a good stock of mediocrity in this world, and that we only light upon genius now and then, at rare angel intervals, handed round like tokay at dessert, in a few houses, and in very small quantities only! Fancy how sick one would grow of it, if one had no other drink!

Now, in this exhibition there are, of course, a certain number of persons who make believe that they are handing you round tokay, — giving you the real imperial stuff, with the seal of genius stamped on the cork. There are numbers of ambitious pictures, in other words, chiefly upon sacred subjects, and in what is called a severe style of art.

The severe style of art consists in drawing your figures in the first place very big and very neat, in which there is no harm; and in dressing them chiefly in stiff, crisp, old-fashioned draperies, such as one sees in the illuminated missals and the old masters. The old masters, no doubt, copied the habits of the people about them; and it has always appeared as absurd to me to imitate these antique costumes, and to dress up saints and virgins after the fashion of the fifteenth century, as it would be to adorn them with hoops and red-heels such as our grandmothers wore; and to make a Magdalen, for instance, taking off her patches, or an angel in powder and a hoop.

It is, or used to be, the custom at the theatres for the grave-digger in "Hamlet" always to wear fifteen or sixteen waistcoats, of which he leisurely divested himself, the audience roaring at each change of raiment. Do the Denmark grave-diggers always wear fifteen waistcoats? Let anybody answer who has visited the country. But the probability is that the custom on the stage is a very ancient one, and that the public would not be satisfied at a departure from the legend. As in the matter of grave-diggers, so it is with angels; they have — and Heaven knows why — a regular costume, which every "serious" painter follows; and which has a great deal more to do with serious art than people at first may imagine. They have large white wings, that fill up a quarter of the picture in which they have the good fortune to be; they have white gowns that fall round their feet in pretty, fantastical draperies; they have fillets round their brows, and their hair combed and neatly pomatumed down the middle; and if they have not a sword, have an elegant portable harp of a certain angelic shape. Large rims of gold-leaf they have round their heads always, — a pretty business it would be if such adjuncts were to be left out.

Now, suppose the legend ordered that every grave-digger should be represented with a gold-leaf halo round his head, and every angel with fifteen waistcoats, artists would have followed serious art just as they do now, most probably, and looked with scorn at the miserable creature who ventured to scoff at the waistcoats. Ten to one but a certain newspaper would have called a man flippant who did not respect the waistcoats, — would have said that he was irreverent for not worshipping the waistcoats. But why talk of it? The fact is, I have rather a desire to set up for a martyr, like my neighbors in the literary trade: it is not a little comforting to undergo such persecutions courageously. "O Socrate! je boirai la cigue avec toi!" as David said to Robespierre. You, too, were accused of blasphemy in your time; and the world has been treating us poor literary gents in the same way ever since. There, now, is Bulw——

But to return to the painters. In the matter of canvas covering, the French artists are a great deal more audacious than ours; and I have known a man starve all the winter through, without fire and without beef, in order that he might have the honor of filling five-and-twenty feet square of canvas with some favorite subject of his

It is curious to look through the collection, and see how for the most part the men draw their ideas. There are caricatures of the late and early style of Raphael; there are caricatures of Masaccio; there is a picture painted in the very pyramidical form, and in the manner of Andrea del Sarto; there is a Holy Family, the exact counterpart of Leonardo da Vinci; and, finally, there is Achille Deveria, — it is no use to give the names and numbers of the other artists, who are not known in England, — there is Achille Deveria, who, having nothing else to caricature, has caricatured a painted window, and designed a Charity, of which all the outlines are half an inch thick.

Then there are numberless caricatures in color as in form. There is a Violet Entombment, — a crimson one, a green one; a light emerald and gamboge Eve; all huge pictures, with talent enough in their composition, but remarkable for this strange, mad love of extravagance, which belongs to the nation. Titian and the Venetians have loved to paint lurid skies and sunsets of purple and gold; here, in consequence, is a piebald picture of crimson and yellow, laid on in streaks from the top to the bottom.

Who has not heard a great, comfortable, big-chested man, with bands round a sleek double chin, and fat white cushion-squeezers of hands, and large red whiskers, and a soft roaring voice, the delight of a congregation, preaching for an hour with all the appearance and twice the emphasis of piety, and leading audiences captive? And who has not seen a humble individual, who is quite confused to be conducted down the aisle by the big beadle with his silver staff (the stalwart "drum-major ecclesiastic"); and when in his pulpit, saying his say in the simplest manner possible, uttering what are very likely commonplaces, without a single rhetorical grace or emphasis ?

The great, comfortable, red-whiskered, roaring cushion-thumper, is most probably the favorite with the public. But there are some persons who, nevertheless, prefer to listen to the man of timid, mild commonplaces, because the simple words he speaks comes from *his* heart, and so find a way directly to yours ; where, if perhaps you can't find belief for them, you still are sure to receive them with respect and sympathy.

There are many such professors at the easel as well as the pulpit ; and you see many painters with a great vigor and dexterity, and no sincerity of heart ; some with little dexterity, but plenty of sincerity ; some one or two in a million who have both these qualities, and thus become the great men of their art. I think there are instances of the two former kinds in this present exhibition of the Louvre. There are fellows who have covered great swaggering canvases with all the attitudes and externals of piety ; and some few whose humble pictures cause no stir, and remain in quiet nooks, where one finds them, and straightway acknowledges the simple, kindly appeal, which they make.

Of such an order is the picture entitled " La Prière," by M. Trimolet. A man and his wife are kneeling at an old-fashioned praying-desk, and the woman clasps a little sickly-looking child in her arms, and all three are praying as earnestly as their simple hearts will let them. The man is a limner, or painter of missals, by trade, as we fancy. One of his works lies upon the praying-desk, and it is evident that he can paint no more that day, for the sun is just set behind the old-fashioned roofs of the houses in the narrow street of the old city where he lives. Indeed, I have had a great deal of pleasure in looking at this little quiet painting, and in the course of half a dozen visits that I have paid to it, have become perfectly acquainted with all the circumstances of the life of the honest missal illuminator and his wife, here praying at the end of their day's work in the calm summer evening.

Very likely M. Trimolet has quite a different history for his little personages, and so has everybody else who examines the picture. But what of that? There is the privilege of pictures. A man does not know all that lies in his picture, any more than he understands all the character of his children. Directly one or the other makes its appearance in the world, it has its own private existence, independent of the progenitor. And in respect of works of art, if the same piece inspire one man with joy, that fills another with compassion, what are we to say of it, but that it has sundry properties of its own which its author even does not understand? The fact is, pictures "are as they seem to all," as Mr. Alfred Tennyson sings, in the first volume of his poems.

Some of this character of holiness and devotion that I fancy I see in M. Trimolet's pictures is likewise observable in a piece by Madame Juillerat, representing Saint Elizabeth, of Hungary, leading a little beggar-boy into her house, where the holy dame of Hungary will, no doubt, make him comfortable with a good plate of victuals. A couple of young ladies follow behind the princess, with demure looks, and garlands in their hair, that hangs straight on their shoulders, as one sees it in the old illuminations. The whole picture has a pleasant, mystic, innocent look; and one is all the better for regarding it. What a fine instinct or task it was in the old missal illuminators to be so particular in the painting of the minor parts of their pictures! the precise manner in which the flowers and leaves, birds and branches, are painted, give an air of truth and simplicity to the whole performance, and make nature, as it were, an accomplice and actor in the scene going on. For instance, you may look at a landscape with certain feelings of pleasure; but if you have pulled a rose, and are smelling it, and if of a sudden a blackbird in a bush hard by begins to sing and chirrup, your feeling of pleasure is very much enhanced, most likely; the senses with which you examine the scene become brightened as it were, and the scene itself becomes more agreeable to you. It is not the same place as it was before you smelt the rose, or before the blackbird began to sing. Now, in Madame Juillerat's picture of the Saint of Hungary and the hungry boy, if the flowers on the young ladies' heads had been omitted, or not painted with their pleasing minuteness and circumstantiality, I fancy that the effect of the piece would have been by no means the same. Another artist of the mystical school, Monsieur Servan, has employed the same adjuncts in a similarly successful manner. One of his pictures represents St. Augustin meditating in a garden. A great cluster of rose-bushes, hollyhocks, and other plants, are in the foreground, most accurately delineated; and a fine rich landscape and river stretch behind the saint, round whom the flowers seem to keep up a mysterious waving and whispering that fill one with a sweet, pleasing, indescribable kind of awe,—a great perfection in this style of painting.

In M. Aguado's gallery there is an early Raphael (which all the world declares to be a copy,—but no matter). This piece only represents two young people walking hand-in-hand in a garden, and looking at you with a kind of "solemn mirth" (the expression of old Sternhold and Hopkins has always struck me as very fine). A meadow is behind them, at the end of which is a cottage, and by which flows a river, environed by certain very prim-looking trees; and that is all. Well; it is impossible for any person who has a sentiment for the art to look at this picture without feeling indescribably moved and pleased by it. It acts upon you — how? How does a beautiful, pious, tender air of Mozart act upon you? What is there in it that should make you happy and gentle, and fill you with all sorts of good thoughts and kindly feelings? I fear that what Dr. Thumpcushion says at church is correct, and that these indulgences are only carnal, and of the earth earthy; but the sensual effort in this case carries one quite away from the earth, and up to something that is very like heaven.

Now the writer of this has already been severely reprehended for saying that Raphael at thirty had lost that delightful innocence and purity which rendered the works of Raphael of twenty so divine; and perhaps it may be the critic's fault and not the painter's (I 'm not proud, and will allow that even a magazine critic may be mistaken). Perhaps by the greatest stretch of the perhaps, it may be that Raphael was every whit as divine at thirty as at eighteen; and that the very quaintnesses and imperfections of manner observable in his early works are the reasons why they appear so singularly pleasing to me. At least, among painters of the present day, I feel myself more disposed to recognize spiritual beauties in those whose powers of execution are manifestly incomplete, than in artists whose hands are skilful and manner formed. Thus there are scores of large pictures here, hanging in the Louvre, that represent subjects taken from Holy Writ, or from the lives of the saints,—pictures skilfully enough painted and intended to be religious, that have not the slightest effect upon me, no more than Dr. Thumpcushion's loudest and glibbest sermon.

Here is No. 1475, for instance,—a "Holy Family," painted in the antique manner, and with all the accessories before spoken of, viz. large flowers, fresh roses, and white stately lilies; curling tendrils of vines forming fantastical canopies for the heads of the sacred personages, and rings of gold-leaf drawn neatly round the same. Here is the Virgin, with long, stiff, prim draperies of blue, red, and white; and old Saint Anne in a sober dress, seated gravely at her side; and Saint Joseph in a becoming attitude; and all very cleverly treated, and pleasing to the eye. But though this picture is twice as well painted as any of those before mentioned, it does not touch my heart in the least; nor do any of the rest of the sacred pieces.

Opposite the "Holy Family" is a great "Martyrdom of Polycarp," and the Catalogue tells you how the executioners first tried to burn the saint; but the fire went out, and the executioners were knocked down; then a soldier struck the saint with a sword, and so killed him. The legends recount numerous miracles of this sort, which I confess have not any very edifying effect upon me. Saints are clapped into boiling oil, which immediately turns cool; or their heads are chopped off, and their blood turns to milk; and so on. One can't understand why these continual delays and disappointments take place, especially as the martyr is always killed at the end; so that it would be best at once to put him out of his pain. For this reason, possibly, the execution of Saint Polycarp did not properly affect the writer of this notice.

M. Laemlein has a good picture of the "Waking of Adam," so royally described by Milton, — a picture full of gladness, vigor, and sunshine. There is a very fine figure of a weeping woman in a picture of the "Death of the Virgin"; and the Virgin falling in M. Steuben's picture of "Our Saviour going to Execution," is very pathetic. The mention of this gentleman brings us to what is called the *bourgeois* style of art, of which he is one of the chief professors. He excels in depicting a certain kind of sentiment, and in the vulgar, which is often too the true, pathetic.

Steuben has painted many scores of Napoleons; and his picture of Napoleon this year brings numbers of admiring people round it. The emperor is seated on a sofa, reading despatches; and the little King of Rome, in a white muslin frock, with his hair beautifully curled, slumbers on his papa's knee. What a contrast! The conqueror of the world, the stern warrior, the great giver of laws and ruler of nations, he dare not move because the little baby is asleep; and he would not disturb him for all the kingdoms he knows so well how to conquer. This is not art, if you please; but it is pleasant to see fat, good-natured mothers and grandmothers clustered round this picture, and looking at it with solemn eyes. The same painter has an Esmeralda dancing and frisking in her night-gown, and playing the tambourine to her goat, capering likewise. This picture is so delightfully bad, the little gypsy has such a killing ogle, that all the world admires it. M. Steuben should send it to London, where it would be sure of a gigantic success.

M. Grenier has a piece much looked at, in the *bourgeois* line. Some rogues of gypsies or mountebanks have kidnapped a fine fat child, and are stripping it of its pretty clothes; and poor baby is crying; and the gypsy-woman holding up her finger, and threatening; and the he-mountebank is lying on a bank, smoking his pipe, — the callous monster! Preciously they will illtreat that dear little darling, if justice do not overtake them, — if, ay, *if*. But, thank Heaven! there in the corner come the police, and they will have that pipe-smoking scoundrel off to the galleys before five minutes are over.

1056. A picture of the galleys. Two galley-slaves are before you, and the piece is called, "A Crime and a Fault." The poor "Fault" is sitting on a stone, looking very repentant and unhappy indeed. The great "Crime" stands grinning you in the face, smoking his pipe. The ruffian! That pipe seems to be a great mark of callosity in ruffians. I heard one man whisper to another, as they were looking at these galley-slaves, "*They are portraits*," and very much affected his companion seemed by the information.

Of a similar virtuous interest is 705, by M. Finart. "A Family of African Colonists carried off by Abdel-Kader." There is the poor male colonist without a single thing on but a rope round his wrists. His silver skin is dabbled with his golden blood, and he looks up to heaven as the Arabs are poking him on with the tips of their horrid spears. Behind him come his flocks and herds, and other members of his family. In front, principal figure, is his angelic wife, in her night-gown, and in the arms of an odious blackamoor on horseback. Poor thing, — poor thing! she is kicking, and struggling, and resisting as hard as she possibly can.

485. "The Two Friends." Debay.

"Deux jeunes femmes se donnent le gage le plus sacré d'une amitié sincère, dans un acte de dévoûment et de reconnaissance.

"L'une d'elles, faible, exténuée d'efforts inutilement tentés pour allaiter, découvre son sein tari, cause du dépérissement de son enfant. Sa douleur est comprise par son amie, à qui la santé permet d'ajouter au bonheur de nourrir son propre enfant, celui de rappeler à la vie le fils mourant de sa compagne."

M. Debay's pictures are not bad, as most of the others here mentioned as appertaining to the bourgeois class; but, good or bad, I can't but own that I like to see these honest, hearty representations, which work upon good simple feeling in a good downright way; and, if not works of art, are certainly works that can do a great deal of good, and make honest people happy. Who is the man that despises melodramas? I swear that T. P. Cooke is a benefactor to mankind. Away with him who has no stomach for such kind of entertainments, where vice is always punished, where virtue always meets its reward; where Mrs. James Vining is always sure to be made comfortable somewhere at the end of the third act; and if O. Smith is lying in agonies of death, in red breeches, on the front of the stage, or has just gone off in a flash of fire down one of the traps, I know it is only make-believe on his part, and believe him to be a good, kind-hearted fellow, that would not do harm to mortal! So much for pictures of the serious melo-dramatic sort.

M. Biard, whose picture of the "Slave-trade" made so much noise in London last year, — and indeed it is as fine as Hogarth, — has this year many comic pieces, and a series representing the present majesty of France, when Duke of Orleans, undergoing various perils by land and by water. There is much good in these pieces; but I mean no disrespect in saying I like the comic ones best. There is one entitled "Une Distraction." A National Guard is amusing himself by catching flies. You can't fail to laugh when you see it. There is "Le Gros Péché," and the biggest of all sins, no less than a drum-major confessing. You can't see the monster's face, which the painter has wisely hidden behind the curtain, as beyond the reach of art; but you see the priest's, and, murder! what a sin it must be that the big tambour has just imparted to him! All the French critics sneer at Biard, as they do at Paul de Kock, for not being artistical enough; but I do not think these gentlemen need mind the sneer: they have the millions with them, as Feargus O'Connor says, and they are good judges, after all.

A great comfort it is to think that there is a reasonable prospect that, for the future, very few more battle-pieces will be painted. They have used up all the victories, and Versailles is almost full. So this year, much to my happiness, only a few yards of warlike canvas are exhibited in place of the furlongs which one was called upon to examine in former exhibitions. One retreat from Moscow is there, and one storming of El Gibbet, or El Arish, or some such place, in Africa. In the latter picture you see a thousand fellows, in loose red pantaloons, rushing up a hill with base heathen Turks on the top, who are firing off guns, carabines, and other pieces of ordnance, at them. All this is very well painted by Monsieur Bollangé, and the rush of red breeches has a queer and pleasing appearance. In the Russian piece, you have frozen men and cattle; mothers embracing their offspring; grenadiers scowling at the enemy, and especially one fellow standing on a bank with his bayonet placed in the attitude for receiving the charge, and actually charged by a whole regiment of Cossacks, — a complete pulk, my dear madam, coming on in three lines, with their lances pointed against this undaunted warrior of France. I believe Monsieur Thiers sat for the portrait, or else the editor of the "Courrier Français," — the two men in this belligerent nation who are the belligerentest. *A propos* of Thiers; the "Nouvelles à la Main" have a good story of this little sham Napoleon. When the second son of the Duke of Orleans was born (I forget his royal highness's title), news was brought to Monsieur Thiers. He was told the princess was well, and asked the courier who brought the news, "Comment se portait *le Roi de Rome?*" It may be said, in confidence, that there is not a single word of truth in the story. But what of that? Are not sham stories as good as real ones? Ask M. Leullier; who, in spite of all that has been said and written upon a certain sea-fight, has actually this year come forward with his

"1311 — *Héroïsme de l'Equipage du Vaisseau le Vengeur,* 4 Juin, 1794.

"Après avoir soutenu longtemps un combat acharné contre trois vaisseaux Anglais, le vaisseau le Vengeur avait perdu la moitié de son équipage, le reste était blessé pour la plupart: le second capitaine avait été coupé en deux par un boulet; le vaisseau était rasé par le feu de l'ennemi, sa mâture abattue, ses flancs criblés par les boulets étaient ouverts de toutes parts; sa cale se remplissait à vue d'œil; il s'enfonçait dans la mer. Les marins qui restent sur son bord servent la batterie basse jusqu'à ce qu'elle se trouve au niveau de la mer; quand elle va disparaître, ils s'élancent dans la seconde, où ils répètent la même manœuvre; celle-ci engloutie, ils montent sur le pont. Un tronçon de mât d'artimon restait encore debout; leurs pavillons en lambeaux y sont cloués; puis, réunissant instinctivement leurs volontés en une seule pensée, ils veulent périr avec le navire qui leur a été confié. Tous, combattants, blessés, mourants, se raniment: un cri immense s'élève, répété sur toutes les parties du tillac: *Vive la République! Vive la France*.. *Le Vengeur* coule.. les cris continuent; tous.. les bras sont dressés au ciel, et ces braves, préférant la mort à la captivité, emportent triomphalement leur pavillon dans ce glorieux tombeau." — *France Maritime.*

I think Mr. Thomas Carlyle is in the occasional habit of calling lies wind-bags. *This* wind-bag, one would have thought, exploded last year; but no such thing. You *can't* sink it, do what you will; it always comes bouncing up to the surface again, where it swims and bobs about gayly for the admiration of all. This lie the Frenchman will believe; all the papers talk gravely about the affair of the Vengeur, as if an established fact: and I heard the matter disposed of by some artists the other day in a very satisfactory manner. One has always the gratification, in all French societies where the matter is discussed, of telling the real story (or, if the subject be not discussed, of bringing the conversation round to it, and then telling the real story); one has always this gratification, and a great, wicked, delightful one it is, — you make the whole company uncomfortable at once; you narrate the history in a calm, good-humored, dispassionate tone; and as you proceed, you see the different personages of the audience looking uneasily at one another, and bursting out occasionally with a "*Mais cependant*"; but you continue your tale with perfect suavity of manner, and have the satisfaction of knowing that you have stuck a dagger into the heart of every single person using it.

Telling, I say, this story to some artists who were examining M. Leullier's picture, — and I trust that many scores of persons besides were listening to the conversation, — one of them replied to my assertion, that Captain Renaudin's letters were extant, and that the whole affair was a humbug, in the following way.

"Sir," said he, "the sinking of the Vengeur is an *established fact of history*. It is completely proved by the documents of the time; and as for the letters of Captain Renaudin, of which you speak, have we not had an example the other day of some pretended letters of Louis Philippe's, which were published in a newspaper here? And what, sir, were those letters? *Forgeries!*"

Q. E. D. Everybody said sans-culotte was right; and I have no doubt that if all the Vengeur's crew could rise from the dead, and that English cox — or boat — swain, who was last *on board the ship*,* of which he and his comrades had possession, and had to swim for his life, could come forward, and swear to the real story, I make no doubt that the Frenchmen would not believe it. Only one I know, my friend Julius, who, ever since the tale has been told to him, has been crying it into all ears and in all societies, and vows he is perfectly hoarse with telling it.

As for M. Leullier's picture, there is really a great deal of good in it. Fellows embracing each other, and holding up hands and eyes to heaven; and in the distance an English ship, with the crew in *red coats*, firing away on the doomed vessel. Possibly, they are only marines whom we see; but as I once beheld several English naval officers in a play habited in top-boots, perhaps the legend in France may be, that the navy, like

* The writer heard of this man from an English captain in the navy, who had him on board his ship.

the army, with us, is caparisoned in scarlet. A good subject for another historical picture would be Cambronne, saying, "*La Garde meurt mais ne se rend pas.*" I have bought a couple of engravings of the Vengeur and Cambronne, and shall be glad to make a little historical collection of facts similarly authenticated.

Accursed, I say, be all uniform coats of blue or of red; all ye epaulets and sabertashes; all ye guns, shrapnels, and musketoons; all ye silken banners, embroidered with bloody reminiscences of successful fights: down, — down to the bottomless pit with you all, and let honest men live and love each other without you! What business have I, forsooth, to plume myself because the Duke of Wellington beat the French in Spain and elsewhere; and kindle as I read the tale, and fancy myself of a heroic stock, because my uncle Tom was at the battle of Waterloo, and because we beat Napoleon there? Who are *we*, in the name of Beelzebub? Did we ever fight in our lives? Have we the slightest inclination for fighting and murdering one another? Why are we to go on hating one another from generation to generation, swelling up our little bosoms with absurd national conceit, strutting and crowing over our neighbors, and longing to be at fisticuffs with them again? As Aristotle remarks, in war there are always two parties; and though it often happens that both declare themselves to be victorious, it still is generally the case that one party beats, and the other is beaten. The conqueror is thus filled with national pride, and the conquered with national hatred, and a desire to do better next time. If he has his revenge, and beats his opponent as desired, these agreeable feelings are reversed, and so Pride and Hatred continue *in sæcula sæculorum*, and ribands and orders are given away, and great men rise and flourish. "Remember you are Britons!" cries our general; "there is the enemy, and d— 'em, give 'em the bayonet!" Hurrah! helter-skelter, load and fire, cut and thrust, down they go! "Soldats! dans ce moment terrible la France vous regarde! Vive l'Empereur!" shouts Jacques Bonhomme, and his sword is through your ribs in a twinkling. "Children!" roars Feld-marechal Sauerkraut, "men of Hohenzollernsigmaringen! remember the eyes of Vaterland are upon you!" and murder again is the consequence. Tomahee-tereboo leads on the Ashantees with the very same war-cry, and they eat all their prisoners with true patriotic cannibalism.

Thus the great truth is handed down from father to son, that

A Briton,
A Frenchman,
An Ashantee,
A Hohenzollernsig-
maringenite, &c.,
} is superior to all the rest of the world;

and by this truth the dullards of the respective nations swear, and by it statesmen govern.

Let the reader say for himself, does he not believe himself to be superior to a man of any other country? We can't help it, — in spite of ourselves we do. But if, by changing the name, the fable applies to yourself, why do you laugh?

Κυιδ ριδης; μυτατω νωμινε δη τη
Φαβυλα ναρρατυρ,

as a certain poet says (in a quotation that is pretty well known in England, and therefore put down here in a new fashion). Why do you laugh, forsooth? Why do you *not* laugh? If donkeys' ears are a matter of laughter, surely we may laugh at them when growing on our own skulls.

Take a couple of instances from "actual life," as the fashionable novel-puffers say.

A little, fat, silly woman, who in no country but this would ever have pretensions to beauty, has lately set up a circulating library in our street. She lends the five-franc editions of the English novels, as well as the romances of her own country, and I have had several of the former works of fiction from her store: Bulwer's "Night and Morning," very pleasant, kind-hearted reading; "Peter Priggins," an astonishing work of slang, that ought to be translated if but to give Europe an idea of what a gay young gentleman in England sometimes is; and other novels — never mind what. But to revert to the fat woman.

She sits all day ogling and simpering behind her little counter; and from the slow, prim, precise way in which she lets her silly sentences slip through her mouth, you see at once that she is quite satisfied with them, and expects that every customer should give her an opportunity of uttering a few of them for his benefit. Going there for a book, I always find myself entangled in a quarter of an hour's conversation.

This is carried on in not very bad French on my part; at least I find that when I say something genteel to the library-woman, she is not at a loss to understand me, and we have passed already many minutes in this kind of intercourse. Two days since, returning "Night and Morning" to the library-lady and demanding the romance of "Peter Priggins," she offered me instead "Ida," par M. le Vicomte Darlincourt, which I refused, having already experienced some of his lordship's works; next she produced "Stella," "Valida," "Eloa," by various French ladies of literary celebrity; but again I declined, declaring respectfully that however agreeable the society of ladies might be, I found their works a little insipid. The fact is, that after being accustomed to such potent mixtures as the French romancers offer you, the mild compositions of the French romanceresses pall on the palate.*

"Madame," says I, to cut the matter short, "je ne demande qu'un roman Anglais, "Peter Priggins": l'avez vous? oui ou non?"

"Ah!" says the library-woman, "Monsieur ne comprend pas nôtre langue c'est dommage."

Now one might, at first sight, fancy the above speech an epigram, and not a bad one, on an Englishman's blundering French grammar and pronunciation; but those who know the library-lady must be aware that she never was guilty of such a thing in her life. It was simply a French bull, resulting from the lady's dulness, and by no means a sarcasm. She uttered the words with a great air of superiority and a prim toss of the head, as much as to say, "How much cleverer I am than you, you silly foreigner! and what a fine thing it is in me to know the finest language in the world!" In this way I have heard donkeys of our two countries address foreigners in broken English or French, as if people who could not understand a language when properly spoken could comprehend it when spoken ill. Why the deuce do people give them-

* In our own country, of course, Mrs. Trollope, Miss Mitford, Miss Pardoe, Mrs. Charles Gore, Miss Edgeworth, Miss Ferrier, Miss Stickney, Miss Barrett, Lady Blessington, Miss Smith, Mrs. Austin, Miss Austin, &c., form exceptions to this rule; and glad am I to offer per favor of this note a humble tribute of admiration to those ladies.

selves these impertinent, stupid airs of superiority, and pique themselves upon the great cleverness of speaking their own language?

Take another instance of this same egregious national conceit. At the English pastry-cook's — (you can't readily find a prettier or more graceful woman than Madame Colombin, nor better plum-cake than she sells) — at Madame Colombin's, yesterday, a huge Briton, with sandy whiskers and a double chin, was swallowing patties and cherry-brandy, and all the while making remarks to a friend similarly employed. They were talking about English and French ships.

"Hang me, Higgins," says Sandy-whiskers, "if *I'd* ever go into one of their cursed French ships! I should be afraid of sinking at the very first puff of wind!"

What Higgins replied does not matter. But think what a number of Sandy-whiskerses there are in our nation, — fellows who are proud of this stupid mistrust, — who think it a mark of national spirit to despise French skill, bravery, cookery, seamanship, and what not. Swallow your beef and porter, you great, fat-paunched man; enjoy your language and your country, as you have been bred to do; but don't fancy yourself, on account of these inheritances of yours, superior to other people of other ways and language. You have luck, perhaps, if you will, in having such a diet and dwelling-place, but no *merit*.

*   *   *   *   And with this little discursive essay upon national prejudices, let us come back to the pictures, and finish our walk through the gallery.

In that agreeable branch of the art for which we have I believe no name, but which the French call *genre*, there are at Paris several eminent professors; and as upon the French stage the costume-pieces are far better produced than with us, so also are French costume-pictures much more accurately and characteristically handled than are such subjects in our own country. You do not see Cimabue and Giotto in the costume of Francis the First, as they appeared (depicted by Mr. Simpson, I think) in the Royal Academy Exhibition of last year; but the artists go to some trouble for collecting their antiquarian stuff, and paint it pretty scrupulously.

M. Jacquard has some pretty small pictures *de genre;* a very good one, indeed, of fat "Monks granting Absolution from Fasting"; of which the details are finely and accurately painted, a task more easy for a French artist than an English one, for the former's studio (as may be seen by a picture in this exhibition) is generally a magnificent curiosity-shop; and for old carvings, screens, crockery, armors, draperies, &c., the painter here has but to look to his own walls and copy away at his ease. Accordingly Jacquard's monks, especially all the properties of the picture, are admirable.

M. Baron has "The Youth of Ribera," a merry Spanish beggar-boy, among a crowd of his like, drawing sketches of them under a garden-wall. The figures are very prettily thought and grouped; there is a fine terrace, and palace, and statues in the background, very rich and luxurious; perhaps too pretty and gay in colors, and too strong in details.

But the king of the painters of small history subjects, is M. Robert Fleury; a great artist indeed, and I trust heartily he may be induced to send one or two of his pieces to London, to show our people what he can do. His mind, judging from his works, is rather of a gloomy turn; and he deals somewhat too much, to my taste, in the horrible. He has this year "A Scene in the Inquisition." A man is howling and writhing with his feet over a fire; grim inquisitors are watching over him; and a dreadful executioner, with fierce eyes peering from under a mysterious capuchin, is doggedly sitting over the coals. The picture is downright horror, but admirably and honestly drawn; and in effect rich, sombre, and simple.

"Benvenuto Cellini" is better still; and the critics have lauded the piece as giving a good idea of the fierce, fantastic Florentine sculptor; but I think M. Fleury has taken him in too grim a mood, and made his ferocity too downright. There was always a dash of the ridiculous in the man, even in his most truculent moments; and I fancy that such simple rage as is here represented scarcely characterizes him. The fellow never cut a throat without some sense of humor, and here we have him greatly too majestic to my taste.

"Old Michael Angelo watching over the Sick-bed of his servant Urbino," is a noble painting; as fine in feeling as in design and color. One can't but admire in all these the *manliness* of the artist. The picture is painted in a large, rich, massive, vigorous manner; and it is gratifying to see that this great man, after resolute seeking for many years, has found the full use of his hand at last, and can express himself as he would. The picture is fit to hang in the very best gallery in the world; and a century hence will no doubt be worth five times as many crowns as the artist asks or has had for it.

Being on the subject of great pictures, let us here mention,

712. "Portrait of a Lady," by Hippolyto Flandrin.

Of this portrait all I can say is, that if you take the best portraits by the best masters, — a head of Sebastian or Michael Angelo, a head of Raphael, or one of those rarer ones of Andria del Sarto, — not one of them, for lofty character and majestic nobleness and simplicity, can surpass this magnificent work.

This seems, doubtless, very exaggerated praise, and people reading it may possibly sneer at the critic who ventures to speak in such a way. To all such I say, Come and see it. You who admire Sir Thomas and the "Books of Beauty" will possibly not admire it; you who give ten thousand guineas for a blowsy Murillo will not possibly relish M. Flandrin's manner; but you who love simplicity and greatness come and see how an old lady, with a black mantilla, and dark eyes, and gray hair, and a few red flowers in her cap, has been painted by M. Flandrin of Lyons. If I were Louis-Philippe, I would send a legion-of-honor cross, of the biggest sort, to decorate the bosom of the painter who has executed this noble piece.

As for portraits (with the exception of this one, which no man in England can equal, not even Mr. Samuel Lawrence, who is trying to get to this point, but has not reached it yet), our English painters keep the lead still, nor is there much remarkable among the hundreds in the gallery. There are vast numbers of English faces staring at you from the canvases; and among the miniatures especially, one can't help laughing at the continual recurrence of the healthy, vacant, simpering, aristocratic English type. There are black velvets and satins, ladies with birds of paradise, deputies on sofas, and generals and marshals in the midst of smoke and cannon-balls. Nothing can be less to my taste than a pot-bellied, swaggering Marshal Soult, who rests his baton on his stomach, and looks at you in the midst of a dim cloud of war. The Duchess de Nemours is done by M. Winterhalter, and has a place of honor, as becomes a good portrait; and, above all, such a pretty lady. She is a pretty, smiling, buxom blonde, with plenty of hair, and rather too much hands, not to speak disrespectfully; and a slice of lace which goes across the middle of her white satin gown seems to cut the picture very disagreeably in two. There is a beautiful head in a large portrait of a lad of eighteen, painted by himself; and here may be mentioned two single figures in pastel by an architect, remarkable for earnest, *spirituel* beauty; likewise two heads in chalk by De Rudder; most charming sketches, full of delicacy, grace, and truth.

The only one of the acknowledged great who has exhibited this year is M. Delacroix, who has a large picture relative to the siege of Constantinople, that looks very like a piece of crumpled tapestry, but that has, nevertheless, its admirers, and its merits, as what work of his has not?

His two smaller pieces are charming. "A Jewish Wedding at Tangiers," is brilliant with light and merriment; a particular sort of merriment, that is, that makes you gloomy in the very midst of the hey-day: and his "Boat" is awful. A score of shipwrecked men are in this boat, on a great, wide, swollen, interminable sea, — no hope, no speck of sail, — and they are drawing lots which shall be killed and eaten. A burly seaman, with a red beard, has just put his hand into the hat, and is touching his own to the officer. One fellow sits with his hands clasped, and gazing, — gazing into the great void before him. By Jupiter, his eyes are unfathomable! he is looking at miles and miles of lead-colored, bitter, pitiless brine! Indeed one can't bear to look at him long; nor at that poor woman, so sickly and so beautiful, whom they may as well kill at once, or she will save them the trouble of drawing straws; and give up to their maws that poor, white, faded, delicate, shrivelled carcass. Ah, what a thing it is to be hungry! O, Eugenius Delacroix! how can you manage, with a few paint-bladders, and a dirty brush, and a careless hand, to dash down such savage histories as these, and fill people's minds with thoughts so dreadful? Ay, there it is; whenever I go through that part of the gallery where M. Delacroix's picture is, I always turn away now, and look at a fat woman with a parroquet opposite. For what's the use of being uncomfortable?

Another great picture is one of about four inches square, — "The Chess-players," by M. Meissonnier, — truly an astonishing piece of workmanship. No silly tricks of effect, and abrupt startling shadow and light, but a picture painted with the minuteness and accuracy of a daguerreotype, and as near as possible perfect in its kind. Two men are playing at chess, and the chess-men are no bigger than pin-heads; every one of them an accurate portrait, with all the light, shadow, roundness, character, and color belonging to it.

Of the landscapes it is very hard indeed to speak, for professors of landscapes almost all execute their art well; but few so well as to strike one with especial attention, or to produce much remark. Constable has been a great friend to the new landscape-school in France, who have laid aside the slimy, weak manner formerly in vogue, and, perhaps, have adopted in its place a method equally reprehensible, — that of plastering their pictures excessively. When you wish to represent a piece of old timber, or a crumbling wall, or the ruts and stones in a road, this impasting method is very successful, but here the skies are trowelled on; the light vaporing distances are as thick as plum-pudding, the cool clear shadows are mashed-down masses of sienna and indigo. But it is undeniable that by these violent means a certain power is had, and noon-day effects of strong sunshine are often dashingly rendered.

How much pleasanter is it to see a little quiet gray waste of David Cox than the very best and smartest of such works! Some men from Düsseldorf have sent very fine, scientific, faithful pictures, that are a little heavy, but still you see that they are portraits drawn respectfully from the great, beautiful, various, divine face of Nature.

In the statue-gallery there is nothing worth talking about; and so let us make an end of the Louvre, and politely wish a good morning to everybody.

PICTURE GOSSIP:

IN A LETTER FROM MICHAEL ANGELO TITMARSH,

ALL ILLUSTRISSIMO SIGNOR, IL MIO SIGNOR COLENDISSIMO AUGUSTO HA ARVÉ, PITTORE IN ROMA.

AM going to fulfil the promise, my dear Augusto, which I uttered with a faltering voice and streaming eyes, before I stepped into the jingling old courier's vehicle, which was to bear me from Rome to Florence. Can I forget that night, — that parting? Gaunter stood by so affected, that for the last quarter of an hour he did not swear once; Flake's emotion exhibited itself in audible sobs; Jellyson said naught, but thrust a bundle of Torlonia's four-baiocchi cigars into the hand of the departing friend; and you yourself were so deeply agitated by the event, that you took four glasses of absinthe to string up your nerves for the fatal moment. Strange vision of past days! — for vision it seems to me now. And have I been in Rome really and truly? Have I seen the great works of my Christian namesake of the Buonarotti family, and the light arcades of the Vatican? Have I seen the glorious Apollo, and that other divine fiddle-player whom Raphael painted? Yes, — and the English dandies swaggering on the Pincian Hill! Yes, — and have eaten woodcocks, and drank Ovieto hard by the huge, broad-shouldered Pantheon Portico, in the comfortable parlors of the Falcone. Do you recollect that speech I made at Bertini's in proposing the health of the Pope of Rome on Christmas day? — do you remember it? *I* don't. But his Holiness, no doubt, heard of the oration, and was flattered by the compliment of the illustrious English traveller.

I went to the exhibition of the Royal Academy lately, and all these reminiscences rushed back on a sudden with affecting volubility; not that there was anything in or out of the gallery which put me specially in mind of sumptuous and liberal Rome; but in the great room was a picture of a fellow in a broad Roman hat, in a velvet Roman coat, and large yellow mustachios, and that prodigious scowl which young artists assume when sitting for their portraits, — he was one of our set at Rome; and the scenes of the winter came back pathetically to my mind, and all the friends of that season, — Orifice, and his sentimental songs; Father Giraldo, and his poodle, and MacBrick, the trump of bankers. Hence the determination to write this letter. But the hand is crabbed, and the postage is dear, and, instead of despatching it by the mail, I shall send it to you by means of the printer, knowing well that "Fraser's Magazine" is eagerly read at Rome, and not (on account of its morality) excluded in the *Index Expurgatorius.*

And it will be doubly agreeable to me to write to you regarding the fine arts in England, because I know, my dear Augusto, that you have a thorough contempt for my opinion, — indeed, for that of all persons, excepting, of course, one whose name is already written in this sentence. Such, however, is not the feeling respecting my critical powers in this country; *here* they know the merit of Michael Angelo Titmarsh better, and they say, "He paints so badly, that, hang it! he *must* be a good judge"; in the latter part of which opinion, of course, I agree.

You should have seen the consternation of the fellows at my arrival! — of our dear brethren who thought I was safe at Rome for the season, and that their works, exhibited in May, would be spared the dreadful ordeal of my ferocious eye. When I entered the club-room in St. Martin's Lane, and called for a glass of brandy-and-water like a bombshell, you should have seen the terror of some of the artists assembled! They knew that the frightful projectile just launched into their club-room must *burst* in the natural course of things. Who would be struck down by the explosion? was the thought of every one. Some of the hypocrites welcomed me meanly back, some of the timid trembled, some of the savage and guilty muttered curses at my arrival. You should have seen the ferocious looks of Daggerly, for example, as he scowled at me from the supper-table, and clutched the trenchant weapon with which he was dissevering his toasted cheese.

From the period of my arrival until that of the opening of the various galleries, I maintained with the artists every proper affability, but still was not too familiar. It is the custom of their friends, before their pictures are sent in to the exhibitions, to visit the painter's works at their private studios, and there encourage them by saying, "Bravo, Jones!" (I don't mean Jones, R. A., for I defy any man to say bravo to *him*, but Jones in general,) "Tomkins, this is your greatest work!" "Smith, my boy, they must elect you an associate for this!" — and so forth. These harmless banalities of compliment pass between the painters and their friends on such occasions. I myself have uttered many such civil phrases in former years under like circumstances. But it is different now. Fame has its privations as well as its pleasures. The friend may see his companions in private, but the JUDGE must not pay visits to his clients. I stayed away from the *ateliers* of all the artists (at least, I only visited one, kindly telling him that he did n't count as an artist at all), would only see their pictures in the public galleries, and judge them in the fair race with their neighbors. This announcement and conduct of mine filled all the Berners Street and Fitzroy Square district with terror.

As I am writing this after having had my fill of their works, so publicly exhibited in the country, at a distance from catalogues, my only book of reference being an orchard whereof the trees are now bursting into full blossom, — it is probable that my remarks will be rather general than particular, that I shall only discourse about those pictures which I especially remember, or, indeed, upon any other point suitable to my honor, and your delectation.

I went round the galleries with a young friend of mine, who, like yourself at present, has been a student of "High Art" at Rome. He had been a pupil of Monsieur Ingres, at Paris. He could draw rude figures of eight feet high to a nicety, and had produced many heroic compositions of that pleasing class and size, to the great profit of the paper-stretchers both in Paris and Rome. He came back from the latter place a year since, with his beard and mustachios, of course. He could find no room in all Newman Street and Soho big enough to hold him and his genius, and was turned out of a decent house, because, for the purposes of art, he wished to batter down the partition wall between the two drawing-rooms he had. His great cartoon last year (whether it was Caractacus before Claudius, or a scene from the "Vicar of Wakefield," I won't say) failed somehow. He was a good deal cut up by the defeat, and went into the country to his relations, from whom he returned after a while, with his mustachios shaved, clean linen, and other signs of depression. He said (with a hollow laugh) he should not commence on his great canvas this year, and so gave up the completion of his composition of "Boadicea addressing the Iceni": quite a novel subject, which, with that ingenuity and profound reading which distinguishes his brethren, he had determined to take up.

Well, sir, this youth and I went to the exhibitions together, and I watched his behavior before the pictures. At the tragic, swaggering, theatrical, historical pictures, he yawned; before some of the grand, flashy landscapes, he stood without the least emotion; but before some quiet scenes of humor or pathos, or some easy little copy of nature, the youth stood in pleased contemplation, the nails of his high-lows seemed to be screwed into the floor there, and his face dimpled over with grins.

"These little pictures," said he, on being questioned, "are worth a hundred times more than the big ones. In the latter you see signs of ignorance of every kind, weakness of hand, poverty of invention, carelessness of drawing, lamentable imbecility of thought. Their heroism is borrowed from the theatre, their sentiment is so maudlin that it makes you sick. I see no symptoms of thought, or of minds strong and genuine enough to cope with elevated subjects. No individuality, no novelty, the decencies of costume (my friend did not mean that the figures we were looking at were naked, like Mr. Etty's, but that they were dressed out of all historical propriety) are disregarded; the people are striking attitudes, as at the Coburg. There is something painful to me in this *naïve* exhibition of incompetency, this imbecility that is so unconscious of its own failure. If, however, the aspiring men don't succeed, the modest do; and what they have really seen or experienced, our artist can depict with successful accuracy and delightful skill. Hence," says he, "I would sooner have So-and-so's little sketch ('A Donkey on a Common') than What-d 'ye-call-'em's enormous picture ('Sir Walter Manny and the Crusaders discovering Nova Scotia'), and prefer yonder unpretending sketch, 'Shrimp-Catchers, Morning,' (how exquisitely the long and level sands are touched off! how beautifully the morning light touches the countenances of the fishermen, and illumines the rosy features of the shrimps!) to yonder pretentious illustration from Spenser, 'Sir Botibol rescues Una from Sir Uglimore in the Cave of the Enchantress Ichthyosaura.'"

I am only mentioning another's opinion of these pictures, and would not of course, for my own part, wish to give pain by provoking comparisons that must be disagreeable to some persons. But I could not help agreeing with my young friend, and saying, "Well, then, in the name of goodness, my dear fellow, if you only like what is real, and natural, and unaffected, — if upon such works you gaze with delight, while from more pretentious performers you turn away with weariness, why the deuce must *you* be in the heroic vein? Why don't you *do* what you like?" The young man turned round on the iron-heel of his high-lows, and walked down stairs clinking them sulkily.

There are a variety of classes and divisions into which

the works of our geniuses may be separated. There are the heroic pictures, the theatrical-heroic, the religious, the historical-sentimental, the historical-familiar, the namby-pamby, and so forth.

Among the heroic pictures of course Mr. Haydon's ranks the first, its size and pretensions call for that place. It roars out to you as it were with a Titanic voice from among all the competition to public favor, "Come and look at me." A broad-shouldered, swaggering, hulking archangel, with those rolling eyes and distending nostrils which belong to the species of sublime caricature, stands scowling on a sphere from which the Devil is just descending, bound earthwards. Planets, comets, and other astronomical phenomena, roll and blaze round the pair and flame in the new blue sky. There is something burly and bold in this resolute genius which will attack only enormous subjects, which will deal with nothing but the epic, something respectable even in the defeats of such characters. I was looking the other day at Southampton at a stout gentleman in a green coat and white hat, who a year or two since fully believed that he could walk upon the water, and set off in the presence of a great concourse of people upon his supermarine journey. There is no need to tell you that the poor fellow got a wetting and sank amidst the jeers of all his beholders. I think somehow they should not have laughed at that honest ducked gentleman, they should have respected the faith and simplicity which led him unhesitatingly to venture upon that watery experiment; and so, instead of laughing at Haydon, which you and I were just about to do, let us check our jocularity, and give him credit for his great earnestness of purpose. I begin to find the world growing more pathetic daily, and laugh less every year of my life. Why laugh at idle hopes, or vain purposes, or utter blundering self-confidence? Let us be gentle with them henceforth, — who knows whether there may not be something of the sort *chez nous?* But I am wandering from Haydon and his big picture. Let us hope somebody will buy. Who, I cannot tell; it will not do for a chapel; it is too big for a house: I have it, — it might answer to hang up over a caravan at a fair, if a travelling orrery were exhibited inside.

This may be sheer impertinence and error, the picture may suit some tastes, it does "The Times" for instance, which pronounces it to be a noble work of the highest art; whereas the "Post" won't believe a bit, and passes it by with scorn. What a comfort it is that there are different tastes then, and that almost all artists have thus a chance of getting a livelihood somehow! There is Martin, for another instance, with his brace of pictures about Adam and Eve, which I would venture to place in the theatrical-heroic class. One looks at those strange pieces and wonders how people can be found to admire, and yet they do. Grave old people with chains and seals, look dumb-foundered into those vast perspectives, and think the apex of the sublime is reached there. In one of Sir Bulwer Lytton's novels there is a passage to that effect. I forget where, but there is a new edition of them coming out in single volumes, and am positive you will find the sentiment somewhere. They come up to his conceptions of the sublime, they answer his ideas of beauty of the Beautiful, as he writes with a large B. He is himself an artist and a man of genius. What right have we poor devils to question such an authority? Do you recollect how we used to laugh in the Capitol at the Domenichino Sibyl which this same author praises so enthusiastically?

a wooden, pink-faced, goggle-eyed, ogling creature, we said it was, with no more beauty or sentiment than a wax doll. But this was our conceit, dear Augusto; on subjects of art, perhaps, there is no reasoning after all: or who can tell why children have a passion for lollypops, and this man worships beef while t' other adores mutton? To the child, lollypops may be the truthful and beautiful, and why should not some men find Martin's pictures as much to their taste as Milton?

Another instance of the blessed variety of tastes may be mentioned here advantageously; while, as you have seen, "The Times" awards the palm to Haydon, and Sir Lytton exalts Martin as the greatest painter of the English school, "The Chronicle," quite as well informed, no doubt, says that Mr. Eddis is the great genius of the present season, and that his picture of Moses's mother parting with him before leaving him in the bulrushes is a great and noble composition.

This critic must have a taste for the neat and agreeable, that is clear. Mr. Eddis's picture is nicely colored; the figures in fine clean draperies, the sky a bright clean color; Moses's mother is a handsome woman; and as she holds her child to her breast for the last time, and lifts up her fine eyes to heaven, the beholder may be reasonably moved by a decent *bourgeois* compassion, — a handsome woman parting from her child is always an object of proper sympathy, — but as for the greatness of the picture as a work of art, that is another question of tastes again. This picture seemed to me to be essentially a prose composition, not a poetical one. It tells you no more than you can see. It has no more wonder or poetry about it than a police report or a newspaper paragraph, and should be placed, as I take it, in the historic-sentimental school, which is pretty much followed in England,—nay, as close as possible to the namby-pamby quarter.

Of the latter sort there are some illustrious examples; and as it is the fashion for critics to award prizes, I would for my part cheerfully award the prize of a new silver teaspoon to Mr. Redgrave, that champion of suffering female innocence, for his "Governess." That picture is more decidedly *spooney* than, perhaps, any other of this present season; and the subject seems to be a favorite with the artist. We have had the "Governess" one year before, or a variation of her under the name of "The Teacher," or *vice versa*. The Teacher's young pupils are at play in the garden, she sits sadly in the school-room, there she sits, poor dear!—the piano is open beside her, and (O, harrowing thought!) "Home, sweet home!" is open in the music-book. She sits and thinks of that dear place, with a sheet of black-edged note-paper in her hand. They have brought her her tea and bread and butter on a tray. She has drunk the tea, *she has not tasted the bread and butter.* There is pathos for you! there is art! This is, indeed, a love for lollypops with a vengeance, a regular babyhood of taste, about which a man with a manly stomach may be allowed to protest a little peevishly, and implore the public to give up such puling food.

There is a gentleman in the Octagon Room who, to be sure, runs Mr. Redgrave rather hard, and should have a silver pap-spoon at any rate, if the teaspoon is irrevocably awarded to his rival. The Octagon Room prize is a picture called the "Arrival of the Overland Mail." A lady is in her bedchamber, a portrait of her husband, Major Jones (cherished lord of that bridal apartment, with its drab-curtained bed), hangs on the wainscot in the distance, and you see his red coat and mustachios gleaming there between the wardrobe and the wash-hand-stand. But where is his lady? She is on her knees by the bedside, her face has sunk into the feather-bed; her hands are clasped agonizingly together; a most tremendous black-edged letter has just arrived by the overland mail. It is all up with Jones. Well, let us hope she will marry again, and get over her grief for poor J.

Is not there something *naïve* and simple in this downright way of exciting compassion? I saw people looking at this pair of pictures evidently with yearning hearts. The great geniuses who invented them have not, you see, toiled in vain. They can command the sympathies of the public, — they have gained Art-Union prizes, let us hope, as well as those humble imaginary ones which I have just awarded, — and yet my heart is not naturally hard, though it refuses to be moved by such means as are here employed.

If the simple statement of a death is to harrow up the feelings, or to claim the tributary tear, *mon Dieu!* a man ought to howl every morning over the newspaper obituary. If we are to cry for every governess who leaves home, what a fund of pathos "The Times" advertisements would afford daily! we might weep down whole columns of close type. I have said before, I am growing more inclined to the pathetic daily, but let us in the name of goodness make a stand somewhere, or the namby-pamby of the world will become unendurable; and we shall melt away in a deluge of blubber. This drivelling, hysterical sentimentality, it is surely the critic's duty to grin down, to shake any man roughly by the shoulder who seems dangerously affected by it, and, not sparing his feelings in the least, tell him he is a fool for his pains, to have no more respect for those who invent it, but expose their error with all the downrightness that is necessary.

By far the prettiest of the maudlin pictures is Mr. Stone's "Premier Pas." It is that old, pretty, rococo, fantastic Jenny and Jessamy couple, whose loves the painter has been chronicling any time these five years, and whom he has spied out at various wells, porches, &c. The lad is making love with all his might, and the maiden is in a pretty confusion, — her heart flutters, and she only seems to spin. She drinks in the warm words of the young fellow with a pleasant conviction of the invincibility of her charms. He appeals nervously, and tugs at a pink which is growing up the porch-side. It is that pink, somehow, which has saved the picture from being decidedly namby-pamby. There is something new, fresh, and delicate about the little incident of the flower. It redeems Jenny, and renders that young prig, Jessamy, bearable. The picture is very nicely painted, according to the careful artist's wont. The neck and hands of the girl are especially pretty. The lad's face, is effeminate and imbecile, but his velveteen breeches are painted with great vigor and strength.

This artist's picture of the "Queen and Ophelia" is in a much higher walk of art. There may be doubts about Ophelia. She is too pretty to my taste. Her dress (especially the black bands round her arms) too elaborately conspicuous and coquettish. The queen is a noble dramatic head and attitude. Ophelia seems to be looking at us, the audience, and in a pretty attitude expressly to captivate us. The queen is only thinking about the crazed girl, and Hamlet, and her own gloomy affairs, and has quite forgotten her own noble beauty and superb presence. The color of the picture struck me as quite new,

— sedate, but bright and very agreeable. The checkered light and shadow is made cleverly to aid in forming the composition, — it is very picturesque and good. It is by far the best of Mr. Stone's works, and in the best line. Good by, Jenny and Jessamy; we hope never to see you again, — no more rococo rustics, no more namby-pamby: the man who can paint the queen of Hamlet must forsake henceforth such fiddle-faddle company.

By the way, has any Shakespearian commentator ever remarked how fond the queen really was of her second husband, the excellent Claudius? How courteous and kind the latter always was towards her? So excellent a family-man ought to be pardoned a few errors in consideration of his admirable behavior to his wife. He *did* go a little far, certainly, but then it was to possess a jewel of a woman.

More pictures indicating a fine appreciation of the tragic sentiment are to be found in the Exhibition. Among them may be mentioned specially Mr. Johnson's picture of "Lord Russell taking the Communion in Prison before Execution." The story is finely told here, the group large and noble. The figure of the kneeling wife, who looks at her husband, meekly engaged in the last sacred office, is very good indeed; and the little episode of the jailer, who looks out into the yard indifferent, seems to me to give evidence of a true dramatic genius. In "Hamlet," how those indifferent remarks of Guildenstern and Rosencrantz, at the end, bring out the main figures and deepen the surrounding gloom of the tragedy!

In Mr. Frith's admirable picture of the "Good Pastor," from Goldsmith, there is some sentiment of a very quiet, refined, Sir-Roger-de-Coverley-like sort, — not too much of it, — it is indicated rather than expressed. "Sentiment, sir," Walker of the "Original" used to say, — "sentiment, sir, is like garlic in made dishes: it should be felt everywhere and seen nowhere."

Now, I won't say that Mr. Frith's sentiment is like garlic, or provoke any other savory comparison regarding it; but say, in a word, this is one of the pictures I would like to have sent abroad to be exhibited at a European congress of painters, to show what an English artist can do. The young painter seems to me to have had a thorough comprehension of his subject and his own abilities. And what a rare quality is this, — to know what you can do! An ass will go and take the grand historic walk, while, with lowly wisdom, Mr. Frith prefers the lowly path where there are plenty of flowers growing, and children prattling along the walks. This is the sort of picture that is good to paint now-a-days, — kindly, beautiful, inspiring delicate sympathies, and awakening tender good-humor. It is a comfort to have such a companion as that in a study to look up at when your eyes are tired with work, and to refresh you with its gentle, quiet good-fellowship. I can see it now, as I shut my own eyes, displayed faithfully on the camera-obscura of the brain, — the dear old parson, with his congregation of old and young clustered round him; the little ones plucking him by the gown, with wondering eyes, half roguery, half terror; the smoke is curling up from the cottage-chimneys, in a peaceful Sabbath-sort of way; the three village quidnuncs are chattering together at the churchyard stile; there 's a poor girl seated there on a stone, who has been crossed in love evidently, and looks anxiously to the parson for a little doubtful consolation. That 's the real sort of sentiment, — there 's no need of a great, clumsy, black-edged letter to placard her misery, as it were, after Mr.

Redgrave's fashion. The sentiment is only the more sincere for being unobtrusive; and the spectator gives his compassion the more readily, because the unfortunate object makes no coarse demands upon his pity.

The painting of this picture is exceedingly clever and dexterous. One or two of the foremost figures are painted with the breadth and pearly delicacy of Greuze. The three village politicians, in the background, might have been touched by Teniers, so neat, brisk, and sharp is the execution of the artist's facile brush.

Mr. Frost (a new name, I think, in the Catalogue) has given us a picture of "Sabrina," which is so pretty that I heartily hope it has not been purchased for the collection from "Comus," which adorns the Buckingham Palace summerhouse. It is worthy of a better place and price than our royal patrons appear to be disposed to give for the works of English artists. What victims have those poor fellows been of this awful patronage! Great has been the commotion in the pictorial world, dear Augusto, regarding the fate of those frescos which royalty was pleased to order, which it condescended to purchase at a price that no poor amateur would have the face to offer. Think of the greatest patronage in the world giving forty pounds for pictures worth four hundred, — condescending to buy works from humble men who could not refuse, and paying for them below their value! Think of august powers and principalities ordering the works of such a great man as Etty to be hacked out of the palace-wall! That was a slap in the face to every artist in England; and I can agree with the conclusion come to by an indignant poet of *Punch's* band, who says, for his part, —

"I will not toil for queen and crown,
If princely patrons spurn me down;

I will not ask for royal job, —
Let my Mæcenas be A SNOB !"

This is, however, a delicate, an awful subject, over which loyal subjects like you and I had best mourn in silence: but the fate of Etty's noble picture of last year made me tremble lest Frost should be similarly nipped; and I hope more genuine patronage for this promising young painter. His picture is like a mixture of very good Hilton and Howard, raised to a state of genius. There is sameness in the heads, but great grace and beauty, — a fine sweeping movement in the composition of the beautiful fairy figures, undulating gracefully through the stream, while the lilies lie gracefully overhead. There is another submarine picture of "Nymphs cajoling Young Hylas," which contains a great deal of very clever imitations of Boucher.

That youthful Goodall, whose early attempts promised so much, is not quite realizing those promises, I think, and is cajoled, like Hylas before mentioned, by dangerous beauty. His "Connemara Girls going to Market" are a vast deal too clean and pretty for such females. They laugh and simper in much too genteel a manner; they are washing such pretty white feet as I don't think are common about Leenane or Ballynalinch, and would be better at ease in white satin slippers than trudging up Croaghpatrick. There is a luxury of geographical knowledge for you! I have not done with it yet. Stop till we come to Roberts's "View of Jerusalem," and Muller's pictures of "Rhodes," and "Xanthus," and "Telmessus." This artist's sketches are excellent, — like nature, and like Decamps, that best of painters of Oriental life and colors. In the pictures, the artist forgets the brilliancy of color which is so conspicuous in his sketches, and "Telmessus" looks as gray and heavy as Dover in March.

Mr. Pickersgill (not the Academician, by any means) deserves great praise for two very poetical pieces; one from Spenser, I think (Sir Botibol, let us say, as before, with somebody in some hag's cave); another called the "Four Ages," which has still better grace and sentiment. This artist, too, is evidently one of the disciples of Hilton; and another, who has, also, as it seems to me, studied with advantage that graceful and agreeable English painter, Mr. Hook, whose "Song of the Olden Time" is hung up in the Octagon Closet, and makes a sunshine in that exceedingly shady place. The female figure is faulty, but charming (many charmers have their little faults, it is said); the old bard who is singing the song of the olden time, a most venerable, agreeable, and handsome old minstrel. In Alnaschar-like moods a man fancies himself a noble patron, and munificent rewarder of artists; in which case I should like to possess myself of the works of these two young men, and give them four times as large a price as the —— gave for pictures five times as good as theirs.

I suppose Mr. Eastlake's composition from "Comus" is the contribution in which *he* has been mulcted, in company with his celebrated brother artists, for the famous Buckingham Palace pavilion. Working for nothing is very well; but to work for a good, honest, remunerating price is, perhaps, the best way, after all. I can't help thinking that the artist's courage has failed him over his "Comus" picture. Time and pains he has given, that is quite evident. The picture is prodigiously labored, and hatched, and tickled up with a Chinese minuteness; but there is a woful lack of *vis* in the work. That poor laborer has kept his promise, has worked the given number of hours; but he has had no food all the while, and has executed his job in a somewhat faint manner. This face of the lady is pure and beautiful; but we have seen it at any time these ten years, with its red transparent shadows, its mouth in which butter would n't melt, and its beautiful brown madder hair. She is getting rather tedious, that sweet, irreproachable creature, that is the fact. She may be an angel; but sky-blue, my wicked senses tell me, is a feeble sort of drink, and men require stronger nourishment.

Mr. Eastlake's picture is a prim, mystic, cruciform composition. The lady languishes in the middle; an angel is consoling her, and embracing her with an arm out of joint; little rows of cherubs stand on each side the angels and the lady, — wonderful little children, with blue or brown beady eyes, and sweet little flossy curly hair, and no muscles or bones, as becomes such supernatural beings, no doubt. I have seen similar little darlings in the toy-shops in the Lowther Arcade for a shilling, with just such pink cheeks and round eyes, their bodies formed out of cotton wool, and their extremities veiled in silver paper. Well; it is as well, perhaps, that Etty's jovial nymphs should not come into such a company. Good Lord! how they would astonish the weak nerves of Mr. Eastlake's *précieuse* young lady!

Quite unabashed by the squeamishness exhibited in the highest quarter (as the newspapers call it), Mr. Etty goes on rejoicing in his old fashion. Perhaps he is worse than ever this year, and despises *nec dulces amores nec choræas,* because certain great personages are offended. Perhaps, this year, his ladies and Cupids *are* a little *hazardés;* his Venuses expand more than ever in the line of Hottentot beauty; his drawing and coloring are still more audacious than they were; patches of red shine on the cheeks of his blowsy nymphs; his idea of form goes to the verge of monstrosity. If you look at the pictures closely (and, considering all things, it requires some courage to do so), the forms disappear; feet and hands are scumbled away, and distances appear to be dabs and blotches of lakes, and brown, and ultramarine. It must be confessed, that some of these pictures would *not* be suitable to hang up everywhere, — in a young ladies' school, for instance. But how rich and superb is the color! Did Titian paint better, or Rubens as well? There is a nymph and child in the left corner of the Great Room, sitting, without the slightest fear of catching cold, in a sort of moonlight, of which the color appears to me to be as rich and wonderful as Titian's best, — "Bacchus and Ariadne," for instance, — and better than Rubens's. There is a little head of a boy in a blue dress (for once in a way) which kills every picture in the room, out-stares all the red-coated generals, out-blazes Mrs. Thwaites and her diamonds (who has the place of honor); and has that unmistakable, inestimable, indescribable mark of the GREAT painter about it, which makes the soul of a man kindle up as he sees it, and own that there is Genius. How delightful it is to feel that shock, and how few are the works of art that can give it!

The author of that sibylline book of mystic rhymes, the unrevealed bard of the "Fallacies of Hope," is as great as usual, vibrating between the absurd and the sublime, until the eye grows dazzled in watching him, and can't really tell in what region he is. If Etty's color is wild and mysterious, looking here as if smeared with the finger, and there with the palette-knife, what can be said about Turner? Go up and look at one of his pictures, and you laugh at yourself and at him, and at the picture, and that wonderful amateur who is invariably found to give a thousand pounds for it, or more, — some sum wild, prodigious, unheard-of, monstrous, like the picture itself. All about the author of the "Fallacies of Hope" is a mysterious extravaganza; price, poem, purchaser, picture. Look at the latter for a little time, and it begins to affect you too, — to mesmerize you. It is revealed to you; and, as it is said in the East, the magicians make children see the sultauns, carpet-bearers, tents, &c., in a spot of ink in their hands; so the magician, Joseph Mallard, makes you see what he likes on a board, that to the first view is merely dabbed over with occasional streaks of yellow, and flecked here and there with vermilion. The vermilion blotches become little boats full of harpooners and gondolas, with a deal of music going on on board. That is not a smear of purple you see yonder, but a beautiful whale, whose tail has just slapped a half-dozen whale-boats into perdition; and as for what you fancied to be a few zigzag lines spattered on the canvas at hap-hazard, look! they turn out to be a ship with all her sails; the captain and his crew are clearly visible in the ship's bows; and you may distinctly see the oil-casks getting ready under the superintendence of that man with the red whiskers and the cast in his eye; who is, of course, the chief mate. In a word, I say that Turner is a great and awful mystery to me. I don't like to contemplate him too much, lest I should actually begin to believe in his poetry as well as his paintings, and fancy the "Fallacies of Hope" to be one of the finest poems in the world.

Now Stanfield has no mysticism or oracularity about him. You can see what he means at once. His style is as simple and manly as a seaman's song. One of the most dexterous, he is also one of the most careful of painters. Every year his works are more elaborated, and you are surprised to find a progress in an artist who had seemed to reach his acmé before. His battle of frigates this year is a brilliant, sparkling pageant of naval war. His great picture of the "Mole of Ancona," fresh, healthy, and bright as breeze and sea can make it. There are better pieces still by this painter, to my mind; one in the first room, especially,—a Dutch landscape, with a warm, sunny tone upon it, worthy of Cuyp and Callcott. Who is G. Stanfield, an exhibitor and evidently a pupil of the Royal Academician? Can it be a son of that gent? If so, the father has a worthy heir to his name and honors. G. Stanfield's Dutch picture may be looked at by the side of his father's.

Roberts has also distinguished himself and advanced in skill, great as his care had been and powerful his effects before. "The Ruins of Karnac" is the most poetical of this painter's works, I think. A vast and awful scene of gloomy Egyptian ruin! The sun lights up tremendous lines of edifices, which were only parts formerly of the enormous city of the hundred gates; long lines of camels come over the reddening desert, and camps are set by the side of the glowing pools. This is a good picture to gaze at, and to fill your eyes and thoughts with grandiose ideas of Eastern life.

This gentleman's large picture of "Jerusalem" did not satisfy me so much. It is yet very faithful. Anybody who had visited this place must see the careful fidelity with which the artist has mapped the rocks and valleys, and laid down the lines of the buildings; but the picture has, to my eyes, too green and trim a look; the mosques and houses look fresh and new, instead of being mouldering, old, sun-baked edifices of glaring stone rising amidst wretchedness and ruin. There is not, to my mind, that sad, fatal aspect, which the city presents from whatever quarter you view it, and which haunts a man who has seen it ever after with an impression of terror. Perhaps in the spring for a little while, at which season the sketch for this picture was painted, the country round about may look very cheerful. When we saw it in autumn, the mountains that stand round about Jerusalem were not green, but ghastly piles of hot rock, patched here and there with yellow, weedy herbage. A cactus or a few bleak olive-trees made up the vegetation of the wretched, gloomy landscape; whereas, in Mr. Roberts's picture, the valley of Jehoshaphat looks like a glade in a park, and the hills, up to the gates, are carpeted with verdure.

Being on the subject of Jerusalem, here may be mentioned with praise Mr. Hart's picture of a Jewish ceremony, with a Hebrew name I have forgotten. This piece is exceedingly bright and pleasing in color, odd and novel as a representation of manners and costume, — a striking and agreeable picture. I don't think as much can be said for the same artist's "Sir Thomas More going to Execution." Miss More is crying on papa's neck, pa looks up to heaven, halberdiers look fierce, &c.: all the regular adjuncts and property of pictorical tragedy are here brought into play. But nobody cares, that is the fact; and one fancies the designer himself cannot have cared much for the orthodox historical group whose misfortunes he was depicting.

These pictures are like boy's hexameters at school. Every lad of decent parts in the sixth form has a knack of turning out great quantities of respectable verse, without blunders, and with scarce any mental labor; but these verses are not the least like poetry, any more than the great Academical paintings of the artists are like great painting. You want something more than a composition, and a set of costumes and figures decently posed and studied. If these were all, for instance, Mr. Charles Landseer's picture of "Charles I. before the Battle of Edge Hill," would be a good work of art. Charles stands at a tree before the inn door, officers are round about, the little princes are playing with a little dog, as becomes their youth and innocence, rows of soldiers appear in red coats, nobody seems to have anything particular to do, except the royal martyr, who is looking at a bone of ham that a girl out of the inn has hold of.

Now this is all very well, but you want something more than this in an historic picture, which should have its parts, characters, varieties, and climax, like a drama. You don't want the *Deus intersit* for no other purpose than to look at a knuckle of ham; and here is a piece well composed, and (bating a little want of life in the figures) well drawn, brightly and pleasantly painted, as all this artist's works are, all the parts and accessories studied and executed with care and skill, and yet meaning nothing, — the part of Hamlet omitted. The king in this attitude (with the baton in his hand, simpering at the bacon aforesaid) has no more of the heroic in him than the pork he contemplates, and he deserves to lose every battle he fights. I prefer the artist's other still-life pictures to this. He has a couple more, professedly so called, very cleverly executed, and capital cabinet pieces.

Strange to say, I have not one picture to remark upon taken from the "Vicar of Wakefield." Mr. Ward has a very good Hogarthian work, with some little extravagance and caricature, representing Johnson waiting in Lord Chesterfield's ante-chamber, among a crowd of hangers-on and petitioners, who are sulky, or yawning, or neglected, while a pretty Italian singer comes out, having evidently had a very satisfactory interview with his lordship, and who (to lose no time) is arranging another rendezvous with another admirer. This story is very well, coarsely, and humorously told, and is as racy as a chapter out of Smollett. There is a yawning chaplain, whose head is full of humor; and a pathetic episode of a widow and pretty child, in which the artist has not succeeded so well.

There is great delicacy and beauty in Mr. Herbert's picture of "Pope Gregory teaching Children to Sing." His Holiness lies on his sofa, languidly beating time over his book. He does not look strong enough to use the scourge in his hands, and with which the painter says he used to correct his little choristers. Two ghostly aides-de-camp in the shape of worn, handsome, shaven ascetic friars, stand behind the pontiff demurely; and all the choristers are in full song, with their mouths as wide open as a nest of young birds when the mother comes. The painter seems to me to have acquired the true spirit of the Middle-Age devotion. All his works have unction; and the prim, subdued, ascetic race, which forms the charm and mystery of the missal-illuminations, and which has operated to convert some imaginative minds from the new to the old faith.

And, by way of a wonder, behold a devotional picture from Mr. Edwin Landseer, "A Shepherd Praying at a Cross in the Fields." I suppose the Sabbath church-bells are ringing from the city far away in the plain. Do you remember the beautiful lines of Uhland?

"Es ist der tag des Herrn
Ich bin allein auf weitern Flur
Noch eine Morgen-glocke nur
Und stille nah und fern.

"Anbetend knie ich hier
O süsses Graun geheimes Wehn
Als knieten viele Ungesehn
Und beteten mit mir."

Here is a noble and touching pictorial illustration of them, — of Sabbath repose and *recueillement*, — an almost endless flock of sheep lies around the pious pastor; the sun shines peacefully over the vast fertile plain; blue mountains keep watch in the distance; and the sky above is serenely clear. I think this is the highest flight of poetry the painter has dared to take yet. The numbers and variety of attitude and expression in that flock of sheep quite startle the spectator as he examines them. The picture is a wonder of skill.

How richly the good pictures cluster at this end of the room! There is a little Mulready, of which the color blazes out like sapphires and rubies; a pair of Leslies, — one called the "Heiress," — one a scene from Molière, — both delightful: these are flanked by the magnificent nymphs of Etty, before mentioned. What school of art in Europe, or what age, can show better painters than these in their various lines? The young men do well, but the elders do best still. No wonder the English pictures are fetching their thousands of guineas at the sales. They deserve these great prices as well as the best works of the Hollanders.

I am sure that three such pictures as Mr. Webster's "Dame's School" ought to entitle the proprietor to pay the income-tax. There is a little caricature in some of the children's faces; but the schoolmistress is a perfect figure, most admirably natural, humorous, and sentimental. The picture is beautifully painted, — full of air, of delightful harmony and tone.

There are works by Creswick that can hardly be praised too much. One particularly, called " A Place to be Remembered;" which no lover of pictures can see and forget. Danby's great " Evening Scene " has portions which are not surpassed by Cuyp or Claude ; and a noble landscape of Lee's, among several others, — a height, with some trees and a great expanse of country beneath.

From the fine pictures you come to the class which are very nearly being fine pictures. In this I would enumerate a landscape or two by Collins. Mr. Leigh's " Polyphemus," of which the landscape part is very good, and only the figure questionable; and, let us say, Mr. Elmore's " Origin of the Guelf and Ghibelline Factions," which contains excellent passages, and admirable drawing and dexterity, but fails to strike as a whole somehow. There is not sufficient purpose in it, or the story is not enough to interest, or, though the parts are excellent, the whole is somewhere deficient.

There is very little comedy in the Exhibition, most of the young artists tending to the sentimental rather than the ludicrous. Leslie's scene from Molière is the best comedy. Collins's " Fetching the Doctor " is also delightful fun. The greatest farce, however, is Chalon's picture with an Italian title, " B. Virgine col," &c. Impudence never went beyond this. The infant's hair has been curled into ringlets, the mother sits on her chair with painted cheeks and a Haymarket leer. The picture might serve for the oratory of an opera girl.

Among the portraits, Knight's and Watson Gordon's are the best. A " Mr. Pigeon " by the former hangs in the place of honor usually devoted to our gracious Prince, and is a fine rich state picture. Even better are there by Mr. Watson Gordon: one representing a gentleman in black silk stockings, whose name has escaped the memory of your humble servant; another, a fine portrait of Mr. De Quincey, the opium-eater. Mr. Lawrence's heads, solemn and solidly painted, look out at you from their frames, though they be ever so high placed, and push out of sight the works of more flimsy but successful practitioners. A portrait of great power and richness of color is that of Mr. Lopez, by Linnell. Mr. Grant is the favorite; but a very unsound painter, to my mind, — painting like a brilliant and graceful amateur rather than a serious artist. But there is a quiet refinement and beauty about his female heads, which no other painter can perhaps give, and charms in spite of many errors. Is it Count D'Orsay, or is it Mr. Ainsworth, that the former has painted? Two peas are not more alike than these two illustrious characters.

In the miniature-room, Mr. Richmond's drawings are of so grand and noble a character, that they fill the eye as much as full-length canvases. Nothing can be finer than Mrs. Fry and the gray-haired lady in black velvet. There is a certain severe, respectable, Exeter-Hall look about most of this artist's pictures, that the observer may compare with the Catholic physiognomies of Mr. Herbert: see his picture of Mr. Pugin, for instance; it tells of chants and cathedrals, as Mr. Richmond's work somehow does of Clapham Common and the May meetings. The genius of May Fair fires the bosom of Chalon, the tea party, the quadrille, the hair-dresser, the tailor, and the flunky. All Ross's miniatures sparkle with his wonderful and minute skill; Carrick's are excellent; Thorburn's almost take the rank of historical pictures. In his picture of two sisters, one has almost the most beautiful head in the world; and his picture of Prince Albert, clothed in red and leaning on a turquoise sabre, has ennobled that fine head, and given his royal highness's pale features an air of sunburnt and warlike vigor. Miss Corbaux, too, has painted one of the loveliest heads ever seen. Perhaps this is the pleasantest room of the whole, for you are sure to meet your friends here; kind faces smile at you from the ivory; and features of fair creatures, O, how * *

* * * * *

Here the eccentric author breaks into a rhapsody of thirteen pages regarding No. 2576, Mrs. Major Blogg, who was formerly Miss Poddy of Cheltenham, whom it appears that Michael Angelo knew and admired. The feelings of the Poddy family might be hurt, and the jealousy of Major Blogg aroused, were we to print Titmarsh's rapturous description of that lady; nor, indeed, can we give him any further space. He concludes by a withering denunciation of most of the statues, in the vault where they are buried; praising, however, the children, Paul and Virginia, the head of Bayly's nymph, and M'Dowall's boy. He remarks the honest character of the English countenance as exhibited in the busts, and contrasts it with Louis Philippe's head by Jones, on whom, both as a sculptor and a singer, he bestows great praise. He indignantly remonstrates with the committee for putting by far the finest female bust in the room, No. 1434, by Powers of Florence, in a situation where it cannot be seen; and, quitting the gallery finally, says he must go before he leaves town and give one more look at Hunt's "Boy at Prayers," in the Water-Color Exhibition, which he pronounces to be the finest serious work of the year.

THE ANONYMOUS IN PERIODICAL LITERATURE.

MY rising young friend Hitchings, the author of "Randolph the Robber," "The Murderers of May Fair," and other romances, and one of the chief writers in the Lictor newspaper, — a highly liberal, nay, seven-leagued boots progressional journal, — was discoursing with the writer of the present lines upon the queer decision to which the French Assembly has come, and which enforces a signature henceforth to all the leading articles in the French papers. As an act of government, Hitchings said he thought the measure most absurd and tyrannous, but he was not sorry for it, as it would infallibly increase the importance of the profession of letters, to which we both belonged. The man of letters will no longer be the anonymous slave of the newspaper-press proprietor, Hitchings said; the man of letters will no longer be used and flung aside in his old days; he will be rewarded according to his merits, and have the chance of making himself a name. And then Hitchings spoke with great fervor regarding the depressed condition of literary men, and said the time was coming when their merits would get them their own.

On this latter subject, which is a favorite one with

many gentlemen of our profession, I, for one, am confessedly incredulous. I am resolved not to consider myself a martyr. I never knew a man who had written a good book (unless, indeed, it were a Barrister with Attorneys) hurt his position in society by having done so. On the contrary, a clever writer, with decent manners and conduct, makes more friends than any other man. And I do not believe (parenthetically) that it will make much difference to my friend Hitchings whether his name is affixed to one, twenty, or two thousand articles of his composition. But what would happen in England if such a regulation as that just passed in France were to become law; and the House of Commons omnipotent, — which can shut up our parks for us, which can shut up our post-office for us, which can do anything it will, — should take a fancy to have the signature of every writer of a newspaper article?

Have they got any secret ledger at the "Times," in which the names of the writers of all the articles in that journal are written down? That would be a curious book to see. Articles in that paper have been attributed to every great man of the day. At one time it was said Brougham wrote regularly; at another, Canning was a known contributor; at some other time, it was Sir Robert Peel, Lord Aberdeen. It would be curious to see the real names. The Chancellor's or the Foreign Secretary's articles would most likely turn out to be written by Jones or Smith. I mean no disrespect to the latter, but the contrary, — to be a writer for a newspaper requires more knowledge, genius, readiness, scholarship, than you want in Saint Stephen's. Compare a good leading article and a speech in the House of Commons: compare a House of Commons orator with a writer, psha!

Would Jones or Smith, however, much profit by the publication of their names to their articles? That is doubtful. When the Chronicle or the Times speaks now, it is "we" who are speaking, — we the Liberal Conservatives, we the Conservative Sceptics; when Jones signs the article it is we no more, but Jones. It goes to the public with no authority. The public does not care very much what Jones's opinions are. They don't purchase the Jones organ any more, — the paper droops; and, in fact, I can conceive nothing more wearisome than to see the names of Smith, Brown, Jones, Robinson, and so forth, written in capitals every day, day after day, under the various articles of the paper. The public would begin to cry out at the poverty of the literary *dramatis personæ.* We have had Brown twelve times this month it would say. That Robinson's name is always coming up. As soon as there is a finance question, or a foreign question, or what not, it is Smith who signs the article. Give us somebody else.

Thus Brown and Robinson would get a doubtful and precarious bread instead of the comfortable and regular engagement which they now have. The paper would not be what it is. It would be impossible to employ men on trial, and see what their talents were worth. Occasion is half a public writer's battle. To sit down in his study and compose an article that *might* be suitable, is a hard work for him, — twice as hard as the real work, and yet not the real work, which is to fight the battle at two hours' notice, at the given place and time. The debate is over at twelve o'clock at night, let us say. Mr. Editor looks round, and fixes on his man. "Now 's your time, Captain Smith," says he, "charge the enemy, and rout them," — or "advance, Colonel Jones, with your column, and charge."

Now there may be men who are Jones's or Robinson's superiors in intellect, and who — give them a week or ten days to prepare — would turn out such an article as neither of the two men named could ever have produced, — that is very likely. I have often, for my part, said the most brilliant thing in the world, and one that would utterly upset that impudent Jenkins, whose confounded jokes and puns spare nobody; but then it has been three hours after Jenkins's pun, when I was walking home very likely, — and so it is with writers; some of them possess the amazing gift of the impromptu, and can always be counted upon in a moment of necessity; whilst others, slower coaches or leaders, require to get all their heavy guns into position, and laboriously to fortify their camp before they begin to fire.

Now, saying that Robinson is the fellow chiefly to be intrusted with the quick work of the paper, it would be a most unkind and unfair piece of tyranny on the newspaper proprietor to force him to publish Robinson's name as the author of all the articles *d'occasion.* You have no more right to call for this publicity from the newspaper owner, who sells you three yards of his printed fabric, than to demand from the linen-draper from what wholesale house he got his calico, — who spun it, who owned the cotton, and who cropped it in America. It is the article, and not the name and pedigree of the artificer, which a newspaper or any other dealer has a right to sell to the public. If I get a letter (which Heaven forbid!) from Mr. Tapes, my attorney, I know it is not in Tapes's own handwriting; I know it is a clerk writes it. So a newspaper is a composite work, got up by many hireling hands, of whom it is necessary to know no other name than the printer's or proprietor's.

It is not to be denied that men of signal ability will write for years in papers, and perish unknown, — and in so far their lot is a hard one, and the chances of life are against them. It is hard upon a man, with whose work the whole town is ringing, that not a soul should know or care who is the author who so delights the public.

But, on the other hand, if your article is excellent, would you have had any great renown from it, supposing the paper had not published it? Would you have had a chance at all but for that paper? Suppose you had brought out that article on a broad sheet, who would have bought it? Did you ever hear of an unknown man making a fortune by a pamphlet?

Again, it may so happen to a literary man that the stipend which he receives from one publication is not sufficient to boil his family pot, and that he must write in some other quarter. If Brown writes articles in the daily papers, and articles in the weekly and monthly periodicals, too, and signs the same, he surely weakens his force by extending his line. It would be better for him to write incognito than to placard his name in so many quarters, — as actors understand, who do not perform in too many pieces on the same night; and painters, who know that it is not worth their while to exhibit more than a certain number of pictures.

Besides, if to some men the want of publicity is an evil, to many others the privacy is most welcome. Many a young barrister is a public writer, for instance, to whose future prospects his fame as a literary man would give no possible aid, and whose intention it is to put away the pen, when the attorneys begin to find out his juridical merits. To such a man it would only be a misfortune to be known as a writer of leading articles. *His* battle for fame and fortune is to be made with other weapons than the pen. Then, again, a man without ambition, — and there are very many such sensible persons, or whose ambition does not go beyond his *pot au feu*, is happy to have the opportunity of quietly and honorably adding to his income, — of occupying himself, — of improving himself, — of paying for Tom at college, or for Mamma's carriage, and what not. Take away this modest mask, — force every man upon the public stage to appear with his name placarded, and we lose some of the best books, some of the best articles, some of the pleasantest wit that we have ever had.

On the whole, then, in this controversy I am against Hitchings; and although he insists upon it that he is a persecuted being, I do not believe it; and although he declares that I ought to consider myself trampled on by the world, I decline to admit that I am persecuted, and protest that it treats me and my brethren kindly in the main.

GOETHE:

A LETTER TO G. H. LEWES.

LONDON, 28th April, 1855.

EAR LEWES:—I wish I had more to tell you regarding Weimar and Goethe. Five-and-twenty years ago, at least a score of young English lads used to live at Weimar for study, or sport, or society; all of which were to be had in the friendly little Saxon capital. The Grand Duke and Duchess received us with the kindliest hospitality. The Court was splendid, but yet most pleasant and homely. We were invited in our turns to dinners, balls, and assemblies there. Such young men as had a right, appeared in uniforms, diplomatic and military. Some, I remember, invented gorgeous clothing,—the kind old Hof Marschall of those days, M. de Spiegel (who had two of the most lovely daughters eyes ever looked on), being in nowise difficult as to the admission of these young Englanders. Of the winter nights we used to charter sedan-chairs, in which we were carried through the snow to those pleasant Court entertainments. I, for my part, had the good luck to purchase Schiller's sword, which formed a part of my Court costume, and still hangs in my study, and puts me in mind of days of youth the most kindly and delightful.

We knew the whole society of the little city, and but that the young ladies, one and all, spoke admirable English, we surely might have learned the very best German. The society met constantly. The ladies of the Court had their evenings. The theatre was open twice or thrice in the week, where we assembled, a large family party. Goethe had retired from the direction, but the great traditions remained still. The theatre was admirably conducted; and besides the excellent Weimar company, famous actors and singers from various parts of Germany performed "Gastrolle"* through the winter. In that winter, I remember we had Ludwig Devrient in Shylock, Hamlet, Falstaff, and the "Robbers"; and the beautiful Schröder in "Fidelio."

After three-and-twenty years' absence I passed a couple of summer days in the well-remembered place, and was fortunate enough to find some of the friends of my youth. Madame de Goethe was there, and received me and my daughters with the kindness of old days. We drank tea in the open air at the famous cottage in the Park,† which still belongs to the family, and had been so often inhabited by her illustrious father.

In 1831, though he had retired from the world, Goethe would nevertheless very kindly receive strangers. His daughter-in-law's tea-table was always spread for us. We passed hours after hours there, and night after night with the pleasantest talk and music. We read over endless novels and poems in French, English, and German. My delight in those days was to make caricatures for children. I was touched to find that they were remembered, and some even kept until the present time; and very

* What in England are called "starring engagements."

† The *Gartenhaus.*

proud to be told, as a lad, that the great Goethe had looked at some of them.

He remained in his private apartments, where only a very few privileged persons were admitted; but he liked to know all that was happening, and interested himself about all strangers. Whenever a countenance struck his fancy, there was an artist settled in Weimar who made a portrait of it. Goethe had quite a gallery of heads, in black and white, taken by this painter. His house was all over pictures, drawings, casts, statues, and medals.

Of course I remember very well the perturbation of spirit, with which, as a lad of nineteen, I received the long-expected intimation that the Herr Geheimrath would see me on such a morning. This notable audience took place in a little ante-chamber of his private apartments, covered all round with antique casts and bas-reliefs. He was habited in a long gray or drab redingote, with a white neckcloth, and a red ribbon in his button-hole. He kept his hands behind his back, just as in Rauch's statuette. His complexion was very bright, clear and rosy. His eyes extraordinarily dark,* piercing and brilliant. I felt quite afraid before them, and recollect comparing them to the eyes of the hero of a certain romance called "Melmoth the Wanderer," which used to alarm us boys thirty years ago, — eyes of an individual who had made a bargain with a Certain Person, and at an extreme old age retained these eyes in all their awful splendor. I fancied Goethe must have been still more handsome as an old man than even in the days of his youth. His voice was very rich and sweet. He asked me questions about my-

* This must have been the effect of the position in which he sat with regard to the light. Goethe's eyes were dark brown, but not very dark.

self, which I answered as best I could. I recollect I was at first astonished, and then somewhat relieved, when I found he spoke French with not a good accent.

Vidi tantum. I saw him but three times. Once, walking in the garden of his house in the *Frauenplan;* once, going to step into his chariot on a sunshiny day, wearing a cap and a cloak with a red collar. He was caressing at the time a beautiful little golden-haired granddaughter, over whose sweet, fair face the earth has long since closed too.

Any of us who had books or magazines from England sent them to him, and he examined them eagerly. "Fraser's Magazine" had lately come out, and I remember he was interested in those admirable outline portraits which appeared for a while in its pages. But there was one, a very ghastly character of Mr. R——, which, as Madame de Goethe told me, he shut up and put away from him angrily. "They would make me look like that," he said; though in truth I can fancy nothing more serene, majestic, and *healthy* looking than the grand old Goethe.

Though his sun was setting, the sky round about was calm and bright, and that little Weimar illumined by it. In every one of those kind salons the talk was still of Art and letters. The theatre, though possessing no very extraordinary actors, was still conducted with a noble intelligence and order. The actors read books, and were men of letters and gentlemen, holding a not unkindly relationship with the *Adel.* At Court, the conversation was exceedingly friendly, simple, and polished. The Grand Duchess (the present Grand Duchess Dowager), a lady of very remarkable endowments, would kindly borrow our books from us, lend us her own, and graciously talk to us young men about our literary tastes and pursuits. In the respect paid by this Court to the Patriarch of letters, there was something ennobling, I think, alike to the subject and sovereign. With a five-and-twenty years' experience since those happy days of which I write, and an acquaintance with an immense variety of human kind, I think I have never seen a society more simple, more charitable, courteous, gentlemanlike than that of the dear little Saxon city, where the good Schiller and the great Goethe lived and lie buried.

Very sincerely yours,

W. M. Thackeray.

A LEAF OUT OF A SKETCH-BOOK.

IF you will take a leaf out of my sketch-book, you are welcome. It is only a scrap, but I have nothing better to give. When the fishing-boats come in at a watering-place, have n't you remarked that though these may be choking with great fish, you can only get a few herrings or a whiting or two? The big fish are all bespoken in London. As it is with fish, so it is with authors let us hope. Some Mr. Charles, of Paternoster Row, some Mr. Groves, of Cornhill, (or elsewhere,) has agreed for your turbots and your salmon, your soles and your lobsters. Take one of my little fish, — any leaf you like out of the little book, — a battered little book: through what a number of countries, to be sure, it has travelled in this pocket!

The sketches are but poor performances, say you. I don't say no; and value them no higher than you do, except as recollections of the past. The little scrawl helps to fetch back the scene which was present and alive once, and is gone away now, and dead. The past resurges out of its grave: comes up — a sad-eyed ghost sometimes — and gives a wan ghost-like look of recognition, ere it pops down under cover again. Here 's the Thames, an old graveyard, an old church, and some old chestnuts standing behind it. Ah! it was a very cheery place, that old graveyard; but what a dismal, cut-throat, crack-windowed, disreputable residence was that "charming villa on the banks of the Thames," which led me on the day's excursion! Why, the "capacious stabling" was a ruinous wooden old barn, the garden was a mangy potato patch, overlooked by the territories of a neighboring washerwoman. The housekeeper owned that the water was constantly in the cellars and ground-floor rooms in winter. Had I gone to live in that place, I should have perished like a flower in spring, or a young gazelle, let us say, with dark blue eye. I had spent a day and hired a fly at ever so much charges, misled by an unveracious auctioneer, against whom I have no remedy for publishing that abominable work of fiction which led me to make a journey, lose a day, and waste a guinea.

What is the next picture in the little show-book? It is a scene at Calais. The sketch is entitled "The Little Merchant." He was a dear, pretty little rosy-cheeked merchant, four years old maybe. He had a little scarlet *képi;* a little military frock-coat; a little pair of military red trousers and boots, which did not near touch the ground from the chair on which he sat sentinel. He was a little crockery merchant, and the wares over which he was keeping guard, sitting surrounded by walls and piles of them as in a little castle, were . . . . well, I never saw such a queer little crockery merchant.

Him and his little chair, boots, képi, crockery, you can see in the sketch, — but I see, nay hear, a great deal more. At the end of the quiet little old, old street, which has retired out of the world's business as it were, being quite too aged, feeble, and musty to take any part in life, — there is a great braying and bellowing of serpents and bassoons, a nasal chant of clerical voices, and a pattering of multitudinous feet. We run towards the market. It is a Church fête day. Banners painted and gilt with images of saints are flaming in the sun. Candles are held aloft, feebly twinkling in the noontide shine. A great procession of children with white veils, white shoes, white roses, passes, and the whole town is standing with its hat off to see the religious show. When I look at my little merchant, then, I not only see him, but that procession passing over the place; and as I see those people in their surplices, I can almost see Eustache de St. Pierre and his comrades walking in their shirts to present themselves to Edward and Philippa of blessed memory. And they stand before the wrathful monarch, — poor fellows, meekly shuddering in their chemises, with ropes round their necks; and good Philippa kneels before the royal conqueror, and says, "My King, my Edward, my *beau Sire!* Give these citizens their lives for our Lady's gramercy and the sake of thy Philippa!" And the Plantagenet growls, and scowls, and softens, and he lets those burgesses go. This novel and remarkable historical incident passes through my mind as I see the clergymen and clergyboys pass in their little short white surplices on a mid-August day. The balconies are full, the bells are all in a jangle, and the blue noonday sky quivers overhead.

I suppose other pen and pencil sketchers have the same feeling. The sketch brings back, not only the scene, but the circumstances under which the scene was viewed. In taking up an old book, for instance, written in former days by your humble servant, he comes upon passages which are outwardly lively and facetious, but inspire their writer with the most dismal melancholy. I lose all cognizance of the text sometimes, which is hustled and elbowed out of sight by the crowd of thoughts which throng forward, and which were alive and active at the time that text was born. Ah, my good Sir! a man's books may n't be interesting (and I could mention other authors' works besides this one's which set me to sleep), but if you knew *all* a writer's thoughts how interesting his book would be! Why, a grocer's day-book might be a wonderful history, if alongside of the entries of cheese, pickles, and figs, you could read the circumstances of the writer's life, and the griefs, hopes, joys, which caused the heart to beat, while the hand was writing and the ink flowing fresh. Ah memory! ah the past, ah the sad, sad past! Look under this waistcoat, my dear Madame. There. Over the liver. Don't be frightened. You can't see it. But there, at this moment, I assure you, there is an enormous vulture gnawing, gnawing.

Turn over the page. You can't deny that this is a nice little sketch of a quaint old town, with city towers, and an embattled town gate, with a hundred peaked gables, and ricketty balconies, and gardens sweeping down to the river wall, with its toppling ancient summer-houses under which the river rushes; the rushing river, the talking river, that murmurs all day, and brawls all night over the stones. At early morning and evening under this terrace which you see in the sketch — it is the terrace of the Steinbock or Capricorn Hotel — the cows come; and there, under the walnut-trees before the tannery, is a fountain and pump where the maids come in the afternoon and for some hours make a clatter as noisy as the river. Mountains gird it around, clad in dark green firs, with purple shadows gushing over their sides, and glorious changes and gradations of sunrise and setting. A more picturesque, quaint, kind, quiet little town than this of Coire in the Grisons, I have seldom seen ; or a more comfortable little inn than this of the Steinbock or Capricorn, on the terrace of which we are standing. But quick, let us turn the page. To look at it makes one horribly melancholy. As we are on the inn-terrace one of our party lies ill in the hotel within. When will that doctor come? Can we trust to a Swiss doctor in a remote little town away at the confines of the railway world? He is a good, sensible, complacent doctor, *laus Deo*, — the people of the hotel as kind, as attentive, as gentle, as eager to oblige. But O, the gloom of those sunshiny days ; the sickening languor and doubt which fill the heart as the hand is making yonder sketch, and I think of the invalid suffering within!

Quick, turn the page. And what is here? This picture, ladies and gentlemen, represents a steamer on the Alabama river, plying (or *which plied*), between Montgomery and Mobile. See, there is a black nurse with a cotton handkerchief round her head, dandling and tossing a white baby. Look in at the open door of that cabin, or "state room" as they call the crib yonder. A mother is leaning by a bed-place ; and see, kicking up in the air, are a little pair of white, fat legs, over which that happy young mother is bending in such happy, tender contemplation. That gentleman with a forked beard and a slouched hat, whose legs are sprawling here and there, and who is stabbing his mouth and teeth with his penknife, is quite good-natured, though he looks so fierce. A little time ago, as I was reading in the cabin, having one book in my hand and another at my elbow, he affably took the book at my elbow, read in it a little, and put it down by my side again. He meant no harm. I say he is quite good-natured and kind. His manners are not those of May Fair, but is not Alabama a river as well as Thames? I wish that other little gentleman were in the cabin who asked me to liquor twice or thrice in the course of the morning, but whose hospitality I declined, preferring not to be made merry by wine or strong waters before dinner. After dinner, in return for his hospitality, I asked *him* if he would drink? "No, sir, I have dined," he answered, with very great dignity, and a tone of reproof. Very good. Manners differ. I have not a word to say.

Well, my little Mentor is not in my sketch, but he is in my mind as I look at it: and this sketch, ladies and gentlemen, is especially interesting and valuable, because *the steamer blew up on the very next journey:* blew up, I give you my honor, — burst her boilers close by my state-room, so that I might, had I but waited for a week, have witnessed a celebrated institution of the country, and had the full benefit of the boiling.

I turn a page and who are these little men who appear on it? Jim and Sady are two young friends of mine at Savannah in Georgia. I made Sady's acquaintance on a first visit to America, — a pretty little brown boy with beautiful bright eyes, — and it appears that I presented him with a quarter of a dollar, which princely gift he remembered years afterwards, for never were eyes more bright and kind than the little man's when he saw me, and I dined with his kind masters on my second visit. Jim at my first visit had been a little toddling tadpole of a creature, but during the interval of the two journeys had developed into the full-blown beauty which you see. On the day after my arrival these young persons paid me a visit, and here is a humble portraiture of them, and an accurate account of a conversation which took place between us, as taken down on the spot by the elder of the interlocutors.

Jim is five years old: Sady is seben: only Jim is a great deal fatter. Jim and Sady have had sausage and hominy for breakfast. One sausage, Jim's was the biggest. Jim can sing, but declines on being pressed, and looks at Sady and grins. They both work in de garden. Jim has been licked by Master, but Sady never. These are their best clothes. They go to church in these clothes. Heard a fine sermon yesterday, but don't know what it was about. Never heard of England, never heard of America. Like orangees best. Don't know any old woman who sells orangees. (*A pecuniary transaction takes place.*) Will give that quarter dollar to Pa. That was Pa who waited at dinner. Are hungry, but dinner not cooked yet. Jim all the while is revolving on his axis and when begged to stand still turns round in a fitful manner.

Exeunt Jim and Sady with a cake apiece which the housekeeper gives them. Jim tumbles down stairs.

In his little red jacket, his little — his little? — his immense red trousers.

On my word the fair proportions of Jim are not exaggerated, — such a queer little laughing blackamoorkin I have never seen. Seen? I see him now, and Sady, and a half-dozen more of the good people, creeping on silent bare feet to the drawing-room door when the music begins, and listening with all their ears, with all their eyes. Good night, kind little, warm-hearted little Sady and Jim! May peace soon be within your doors, and plenty within your walls! I have had so much kindness there, that I grieve to think of friends in arms, and brothers in anger.

THE LAST SKETCH.

OT many days since I went to visit a house where in former years I had received many a friendly welcome. We went in to the owner's — an artist's — studio. Prints, pictures, and sketches hung on the walls as I had last seen and remembered them. The implements of the painter's art were there. The light which had shone upon so many, many hours of patient and cheerful toil, poured through the northern window upon print and bust, lay figure and sketch, and upon the easel before which the good, the gentle, the beloved Leslie labored. In this room the busy brain had devised, and the skilful hand executed, I know not how many of the noble works which have delighted the world with their beauty and charming humor. Here the poet called up into pictorial presence, and informed with life, grace, beauty, infinite friendly mirth and wondrous naturalness of expression, the people of whom his dear books told him the stories, — his Shakespeare, his Cervantes, his Molière, his Le Sage. There was his last work on the easel, — a beautiful fresh smiling shape of Titania, such as his sweet guileless fancy imagined the "Midsummer Night's" queen to be. Gracious, and pure, and bright, the sweet smiling image glimmers on the canvas. Fairy elves, no doubt, were to

have been grouped around their mistress in laughing clusters. Honest Bottom's grotesque head and form are indicated. as reposing by the side of the consummate beauty. The darkling forest would have grown around them, with the stars glittering from the midsummer sky: the flowers at the queen's feet, and the boughs and foliage about her, would have been peopled with gambolling sprites and fays. They were dwelling in the artist's mind, no doubt, and would have been developed by that patient, faithful, admirable genius: but the busy brain stopped working, the skilful hand fell lifeless, the loving, honest heart ceased to beat. What was she to have been — that fair Titania — when perfected by the patient skill of the poet, who in imagination saw the sweet innocent figure, and with tender courtesy and caresses, as it were, posed and shaped and traced the fair form? Is there record kept anywhere of fancies conceived, beautiful, unborn? Some day will they assume form in some yet undeveloped light? If our bad unspoken thoughts are registered against us, and are written in the awful account, will not the good thoughts unspoken, the love and tenderness, the pity, beauty, charity, which pass through the breast, and cause the heart to throb with silent good, find a remembrance, too? A few weeks more, and this lovely offspring of the poet's conception would have been complete, — to charm the world with its beautiful mirth. May there not be some sphere unknown to us where it may have an existence? They say our words, once out of our lips, go travelling in *omne ævum*, reverberating for ever and ever. If our words, why not our thoughts? If the Has Been, why not the Might Have Been?

Some day our spirits may be permitted to walk in galleries of fancies more wondrous and beautiful than any achieved works which at present we see, and our minds to behold and delight in masterpieces which poets' and artists' minds have fathered and conceived only.

With a feeling much akin to that with which I looked upon the friend's — the admirable artist's — unfinished work, I can fancy many readers turning to these, — the last pages which were traced by Charlotte Brontë's hand. Of the multitude that has read her books, who has not known and deplored the tragedy of her family, her own most sad and untimely fate? Which of her readers has not become her friend? Who that has known her books has not admired the artist's noble English, the burning love of truth, the bravery, the simplicity, the indignation at wrong, the eager sympathy, the pious love and reverence, the passionate honor, so to speak, of the woman? What a story is that of that family of poets in their solitude yonder on the gloomy northern moors! At nine o'clock at night, Mrs. Gaskell tells, after evening prayers, when their guardian and relative had gone to bed, the three poetesses, — the three maidens, Charlotte, and Emily, and Anne, — Charlotte being the "motherly friend and guardian to the other two," — "began, like restless wild animals, to pace up and down their parlor, "making out" their wonderful stories, talking over plans and projects, and thoughts of what was to be their future life.

One evening, at the close of 1854, as Charlotte Nicholls sat with her husband by the fire, listening to the howling of the wind about the house, she suddenly said to her husband, "If you had not been with me, I must have been writing now." She then ran up stairs and brought down, and read aloud, the beginning of a new tale. When she had finished, her husband remarked, "the critics will accuse you of repetition." She replied, "O, I shall alter that. I always begin two or three times before I can please myself." But it was not to be. The trembling little hand was to write no more. The heart, newly awakened to love and happiness, and throbbing with maternal hope, was soon to cease to beat; that intrepid outspeaker and champion of truth, that eager, impetuous redresser of wrong, was to be called out of the world's fight and struggle, to lay down the shining arms, and to be removed to a sphere where even a noble indignation *cor ulterius nequit lacerare*, and where truth complete, and right triumphant, no longer need to wage war.

I can only say of this lady, *vidi tantum*. I saw her first just as I rose out of an illness from which I had never thought to recover. I remember the trembling little frame, the little hand, the great honest eyes. An impetuous honesty seemed to me to characterize the woman. Twice I recollect she took me to task for what she held to be errors in doctrine. Once about Fielding we had a disputation. She spoke her mind out. She jumped too rapidly to conclusions. (I have smiled at one or two passages in the "Biography," in which my own disposition or behavior forms the subject of talk.) She formed conclusions that might be wrong, and built up whole theories of character upon them. New to the London world, she entered it with an independent, indomitable spirit of her own; and judged of contemporaries, and especially spied out arrogance or affectation, with extraordinary keenness of vision. She was angry with her favorites if their conduct or conversation fell below her ideal. Often she seemed to me to be judging the London folk prematurely: but perhaps the city is rather angry at being judged. I fancied an austere little Joan of Arc marching in upon us, and rebuking our easy lives, our easy morals. She gave me the impression of being a very pure, and lofty, and high-minded person. A great and holy reverence of right and truth seemed to be with her always. Such, in our brief interview, she appeared to me. As one thinks of that life so noble, so lonely, — of that passion for truth, — of those nights and nights of eager study, swarming fancies, invention, depression, elation, prayer; as one reads the necessarily incomplete, though most touching and admirable history of the heart that throbbed in this one little frame, — of this one amongst the myriads of souls that have lived and died on this great earth, — this great earth? — this little speck in the infinite universe of God, — with what wonder do we think of to-day, with what awe await to-morrow, when that which is now but darkly seen shall be clear! As I read this little fragmentary sketch, I think of the rest. Is it? And where is it? Will not the leaf be turned some day, and the story be told? Shall the deviser of the tale somewhere perfect the history of little EMMA's griefs and troubles? Shall TITANIA come forth complete with her sportive court, with the flowers at her feet, the forest around her, and all the stars of summer glittering overhead?

How well I remember the delight, and wonder, and pleasure with which I read "Jane Eyre," sent to me by an author whose name and sex were then alike unknown to me; the strange fascinations of the book; and how, with my own work pressing upon me, I could not, having taken the volumes up, lay them down until they were read through! Hundreds of those who, like myself, recognized and admired that master-work of a great genius, will look with a mournful interest and regard and curiosity upon the last fragmentary sketch from the noble hand which wrote "Jane Eyre."

"STRANGE TO SAY, ON CLUB PAPER."

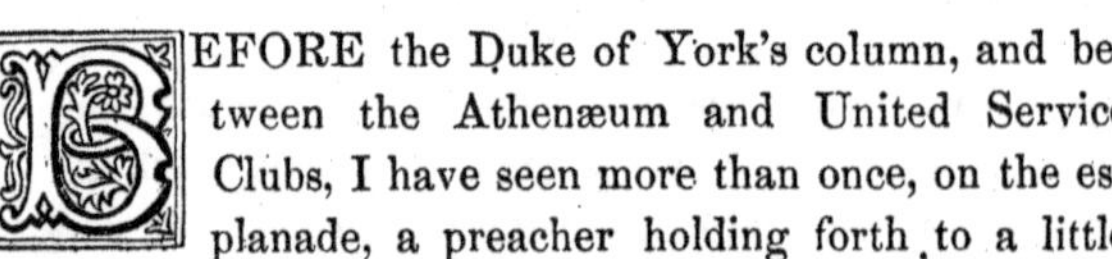EFORE the Duke of York's column, and between the Athenæum and United Service Clubs, I have seen more than once, on the esplanade, a preacher holding forth to a little congregation of *badauds* and street-boys, whom he entertains with a discourse on the crimes of a rapacious aristocracy, or warns of the imminent peril of their own souls. Sometimes this orator is made to "move on" by brutal policemen. Sometimes, on a Sunday, he points to a white head or two visible in the windows of the clubs to the right and left of him, and volunteers a statement that those quiet and elderly Sabbath-breakers will very soon be called from this world to another, where their lot will by no means be so comfortable as that which the reprobates enjoy here, in their arm-chairs, by their snug fires.

At the end of last month, had I been a Pall Mall preacher, I would have liked to send a whip round to all the clubs in St. James's, and convoke the few members remaining in London to hear a discourse *sub Dio* on a text from the Observer newspaper. I would have taken post under the statue of Fame, say, where she stands distributing wreaths to the three Crimean Guardsmen. (The crossing-sweeper does not obstruct the path, and I suppose is away at his villa on Sundays.) And, when the congregation was pretty quiet, I would have begun:—

In the Observer of the 27th September, 1863, in the fifth page and the fourth column, it is thus written:—

"The codicil appended to the will of the late Lord Clyde, executed at Chatham, and bearing the signature of Clyde, F. M., is written, strange to say, on a sheet of paper *bearing the Athenæum Club mark.*"

What the codicil is, my dear brethren, it is not our business to inquire. It conveys a benefaction to a faithful and attached friend of the good field-marshal. The gift may be a lac of rupees, or it may be a house and its contents,—furniture, plate, and wine-cellar. My friends, I know the wine-merchant, and, for the sake of the legatee, hope heartily that the stock is large.

Am I wrong, dear brethren, in supposing that you expect a preacher to say a seasonable word on death here? If you don't, I fear you are but little familiar with the habits of preachers, and are but lax hearers of sermons. We might contrast the vault where the warrior's remains lie shrouded and coffined, with that in which his worldly provision of wine is stowed away. Spain and Portugal and France,—all the lands which supplied his store,—as hardy and obedient subaltern, as resolute captain, as colonel daring but prudent,—he has visited the fields of all. In India and China he marches always unconquered; or at the head of his dauntless Highland brigade he treads the Crimean snow; or he rides from conquest to conquest in India once more; succoring his countrymen in the hour of their utmost need; smiting down the scared mutiny, and trampling out the embers of rebellion; at the head of a heroic army, a consummate chief. And now his glorious old sword is sheathed, and his honors are won; and he has bought him a house, and stored it with modest cheer for his friends (the good old man put water in his own wine, and a glass or two sufficed him), — behold the end comes, and his legatee inherits these modest possessions by virtue of a codicil to his lordship's will, written, "*strange to say, upon a sheet of paper bearing the Athenæum Club mark.*"

It is to this part of the text, my brethren, that I propose to address myself particularly, and if the remarks I make are offensive to any of you, you know the doors of our meeting-house are open, and you can walk out when you will. Around us are magnificent halls and palaces, frequented by such a multitude of men as not even the Roman Forum assembled together. Yonder are the Martium and the Palladium. Next to the Palladium is the elegant Viatorium, which Barry gracefully stole from Rome. By its side is the massive Reformatorium: and the — the Ultratorium rears its granite columns beyond. Extending down the street palace after palace rises magnificent, and under their lofty roofs warriors and lawyers, merchants and nobles, scholars and seamen, the wealthy, the poor, the busy, the idle assemble. Into the halls built down this little street and its neighborhood the principal men of all London come to hear or impart the news; and the affairs of the state or of private individuals, the quarrels of empires or of authors, the movements of the court or the splendid vagaries of fashion, the intrigues of statesmen or of persons of another sex yet more wily, the last news of battles in the great occidental continents, nay, the latest betting for the horse-races, or the advent of a dancer at the theatre, — all that men do is discussed in these Pall Mall agoræ, where we of London daily assemble.

Now among so many talkers, consider how many false reports must fly about: in such multitudes imagine how many disappointed men there must be; how many chatterboxes; how many feeble and credulous (whereof I mark some specimens in my congregation); how many mean, rancorous, prone to believe ill of their betters, eager to find fault; and then, my brethren, fancy how the words of my text must have been read and received in Pall Mall! (I perceive several of the congregation looking most uncomfortable. One old boy with a dyed mustache turns purple in the face, and struts back to the Martium; another, with a shrug of the shoulder and a murmur of "Rubbish," slinks away in the direction of the Togatorium, and the preacher continues.) The will of Field-Marshal Lord Clyde — signed *at Chatham,* mind, where his lordship died — is written, *strange to say,* on a sheet of paper bearing the Athenæum Club mark!

The inference is obvious. A man cannot get Athenæum paper except at the Athenæum. Such paper is not sold at Chatham, where the last codicil to his lordship's will is dated. And so the painful belief is forced upon us, that a Peer, a Field-Marshal, wealthy, respected, illustrious, could pocket paper at his club, and carry it away with him to the country. One fancies the hall porter conscious of the old lord's iniquity, and holding down his head as the marshal passes the door. What is that roll which his lordship carries? Is it his marshal's bâton gloriously won? No; it is a roll of foolscap conveyed from the club. What has he on his breast, under his great-coat? Is it his Star of India? No; it is a bundle of envelopes, bearing the head of Minerva, some sealing-wax, and a half-score of pens.

Let us imagine how in the hall of one or other of these clubs this strange anecdote will be discussed.

"Notorious screw," says Sneer. "The poor old fellow's avarice has long been known."

"Suppose he wishes to imitate the Duke of Marlborough," says Simper.

"Habit of looting contracted in India, you know; ain't so easy to get over, you know," says Snigger.

"When officers dined with him in India," remarks Solemn, "it was notorious that the spoons were all of a different pattern."

"Perhaps it is n't true. Suppose he wrote his paper at the club?" interposes Jones.

"It is dated at Chatham, my good man," says Brown. "A man if he is in London, says he is in London. A man if he is in Rochester, says he is in Rochester. This man happens to forget that he is using the club paper; and he happens to be found out: many men *don't* happen to be found out. I 've seen literary fellows at clubs writing their rubbishing articles; I have no doubt they take away reams of paper. They crib thoughts; why should n't they crib stationery? One of your literary vagabonds who is capable of stabbing a reputation, who is capable of telling any monstrous falsehood to support his party, is surely capable of stealing a ream of paper."

"Well, well, we have all our weaknesses," sighs Robinson. "Seen that article, Thompson, in the Observer, about Lord Clyde and the club paper? You 'll find it up stairs. In the third column of the fifth page, towards the bottom of the page. I suppose he was so poor he could n't afford to buy a quire of paper. Had n't fourpence in the world. O, no!"

"And they want to get up a testimonial to this man's

memory, — a statue or something!" cries Jawkins. "A man who wallows in wealth and takes paper away from his club! I don't say he is not brave: brutal courage most men have. I don't say he was not a good officer: a man with such experience *must* have been a good officer, unless he was born fool. But to think of this man, loaded with honors, — though of a low origin, — so lost to self-respect as actually to take away the Athenæum paper! These parvenus, sir, betray their origin, — betray their origin. I said to my wife this very morning, 'Mrs. Jawkins,' I said, 'there is talk of a testimonial to this man. I will not give one shilling. I have no idea of raising statues to fellows who take away club paper. No, by George, I have not. Why, they will be raising statues to men who take club spoons next! Not one penny of *my* money shall they have!'"

And now, if you please, we will tell the real story which has furnished this scandal to a newspaper, this tattle to club gossips and loungers. The field-marshal, wishing to make a further provision for a friend, informed his lawyer what he desired to do. The lawyer, a member of the Athenæum Club, there wrote the draft of such a codicil as he would advise, and sent the paper by the post to Lord Clyde at Chatham. Lord Clyde, finding the paper perfectly satisfactory, signed it and sent it back: and hence we have the story of "the codicil bearing the signature of Clyde, F. M., and written, strange to say, upon paper bearing the Athenæum Club mark."

Here I have been imagining a dialogue between a half-dozen gossips such as congregate round a club fireplace of an afternoon. I wonder how many people besides, — whether any chance reader of this very page, has read and believed this story about the good old lord? Have the country papers copied the anecdote, and our "own correspondents" made their remarks on it? If, my good sir, or madam, you have read it and credited it, don't you own to a little feeling of shame and sorrow, now that the trumpery little mystery is cleared? To "the new inhabitant of light," passed away and out of reach of our censure, misrepresentation, scandal, dulness, malice, a silly falsehood matters nothing. Censure and praise are alike to him, — "the music warbling to the deafened ear, the incense wasted on the funeral bier," the pompous eulogy pronounced over the gravestone, or the lie that slander spits on it. Faithfully though this brave old chief did his duty, honest and upright though his life was, glorious his renown, — you see he could write at Chatham on London paper; you see men can be found to point out how "strange" his behavior was.

And about ourselves? My good people, do you by chance know any man or woman who has formed unjust conclusions regarding his neighbor? Have you ever found yourself willing, nay, eager to believe evil of some man whom you hate? Whom you hate because he is successful, and you are not: because he is rich, and you are poor: because he dines with great men who don't invite you: because he wears a silk gown, and yours is still stuff: because he has been called in to perform the operation though you lived close by: because his pictures have been bought, and yours returned home unsold: because he fills his church, and you are preaching to empty pews? If your rival prospers, have you ever felt a twinge of anger? If his wife's carriage passes you and Mrs. Tomkins, who are in a cab, don't you feel that those people are giving themselves absurd airs of importance? If he lives with great people, are you not sure he is a sneak? And if you ever felt envy towards another, and if your heart has ever been black towards your brother, if you have been peevish at his success, pleased to hear his merit depreciated, and eager to believe all that is said in his disfavor, — my good sir, as you yourself contritely own that you are unjust, jealous, uncharitable, so you may be sure some men are uncharitable, jealous, and unjust regarding *you.*

The proofs and manuscript of this little sermon have just come from the printer's, and as I look at the writing, I perceive, not without a smile, that one or two of the pages bear, "strange to say," the mark of a club of which I have the honor to be a member. Those lines quoted in a foregoing page are from some noble verses written by one of Mr. Addison's men, Mr. Tickell, on the death of Cadogan, who was amongst the most prominent "of Marlborough's captains and Eugenio's friends." If you are acquainted with the history of those times, you have read how Cadogan had his feuds and hatreds too, as Tickell's patron had his, as Cadogan's great chief had his. "The Duke of Marlborough's character has been so variously drawn" (writes a famous contemporary of the duke's), "that it is hard to pronounce on either side without the suspicion of flattery or detraction. I shall say nothing of his military accomplishments, which the opposite reports of his friends and enemies among the soldiers have rendered problematical. Those maligners who deny him personal valor, seem not to consider that this accusation is charged at a venture, since the person of a general is too seldom exposed, and that fear which is said sometimes to have disconcerted him before action might probably be more for his army than himself." If Swift could hint a doubt of Marlborough's courage, what wonder that a nameless scribe of our day should question the honor of Clyde?

AUTOUR DE MON CHAPEAU.

EVER have I seen a more noble tragic face. In the centre of the forehead there was a great furrow of care, towards which the brows rose piteously. What a deep solemn grief in the eyes! They looked blankly at the object before them, but through it, as it were, and into the grief beyond. In moments of pain, have you not looked at some indifferent object so? It mingles dumbly with your grief, and remains afterwards connected with it in your mind. It may be some indifferent thing, — a book which you were reading at the time when you received her farewell letter (how well you remember the paragraph afterwards, — the shape of the words, and their position on the page!); the words you were writing when your mother came in, and said it was all over, — she was MARRIED, — Emily married, — to that insignificant little rival at whom you have laughed a hundred times in her company. Well, well, my friend and reader, whoe'er you be, — old man or young, wife or maiden, — you have had your grief-pang. Boy, you have lain awake the first night at school, and thought of home. Worse still, man, you have parted from the dear ones with bursting heart: and, lonely boy, recall the bolstering an unfeeling comrade gave you; and, lonely man, just torn from your children,

— their little tokens of affection yet in your pocket, — pacing the deck at evening in the midst of the roaring ocean, you can remember how you were told that supper was ready, and how you went down to the cabin and had brandy-and-water and biscuit. You remember the taste of them. Yes, — forever. You took them whilst you and your Grief were sitting together, and your Grief clutched you round the soul. Serpent, how you have writhed round me, and bitten me! Remorse, Remembrance, &c., come in the night season, and I feel you gnawing, gnawing! . . . . I tell you that man's face was like Laocoon's (which, by the way, I always think overrated. The real head is at Brussels, at the Duke Daremberg's, not at Rome).

That man! What man? That man of whom I said that his magnificent countenance exhibited the noblest tragic woe. He was not of European blood. He was handsome, but not of European beauty. His face white, — not of a Northern whiteness: his eyes protruding somewhat, and rolling in their grief. Those eyes had seen the Orient sun, and his beak was the eagle's. His lips were full. The beard, curling round them, was unkempt and tawny. The locks were of a deep, deep coppery red. The hands, swart and powerful, accustomed to the rough grasp of the wares in which he dealt, seemed unused to the flimsy artifices of the bath. He came from the Wilderness, and its sands were on his robe, his cheek, his tattered sandal, and the hardy foot it covered.

And his grief, — whence came his sorrow? I will tell you. He bore it in his hand. He had evidently just concluded the compact by which it became his. His business was that of a purchaser of domestic raiment. At early dawn, — nay, at what hour when the city is alive, — do we not all hear the nasal cry of "Clo"? In Paris, *Habits Galons, Marchand d'habits*, is the twanging signal with which the wandering merchant makes his presence known. It was in Paris I saw this man. Where else have I not seen him? In the Roman Ghetto, — at the Gate of David, in his fathers' once imperial city. The man I mean was an itinerant vendor and purchaser of wardrobes, — what you call an . . . . Enough! You know his name.

On his left shoulder hung his bag; and he held in that hand a white hat, which I am sure he had just purchased, and which was the cause of the grief which smote his noble features. Of course I cannot particularize the sum, but he had given too much for that hat. He felt he might have got the thing for less money. It was not the amount, I am sure it was the principle involved. He had given fourpence (let us say) for that which threepence would have purchased. He had been done: and a manly shame was upon him, that he, whose energy, acuteness, experience, point of honor, should have made him the victor in any mercantile duel in which he should engage, — had been overcome by a porter's wife, who very likely sold him the old hat, or by a student who was tired of it. I can understand his grief. Do I seem to be speaking of it in a disrespectful or flippant way? Then you mistake me. He had been outwitted. He had desired, coaxed, schemed, haggled, got what he wanted, and now found he had paid too much for his bargain. You don't suppose I would ask you to laugh at that man's grief? It is you, clumsy cynic, who are disposed to sneer, whilst, it may be, tears of genuine sympathy are trickling down this nose of mine. What do you mean by laughing? If you saw a wounded soldier on the field of battle, would you laugh? If you saw a ewe robbed of her lamb, would you laugh, you brute? It is you who are the cynic, and have no feeling: and you sneer because that grief is unintelligible to you which touches my finer sensibility. The OLD CLOTHES' MAN had been defeated in one of the daily battles of his most interesting, checkered, adventurous life.

Have you ever figured to yourself what such a life must be? The pursuit and conquest of twopence must be the most eager and fascinating of occupations. We might all engage in that business if we would. Do not whist-players, for example, toil, and think, and lose their temper over sixpenny points? They bring study, natural genius, long forethought, memory, and careful historical experience to bear upon their favorite labor. Don't tell me that it is the sixpenny points, and five shillings the rub, which keep them for hours over their painted pasteboard. It is the desire to conquer. Hours pass by. Night glooms. Dawn, it may be, rises unheeded; and they sit calling for fresh cards at the Portland, or the Union, while waning candles sputter in the sockets, and languid waiters snooze in the ante-room. Sol rises. Jones has lost four pounds; Brown has won two; Robinson lurks away to his family house and (mayhap, indignant) Mrs. R. Hours of evening, night, morning, have passed away whilst they have been waging this sixpenny battle. What is the loss of four pounds to Jones, the gain of two to Brown? B. is, perhaps, so rich that two pounds more or less are as naught to him; J. is so hopelessly involved that to win four pounds cannot benefit his creditors, or alter his condition; but they play for that stake: they put forward their best energies: they ruff, finesse (what are the technical words, and how do I know?) It is but a sixpenny game if you like; but they want to win it. So as regards my friend yonder with the hat. He stakes his money: he wishes to win the game, not the hat merely. I am not prepared to say that he is not inspired by a noble ambition. Cæsar wished to be first in a village. If first of a hundred yokels, why not first of two? And my friend, the old clothes' man, wishes to win his game, as well as to turn his little sixpence.

Suppose in the game of life — and it is but a twopenny game after all — you are equally eager of winning. Shall you be ashamed of your ambition, or glory in it? There are games, too, which are becoming to particular periods of life. I remember in the days of our youth, when my friend Arthur Bowler was an eminent cricketer. Slim, swift, strong, well-built, he presented a goodly appearance on the ground in his flannel uniform. *Militâsti non sine gloria*, Bowler my boy! Hush! We tell no tales. Mum is the word. Yonder comes Charley, his son. Now Charley his son has taken the field, and is famous among the eleven of his school. Bowler, senior, with his capacious waistcoat, &c., waddling after a ball, would present an absurd object, whereas it does the eyes good to see Bowler, junior, scouring the plain, — a young exemplar of joyful health, vigor, activity. The old boy wisely contents himself with amusements more becoming his age and waist; takes his sober ride; visits his farm soberly, — busies himself about his pigs, his ploughing, his peaches, or what not. Very small *routiniers* amusements interest him; and (thank goodness!) nature provides very kindly for kindly-disposed fogies. We relish those things which we scorned in our lusty youth. I see the young folks of an evening kindling and glowing over their delicious novels. I look up and watch the eager eye flashing down the page, being, for my part, perfectly contented with my twaddling old volume of Howell's Letters or the Gentleman's Magazine. I am actually arrived at such a calm frame of mind that I like batter-pudding. I never should have believed it possible; but it is so. Yet a little while, and I may relish water-gruel. It will be the age of *mon lait de poule et mon bonnet de nuit.* And then,—the cotton extinguisher is pulled over the old noddle, and the little flame of life is popped out.

Don't you know elderly people who make learned notes in Army Lists, Peerages, and the like? This is the batter-pudding, water-gruel of old age. The worn-out old digestion does not care for stronger food. Formerly it could swallow twelve hours' tough reading, and digest an encyclopædia.

If I had children to educate, I would at ten or twelve years of age have a professor or professoress of whist for them, and cause them to be well grounded in that great and useful game. You cannot learn it well when you are old, any more than you can learn dancing or billiards. In our house at home we youngsters did not play whist, because we were dear, obedient children, and the elders said playing at cards was "a waste of time." A waste of time, my good people! *Allons!* What do elderly home-keeping people do of a night after dinner? Darby gets his newspaper; my dear Joan her Missionary Magazine, or her volume of Cumming's Sermons,—and don't you know what ensues? Over the arm of Darby's arm-chair the paper flutters to the ground unheeded, and he performs the trumpet obbligato *que vous savez* on his old nose. My dear old Joan's head nods over her sermon (awakening though the doctrine may be). Ding, ding, ding: can that be ten o'clock? It is time to send the servants to bed, my dear, — and to bed master and mistress go too. But they have not wasted their time playing at cards. O no! I belong to a club where there is whist of a night; and not a little amusing is it to hear Brown speak of Thompson's play, and *vice versâ.* But there is one man — Greatorex let us call him — who is the acknowledged captain and primus of all the whist-players. We all secretly admire him. I, for my part, watch him in private life, hearken to what he says, note what he orders for dinner, and have that feeling of awe for him that I used to have as a boy for the cock of the school. Not play at whist? *Quelle triste vieillesse vous vous préparez!* were the words of the great and good Bishop of Autun. I can't. It is too late now. Too late! too late! Ah! humiliating confession! That joy might have been clutched, but the life-stream has swept us by it, — the swift life-stream rushing to the nearing sea. Too late! too late! Twentystone, my boy! When you read in the papers "Valse à deux temps," and all the fashionable dances taught to adults by "Miss Lightfoots," don't you feel that you would like to go in and learn? Ah, it is too late! You have passed the *choreas,* Master Twentystone, and the young people are dancing without you.

I don't believe much of what my Lord Byron, the poet, says; but when he wrote: "So, for a good old gentlemanly vice, I think I shall put up with avarice," I think his lordship meant what he wrote, and if he practised what he preached, shall not quarrel with him. As an occupation in declining years, I declare I think saving is useful, amusing, and not unbecoming. It must be a perpetual amusement. It is a game that can be played by day, by night, at home and abroad, and at which you must win in the long run. I am tired and want a cab. The fare to my house, say, is two shillings. The cabman will naturally want half-a-crown. I pull out my book. I show him the distance is exactly three miles and fifteen hundred and ninety yards. I offer him my card, — my winning card. As he retires with the two shillings, blaspheming inwardly, every curse is a compliment to my skill. I have played him and beat him; and a sixpence is my spoil, and just reward. This is a game, by the way, which women play far more cleverly than we do. But what an interest it imparts to life! During the whole drive home I know I shall have my game at the journey's end; am sure of my hand, and shall beat my adversary. Or, I can play in another way. I won't have a cab at all; I will wait for the omnibus; I will be one of the damp fourteen in that steaming vehicle. I will wait about in the rain for an hour, and 'bus after 'bus shall pass, but I will not be beat. I *will* have a place, and get it at length, with my boots wet through, and an umbrella dripping between my legs. I have a rheumatism, a cold, a sore-throat, a sulky evening, — a doctor's bill to-morrow, perhaps. Yes, but I have won my game, and am gainer of a shilling on this rubber.

If you play this game all through life, it is wonderful what daily interest it has, and amusing occupation. For instance, my wife goes to sleep after dinner over her volume of sermons. As soon as the dear soul is sound asleep, I advance softly and puff out her candle. Her pure dreams will be all the happier without that light; and, say she sleeps an hour, there is a penny gained.

As for clothes, *parbleu!* There is not much money to be saved in clothes, for the fact is, as a man advances in life — as he becomes an *ancient Briton* (mark the pleasantry) — he goes without clothes. When my tailor proposes something in the way of a change of raiment, I laugh in his face. My blue coat and brass buttons will last these ten years. It is seedy? What then? I don't want to charm anybody in particular. You say that my clothes are shabby? What do I care? When I wished to look well in somebody's eyes, the matter may have been different. But now when I receive my bill of £10 (let us say) at the year's end, and contrast it with old tailors' reckonings, I feel that I have played the game with master tailor, and beat him, and my old clothes are a token of the victory.

I do not like to give servants board wages, though they are cheaper than household bills; but I know they save out of board wages, and so beat me. This shows that it is not the money but the game which interests me. So about wine. I have it good and dear. I will trouble you to tell me where to get it good and cheap. You may as well give me the address of a shop where I can buy meat for fourpence a pound, or sovereigns for fifteen shillings a piece. At the game of auctions, docks, shy wine-merchants, depend on it there is *no* winning; and I would as soon think of buying jewelry at an auction in Fleet Street as of purchasing wine from one of your dreadful needy wine agents such as infest every man's door. Grudge myself good wine? As soon grudge my horse corn. *Merci!* that would be a very losing game indeed, and your humble servant has no relish for such.

But in the very pursuit of saving there must be a hundred harmless delights and pleasures which we who are careless necessarily forego. What do you know about the natural history of your household? Upon your honor and conscience, do you know the price of a pound of butter? Can you say what sugar costs, and how much your family consumes and ought to consume? How much lard do you use in your house? As I think on these subjects I own I hang down the head of shame. I suppose for a moment that you, who are reading this, are a middle-aged gentleman, and *paterfamilias.* Can you answer the above questions? You know, sir, you cannot. Now turn round, lay down the book, and suddenly ask Mrs. Jones and your daughters if *they* can answer? They cannot. They look at one another. They pretend they can answer. They can tell you the plot and principal characters of the last novel. Some of them know something about history, geology, and so forth. But of the natural history of home — *Nichts,* and for shame on you all! *Honnis soyez!* For shame on you? for shame on us!

In the early morning I hear a sort of call or *jodel* under my window, and know 't is the matutinal milkman leaving his can at my gate. O household gods! have I lived all these years and don't know the price or the quantity of the milk which is delivered in that can? Why don't I know? As I live, if I live till to-morrow morning, as soon as I hear the call of Lactantius, I will dash out upon him. How many cows? How much milk, on an average, all the year round? What rent? What cost of food and dairy servants? What loss of animals, and average cost of purchase? If I interested myself properly about my pint (or hogshead, whatever it be) of milk, all this knowledge would ensue; all this additional interest in life. What is this talk of my friend, Mr. Lewes, about objects at the seaside, and so forth? Objects at the seaside? Objects at the area-bell; objects before my nose; objects which the butcher brings me in his tray; which the cook dresses and puts down before me, and over which I say grace! My daily life is surrounded with objects which ought to interest me. The pudding I eat (or refuse, that is neither here nor there, and, between ourselves, what I have said about batter-pudding may be taken *cum grano*,—we are not come to *that* yet, except for the sake of argument or illustration), — the pudding, I say, on my plate, the eggs that made it, the fire that cooked it, the tablecloth on which it is laid, and so forth, — are each and all of these objects a knowledge of which I may acquire, — a knowledge of the cost and production of which I might advantageously learn? To the man who *does* know these things, I say the interest of life is prodigiously increased. The milkman becomes a study to him; the baker a being he curiously and tenderly examines. Go, Lewes, and clap a hideous sea-anemone into a glass; I will put a cabman under mine, and make a vivisection of a butcher. O Lares, Penates, and gentle household gods, teach me to sympathize with all that comes within my doors! Give me an interest in the butcher's book. Let me look forward to the ensuing number of the grocer's account with eagerness. It seems ungrateful to my kitchen-chimney not to know the cost of sweeping it; and I trust that many a man who reads this, and muses on it, will feel, like the writer, ashamed of himself, and hang down his head humbly.

Now, if to this household game you could add a little money interest, the amusement would be increased far beyond the mere money value, as a game at cards for sixpence is better than a rubber for nothing. If you can interest yourself about sixpence, all life is invested with a new excitement. From sunrise to sleeping you can always be playing that game, — with butcher, baker coal-merchant, cabman, omnibus man, — nay, diamond-merchant and stockbroker. You can bargain for a guinea over the price of a diamond necklace, or for a sixteenth per cent in a transaction at the Stock Exchange. We all know men who have this faculty who are not ungenerous with their money. They give it on great occasions. They are more able to help than you and I who spend ours, and say to poor Prodigal, who comes to us out at elbow, "My dear fellow, I should have been delighted; but I have already anticipated my quarter, and am going to ask Screwby if he can do anything for me."

In this delightful, wholesome, ever-novel, twopenny game, there is a danger of excess, as there is in every other pastime or occupation of life. If you grow too eager for your twopence, the acquisition or the loss of it may affect your peace of mind, and peace of mind is better than any amount of twopences. My friend, the old clothes' man, whose agonies over the hat have led to this rambling disquisition, has, I very much fear, by a too eager pursuit of small profits, disturbed the equanimity of a mind that ought to be easy and happy. "Had I stood out," he thinks, "I might have had the hat for threepence," and he doubts whether, having given fourpence for it, he will ever get back his money. My good Shadrach, if you go through life passionately deploring the irrevocable, and allow yesterday's transactions to embitter the cheerfulness of to-day and to-morrow, — as lieve walk down to the Seine, souse in, hats, body, clothes-bag, and all, and put an end to your sorrows and sordid cares. Before and since Mr. Franklin wrote his pretty apologue of the Whistle, have we not all made bargains of which we repented, and coveted and acquired objects for which we have paid too dearly? Who has not purchased his hat in some market or other? There is General M'Clellan's cocked hat for example. I dare say he was eager enough to wear it, and he has learned that it is by no means cheerful wear. There were the military beavers of Messeigneurs of Orleans: they wore them gallantly in the face of battle; but I suspect they were glad enough to pitch them into the James River, and come home in mufti. Ah, *mes amis! à chacun son schakot!* I was looking at a bishop the other day, and thinking: "My right reverend lord, that broad-brim and rosette must bind your great broad forehead very tightly, and give you many a headache. A good easy wide-awake were better for you, and I would like to see that honest face with a cutty pipe in the middle of it." There is my Lord Mayor. My once dear lord, my kind friend, when your two years' reign was over, did not you jump for joy, and fling your chapeau-bras out of window: and has n't *that* hat cost you a pretty bit of money? There, in a splendid travelling chariot, in the sweetest bonnet, all trimmed with orange-blossoms and Chantilly lace, sits my Lady Rosa, with old Lord Snowden by her side. Ah, Rosa! what a price have you paid for that hat which you wear; and is your ladyship's coronet not purchased too dear? Enough of hats. Sir, or Madam, I take off mine, and salute you with profound respect.

ON A PEAL OF BELLS.

S some bells in a church hard by are making a great holiday clanging in the summer afternoon, I am reminded somehow of a July day, a garden, and a great clanging of bells years and years ago, on the very day when George IV. was crowned. I remember a little boy lying in that garden, reading his first novel. It was called "The Scottish Chiefs." The little boy (who is now ancient and not little) read this book in the summer-house of his great grandmamma. She was eighty years of age then. A most lovely and picturesque old lady, with a long tortoise-shell cane, with a little puff, or *tour*, of snow white (or was it powdered?) hair under her cap, with the prettiest little black velvet slippers and high heels you ever saw. She had a grandson, a lieutenant in the navy; son of her son, a captain in the navy; grandson of her husband, a captain in the navy. She lived for scores and scores of years in a dear little old Hampshire town inhabited by the wives, widows, daughters of navy captains, admirals, lieutenants. Dear me! Don't I remember Mrs. Duval, widow of Admiral Duval; and the Miss Dennets, at the Great House at the other end of the town, Admiral Dennet's daughters; and the Miss Barrys, the late Captain Barry's daughters; and the good old Miss Maskews, Ad-

miral Maskews' daughter; and that dear little Miss Norval, and the kind Miss Bookers, one of whom married Captain, now Admiral, Sir Henry Excellent, K. C. B.? Far, far away into the past I look and seek the little town with its friendly glimmer. That town was so like a novel of Miss Austen's, that I wonder was she born and bred there? No, we should have known, and the good old ladies would have pronounced her to be a little idle thing, occupied with her silly books and neglecting her housekeeping. There were other towns in England, no doubt, where dwelt the widows and wives of other navy captains, where they tattled, loved each other, and quarrelled; talked about Betty, the maid, and her fine ribbons, indeed! Took their dish of tea at six, played at quadrille every night till ten, when there was a little bit of supper, after which Betty came with the lantern; and next day came, and next, and next, and so forth, until a day arrived when the lantern was out, when Betty came no more: all that little company sank to rest under the daisies, whither some folks will presently follow them. How did they live to be so old, those good people? *Moi qui vous parle,* I perfectly recollect old Mr. Gilbert, who had been to sea with Captain Cook; and Captain Cook, as you justly observe, dear miss, quoting out of your Mangnall's Questions, was murdered by the natives of Owhyhee, anno 1779. Ah! don't you remember his picture, standing on the sea-shore, in tights and gaiters, with a musket in his hand, pointing to his people not to fire from the boats, whilst a great tattooed savage is going to stab him in the back? Don't you remember those houris dancing before him and the other officers at the great Otaheite ball? Don't you know that Cook was at the siege of Quebec, with the glorious Wolfe, who fought under the Duke of Cumberland, whose royal father was a distinguished officer at Ramillies, before he commanded in chief at Dettingen? Huzzay! Give it them, my lads! My horse is down? Then I know I shall not run away. Do the French run? then I die content. Stop. Wo! *Quo me rapis?* My Pegasus is galloping off, goodness knows where, like his Majesty's charger at Dettingen.

How do these rich historical and personal reminiscences come out of the subject at present in hand? What *is* that subject, by the way? My dear friend, if you look at the last essaykin (though you may leave it alone, and I shall not be in the least surprised or offended), if you look at the last paper where the writer imagines Athos and Porthos, Dalgetty and Ivanhoe, Amelia and Sir Charles Grandison, Don Quixote and Sir Roger, walking in at the garden-window, you will at once perceive that NOVELS and their heroes and heroines are our present subject of discourse, into which we will presently plunge. Are you one of us, dear sir, and do you love novel-reading? To be reminded of your first novel will surely be a pleasure to you. Hush! I never read quite to the end of my first, "The Scottish Chiefs." I could n't. I peeped in an alarmed furtive manner at some of the closing pages. Miss Porter, like a kind, dear, tender-hearted creature, would not have Wallace's head chopped off at the end of Vol. V. She made him die in prison,* and if I remember right (protesting I have not read the book for forty-

* I find, on reference to the novel, that Sir William died on the scaffold, not in prison. His last words were: "'My prayer is heard. Life's cord is cut by Heaven. Helen! Helen! May Heaven preserve my country, and —.' He stopped. He fell. And with that mighty shock the scaffold shook to its foundation."

two or three years), Robert Bruce made a speech to his soldiers, in which he said, "And Bannockburn shall equal Cambuskenneth." * But I repeat, I could not read the end of the fifth volume of that dear delightful book for crying. Good heavens! It was as sad, as sad as going back to school.

The glorious Scott cycle of romances came to me some four or five years afterwards; and I think boys of our year were specially fortunate in coming upon those delightful books at that special time when we could best enjoy them. O, that sunshiny bench on half-holidays, with Claverhouse or Ivanhoe for a companion! I have remarked of very late days some little men in a great state of delectation over the romances of Captain Mayne Reid, and Gustave Aimard's Prairie and Indian Stories, and, during occasional holiday visits, lurking off to bed with the volume under their arms. But are those Indians and warriors so terrible as *our* Indians and warriors were? (I say, are they? Young gentlemen, mind, I do not say they are not.) But as an oldster I can be heartily thankful for the novels of the 1–10 Geo. IV., let us say, and so downward to a period not unremote. Let

* The remark of Bruce (which I protest I had not read for forty-two years), I find to be as follows: "When this was uttered by the English heralds, Bruce turned to Ruthven, with an heroic smile. 'Let him come, my brave barons! and he shall find that Bannockburn shall page with Cambuskenneth!'" In the same amiable author's famous novel of "Thaddeus of Warsaw," there is more crying than in any novel I ever remember to have read. See, for example, the last page . . . . "Incapable of speaking, Thaddeus led his wife back to her carriage. . . . . His tears gushed out in spite of himself, and mingling with hers, poured those thanks, those assurances, of animated approbation through her heart, which made it even ache with excess of happiness." . . . . And a sentence or two further, "Kosciusko did bless him, and embalmed the benediction with a shower of tears."

us see; there is, first, our dear Scott. Whom do I love in the works of that dear old master? Amo —

The Baron of Bradwardine, and Fergus. (Captain Waverley is certainly very mild.)

Amo Ivanhoe; LOCKSLEY; the Templar.

Amo Quentin Durward, and specially Quentin's uncle, who brought the Boar to bay. I forget the gentleman's name.

I have never cared for the Master of Ravenswood, or fetched his hat out of the water since he dropped it there when I last met him (circa 1825).

Amo SALADIN and the Scotch knight in "The Talisman." The Sultan best.

Amo CLAVERHOUSE.

Amo MAJOR DALGETTY. Delightful Major! To think of him is to desire to jump up, run to the book, and get the volume down from the shelf. About all those heroes of Scott, what a manly bloom there is, and honorable modesty! They are not at all heroic. They seem to blush somehow in their position of hero, and as it were to say, "Since it must be done, here goes!" They are handsome, modest, upright, simple, courageous, not too clever. If I were a mother (which is absurd), I should like to be mother-in-law to several young men of the Walter-Scott-hero sort.

Much as I like those most unassuming, manly, unpretending gentlemen, I have to own that I think the heroes of another writer, viz.

LEATHER-STOCKING,
UNCAS,
HARDHEART,
TOM COFFIN,

are quite the equals of Scott's men: perhaps Leather-stocking is better than any one in "Scott's lot." *La Longue Carabine* is one of the great prize-men of fiction. He ranks with your Uncle Toby, Sir Roger de Coverley, Falstaff, — heroic figures, all, — American or British, and the artist has deserved well of his country who devised them.

At school, in my time, there was a public day, when the boys' relatives, an examining bigwig or two from the universities, old school-fellows, and so forth, came to the place. The boys were all paraded; prizes were administered; each lad being in a new suit of clothes, — and magnificent dandies, I promise you, some of us were. O, the chubby cheeks, clean collars, glossy new raiment, beaming faces, glorious in youth, — *fit tueri cœlum*, — bright with truth, and mirth, and honor! To see a hundred boys marshalled in a chapel or old hall; to hear their sweet fresh voices when they chant, and look in their brave calm faces, — I say, does not the sight and sound of them smite you, somehow, with a pang of exquisite kindness? . . . . Well. As about boys, so about Novelists. I fancy the boys of Parnassus School all paraded. I am a lower boy myself in that academy. I like our fellows to look well, upright, gentlemanlike. There is Master Fielding, — he with the black eye. What a magnificent build of a boy! There is Master Scott, one of the heads of the school. Did you ever see the fellow more hearty and manly? Yonder lean, shambling, cadaverous lad, who is always borrowing money, telling lies, leering after the housemaids, is Master Laurence Sterne, — a bishop's grandson, and himself intended for the Church; for shame, you little reprobate! But what a genius the fellow has! Let him have a sound flogging, and as soon as the young scamp is out of the whipping-room, give him a gold medal. Such would be my practice if I were Doctor Birch, and master of the school.

Let us drop this school metaphor, this birch and all pertaining thereto. Our subject, I beg leave to remind the reader's humble servant, is novel heroes and heroines. How do you like your heroes, ladies? Gentlemen, what novel heroines do you prefer? When I set this essay going, I sent the above question to two of the most inveterate novel-readers of my acquaintance. The gentleman refers me to Miss Austen; the lady says Athos, Guy Livingstone, and (pardon my rosy blushes) Colonel Esmond, and owns that in youth she was very much in love with Valancourt.

Valancourt, and who was he? cry the young people. Valancourt, my dears, was the hero of one of the most famous romances which ever was published in this country. The beauty and elegance of Valancourt made your young grandmammas' gentle hearts to beat with respectful sympathy. He and his glory have passed away. Ah, woe is me that the glory of novels should ever decay; that dust should gather round them on the shelves; that the annual checks from Messieurs the publishers should dwindle, dwindle! Inquire at Mudie's, or the London Library, who asks for "The Mysteries of Udolpho" now? Have not even "The Mysteries of Paris" ceased to frighten? Alas, our novels are but for a season; and I know characters, whom a painful modesty forbids me to mention, who shall go to limbo along with Valancourt, and Doricourt, and Thaddeus of Warsaw.

A dear old sentimental friend, with whom I discoursed on the subject of novels yesterday, said that her favorite hero was Lord Orville, in "Evelina," that novel which

Dr. Johnson loved so. I took down the book from a dusty old crypt at a club, where Mrs Barbauld's novelists repose; and this is the kind of thing, ladies and gentlemen, in which your ancestors found pleasure: —

"And here, whilst I was looking for the books, I was followed by Lord Orville. He shut the door after he came in, and approaching me with a look of anxiety, said, 'Is this true, Miss Anville, — are you going?'

"'I believe so, my lord,' said I, still looking for the books.

"'So suddenly, so unexpectedly: must I lose you?'

"'No great loss, my lord,' said I, endeavoring to speak cheerfully.

"'Is it possible,' said he gravely, 'Miss Anville can doubt my sincerity?'

"'I can't imagine,' cried I, 'what Mrs. Selwyn has done with those books.'

"'Would to heaven,' continued he, 'I might flatter myself you would allow me to prove it!'

"'I must run up stairs,' cried I, greatly confused, 'and ask what she has done with them.'

"'You are going, then,' cried he, taking my hand, 'and you give me not the smallest hope of any return! Will you not, my too lovely friend, will you not teach me, with fortitude like your own, to support your absence?'

"'My lord,' cried I, endeavoring to disengage my hand, 'pray let me go!'

"'I will,' cried he, to my inexpressible confusion, dropping on one knee, 'if you wish me to leave you.'

"'O, my lord,' exclaimed I, 'rise, I beseech you; rise. Surely your lordship is not so cruel as to mock me.'

"'Mock you!' repeated he earnestly, 'no, I revere you.

I esteem and admire you above all human beings! You are the friend to whom my soul is attached, as to its better half. You are the most amiable, the most perfect of women; and you are dearer to me than language has the power of telling.'

"I attempt not to describe my sensations at that moment; I scarce breathed; I doubted if I existed; the blood forsook my cheeks, and my feet refused to sustain me. Lord Orville hastily rising supported me to a chair, upon which I sank almost lifeless.

"I cannot write the scene that followed, though every word is engraven on my heart; but his protestations, his expressions, were too flattering for repetition; nor would he, in spite of my repeated efforts to leave him, suffer me to escape; in short, my dear sir, I was not proof against his solicitations, and he drew from me the most sacred secret of my heart!" *

* Contrast this old perfumed, powdered D'Arblay conversation with the present modern talk. If the two young people wished to hide their emotions now-a-days, and express themselves in modest language, the story would run: —

"Whilst I was looking for the books, Lord Orville came in. He looked uncommonly down in the mouth, as he said: 'Is this true, Miss Anville; are you going to cut?'

"'To absquatulate, Lord Orville,' said I, still pretending that I was looking for the books.

"'You 're very quick about it,' said he.

"'Guess it 's no great loss,' I remarked, as cheerfully as I could.

"'You don't think I 'm chaffing?' said Orville, with much emotion.

"'What has Mrs Selwyn done with the books ?' I went on.

"'What, going?' said he, 'and going for good? I wish I was such a good-plucked one as you, Miss Anville,'" &c.

The conversation, you perceive, might be easily written down to this key; and if the hero and heroine were modern, they would not be suffered to go through their dialogue on stilts, but would converse in the natural, graceful way at present customary. By the way, what

Other people may not much like this extract, madam, from your favorite novel, but when you come to read it, *you* will like it. I suspect that when you read that book which you so love, you read it *à deux*. Did you not yourself pass a winter at Bath, when you were the belle of the assembly? Was there not a Lord Orville in your case, too? As you think of him eleven lustres pass away. You look at him with the bright eyes of those days, and your hero stands before you, the brave, the accomplished, the simple, the true gentleman; and he makes the most elegant of bows to one of the most beautiful young women the world ever saw; and he leads you out to the cotillon, to the dear, unforgotten music. Hark to the horns of Elfland, blowing, blowing! *Bonne vieille*, you remember their melody, and your heart-strings thrill with it still.

Of your heroic heroes, I think our friend Monsigneur Athos, Count de la Fère, is my favorite. I have read about him from sunrise to sunset with the utmost contentment of mind. He has passed through how many volumes? Forty? Fifty? I wish for my part there were a hundred more, and would never tire of him rescuing prisoners, punishing ruffians, and running scoundrels through the midriff with his most graceful rapier. Ah, Athos, Porthos, and Aramis, you are a magnificent trio. I think I like d'Artagnan in his own memoirs best. I bought him years and years ago, price fivepence, in a little parchment-

a strange custom that is in modern lady novelists to make the men bully the women! In the time of Miss Porter and Madame D'Arblay, we have respect, profound bows and courtesies, graceful courtesy from men to women. In the time of Miss Brontë, absolute rudeness. Is it true, mesdames, that you like rudeness, and are pleased at being ill-used by men? I could point to more than one lady novelist who so represents you.

covered Cologne-printed volume, at a stall in Gray's-inn-lane. Dumas glorifies him and makes a marshal of him; if I remember rightly, the original D'Artagnan was a needy adventurer, who died in exile very early in Louis XIV.'s reign. Did you ever read the "Chevalier d'Harmenthal"? Did you ever read the "Tulipe Noire," as modest as a story by Miss Edgeworth? I think of the prodigal banquets to which this Lucullus of a man has invited me, with thanks and wonder. To what a series of splendid entertainments he has treated me! Where does he find the money for these prodigious feasts? They say that all the works bearing Dumas's name are not written by him. Well? Does not the chief cook have *aides* under him? Did not Rubens's pupils paint on his canvases? Had not Lawrence assistants for his backgrounds? For myself, being also *du métier*, I confess I would often like to have a competent, respectable, and rapid clerk for the business part of my novels; and on his arrival, at eleven o'clock, would say, "Mr. Jones, if you please, the archbishop must die this morning in about five pages. Turn to article 'Dropsy' (or what you will) in Encyclopædia. Take care there are no medical blunders in his death. Group his daughters, physicians, and chaplains round him. In Wales's 'London,' letter B, third shelf, you will find an account of Lambeth, and some prints of the place. Color in with local coloring. The daughter will come down, and speak to her lover in his wherry at Lambeth Stairs," &c., &c. Jones (an intelligent young man) examines the medical, historical, topographical books necessary; his chief points out to him in Jeremy Taylor (fol., London, MDCLV.) a few remarks, such as might befit a dear old archbishop departing this life. When I come back to dress for dinner, the archbishop is dead on my table in five pages; medicine, topography, theology, all right, and Jones has gone home to his family some hours. Sir Christopher is the architect of St. Paul's. He has not laid the stones or carried up the mortar. There is a great deal of carpenter's and joiner's work in novels which surely a smart professional hand might supply. A smart professional hand? I give you my word, there seem to me parts of novels, — let us say the love-making, the "business," the villain in the cupboard, and so forth, — which I should like to order John Footman to take in hand, as I desire him to bring the coals and polish the boots. Ask *me* indeed to pop a robber under a bed, to hide a will which shall be forthcoming in due season, or at my time of life to write a namby-pamby love conversation between Emily and Lord Arthur! I feel ashamed of myself, and especially when my business obliges me to do the love passages, I blush so, though quite alone in my study, that you would fancy I was going off in an apoplexy. Are authors affected by their own works? I don't know about other gentlemen, but if I make a joke myself I cry; if I write a pathetic scene I am laughing wildly all the time, — at least Tomkins thinks so. You know I am such a cynic!

The editor of the Cornhill Magazine (no soft and yielding character like his predecessor, but a man of stern resolution) will only allow these harmless papers to run to a certain length. But for this veto I should gladly have prattled over half a sheet more, and have discoursed on many heroes and heroines of novels whom fond memory brings back to me. Of these books I have been a diligent student from those early days, which are recorded at the commencement of this little essay. O, delightful novels, well remembered! O, novels, sweet and delicious as the raspberry open-tarts of budding boyhood! Do I forget one night after prayers (when we under-boys were sent to bed), lingering at my cupboard to read one little half page more of my dear Walter Scott, — and down came the monitor's dictionary upon my head? Rebecca, daughter of Isaac of York, I have loved thee faithfully for forty years! Thou wert twenty years old (say), and I but twelve, when I knew thee. At sixty odd, love, most of the ladies of thy Orient race have lost the bloom of youth, and bulged beyond the line of beauty; but to me thou art ever young and fair, and I will do battle with any felon Templar who assails thy fair name.

ON SOME CARP AT SANS SOUCI.

E have lately made the acquaintance of an old lady of ninety, who has passed the last twenty-five years of her old life in a great metropolitan establishment, — the workhouse, namely, of the parish of Saint Lazarus. Stay, — twenty-three or four years ago, she came out once, and thought to earn a little money by hop-picking; but being overworked, and having to lie out at night, she got a palsy which has incapacitated her from all further labor, and has caused her poor old limbs to shake ever since.

An illustration of that dismal proverb which tells us how poverty makes us acquainted with strange bedfellows, this poor old shaking body has to lay herself down every night in her workhouse bed by the side of some other old woman with whom she may or may not agree. She herself can't be a very pleasant bedfellow, poor thing! with her shaking old limbs and cold feet. She lies awake a deal of the night, to be sure, not thinking of happy old times, for hers never were happy; but sleepless with aches, and agues, and rheumatism of old age. "The gentleman gave me brandy-and-water," she said, her old voice shaking with rapture at the thought. I never had a great love for Queen Charlotte, but I like her better now from what this old lady told me. The

Queen, who loved snuff herself, has left a legacy of snuff to certain poorhouses; and, in her watchful nights, this old woman takes a pinch of Queen Charlotte's snuff, "and it do comfort me, sir, that it do!" *Pulveris exigui munus.* Here is a forlorn aged creature, shaking with palsy, with no soul among the great struggling multitude of mankind to care for her, not quite trampled out of life, but past and forgotten in the rush, made a little happy, and soothed in her hours of unrest by this penny legacy. Let me think as I write. (The next month's sermon, thank goodness! is safe to press.) This discourse will appear at the season when I have read that wassail bowls make their appearance; at the season of pantomime, turkey and sausages, plum-puddings, jollifications for schoolboys; Christmas bills, and reminiscences more or less sad and sweet, for elders. If we oldsters are not merry, we shall be having a semblance of merriment. We shall see the young folks laughing round the holly-bush. We shall pass the bottle round cosily as we sit by the fire. That old thing will have a sort of festival too. Beef, beer, and pudding will be served to her for that day, also. Christmas falls on a Thursday. Friday is the workhouse day for coming out. Mary, remember that old Goody Twoshoes has her invitation for Friday, 26th December! Ninety, is she, poor old soul? Ah! what a bonny face to catch under a mistletoe! "Yes, ninety, sir," she says, "and my mother was a hundred, and my grandmother was a hundred and two."

Herself ninety, her mother a hundred, her grandmother a hundred and two? What a queer calculation!

Ninety! Very good, granny; you were bo1n, then, in 1772.

Your mother, we will say, was twenty-seven when you were born, and was born therefore in 1745.

Your grandmother was thirty when her daughter was born, and was born therefore in 1715.

We will begin with the present granny first. My good old creature, you can't of course remember, but that little gentleman for whom your mother was laundress in the Temple was the ingenious Mr. Goldsmith, author of a "History of England," "The Vicar of Wakefield," and many diverting pieces. You were brought almost an infant to his chambers in Brick Court, and he gave you some sugar-candy, for the doctor was always good to children. That gentleman who wellnigh smothered you by sitting down on you as you lay in a chair asleep was the learned Mr. S. Johnson, whose history of "Rasselas" you have never read, my poor soul; and whose tragedy of "Irene" I don't believe any man in these kingdoms ever perused. That tipsy Scotch gentleman who used to come to the chambers sometimes, and at whom everybody laughed, wrote a more amusing book than any of the scholars, your Mr. Burke and your Mr. Johnson, and your Doctor Goldsmith. Your father often took him home in a chair to his lodgings; and has done as much for Parson Sterne in Bond Street, the famous wit. Of course, my good creature, you remember the Gordon Riots, and crying No Popery before Mr. Langdale's house, the Popish distiller's, and that bonny fire of my Lord Mansfield's books in Bloomsbury Square? Bless us, what a heap of illuminations you have seen! For the glorious victory over the Americans at Breed's Hill; for the peace in 1814, and the beautiful Chinese bridge in St. James's Park; for the coronation of his Majesty, whom you recollect as Prince of Wales, Goody, don't you? Yes; and you went in a procession of laundresses to pay your respects to his good lady, the injured Queen of England, at Brandenburg

House; and you remember your mother told you how she was taken to see the Scotch lords executed at the Tower. And as for your grandmother, she was born five months after the battle of Malplaquet. She was; where her poor father was killed, fighting like a bold Briton for the Queen. With the help of a Wade's Chronology, I can make out ever so queer a history for you, my poor old body, and a pedigree as authentic as many in the peerage-books.

Peerage-books and pedigrees? What does she know about them? Battles and victories, treasons, kings, and beheadings, literary gentlemen, and the like, what have they ever been to her? Granny, did you ever hear of General Wolfe? Your mother may have seen him embark, and your father may have carried a musket under him. Your grandmother may have cried huzzay for Marlborough; but what is the Prince Duke to you, and did you ever so much as hear tell of his name? How many hundred or thousand of years had that toad lived who was in the coal at the defunct Exhibition? — and yet he was not a bit better informed than toads seven or eight hundred years younger.

"Don't talk to me your nonsense about Exhibitions, and Prince Dukes, and toads in coals, or coals in toads, or, what is it!" says granny. "I know there was a good Queen Charlotte, for she left me snuff; and it comforts me of a night when I lie awake."

To me there is something very touching in the notion of that little pinch of comfort doled out to granny, and gratefully inhaled by her in the darkness. Don't you remember what traditions there used to be of chests of plate, bulses of diamonds, laces of inestimable value, sent out of the country privately by the old Queen, to enrich certain relations in M-ckl-nb-rg Str-l-tz? Not all the treasure went. *Non omnis moritur.* A poor old palsied thing at midnight is made happy sometimes as she lifts her shaking old hand to her nose. Gliding noiselessly among the beds where lie the poor creatures huddled in their cheerless dormitory, I fancy an old ghost with a snuff-box that does not creak. "There, Goody, take of my rappee. You will not sneeze, and I shall not say, 'God bless you.' But you will think kindly of old Queen Charlotte, won't you? Ah! I had a many troubles, a many troubles. I was a prisoner almost so much as you are. I had to eat boiled mutton every day: *entre nous*, I abominated it. But I never complained. I swallowed it. I made the best of a hard life. We have all our burdens to bear. But hark! I hear the cock-crow, and snuff the morning air." And with this the royal ghost vanishes up the chimney, — if there be a chimney in that dismal harem, where poor old Twoshoes and her companions pass their nights, — their dreary nights, their restless nights, their cold, long nights, shared in what glum companionship, illumined by what a feeble taper!

"Did I understand you, my good Twoshoes, to say that pour mother was seven-and-twenty years old when you were born, and that she married your esteemed father when she herself was twenty-five? 1745, then, was the date of your dear mother's birth. I dare say her father was absent in the Low Countries, with his Royal Highness the Duke of Cumberland, under whom he had the honor of carrying a halberd at the famous engagement of Fontenoy, — or if not there, he may have been at Preston Pans, under General Sir John Cope, when the wild Highlanders broke through all the laws of discipline and the English lines; and, being on the spot, did he see the famous ghost which did n't appear to Colonel Gardiner of the Dragoons? My good creature, is it possible you don't remember that Doctor Swift, Sir Robert Walpole (my Lord Orford, as you justly say), old Sarah Marlborough, and little Mr. Pope, of Twitnam, died in the year of your birth? What a wretched memory you have? What? have n't they a library, and the commonest books of reference at the old convent of Saint Lazarus, where you dwell?"

"Convent of Saint Lazarus, Prince William, Dr. Swift, Atossa, and Mr. Pope, of Twitnam! What is the gentleman talking about?" says old Goody, with a "Ho! ho!" and a laugh like an old parrot, — you know they live to be as old as Methuselah, parrots do, and a parrot of a hundred is comparrotively young (ho! ho! ho!). Yes, and likewise carps live to an immense old age. Some which Frederick the Great fed at Sans Souci are there now, with great humps of blue mould on their old backs; and they could tell all sorts of queer stories, if they chose to speak — but they are very silent, carps are — of their nature *peu communicatives.* O, what has been thy long life, old Goody, but a dole of bread and water and a perch on a cage; a dreary swim round and round a Lethe of a pond? What are Rossbach or Jena to those mouldy ones, and do they know it is a grandchild of England who brings bread to feed them?

No! Those Sans Souci carps may live to be a thousand years old and have nothing to tell but that one day is like another; and the history of friend Goody Two-shoes has not much more variety than theirs. Hard labor, hard fare, hard bed, numbing cold all night, and gnawing hunger most days. That is her lot. Is it lawful in my prayers to say, "Thank heaven, I am not as one of these?" If I were eighty, would I like to feel the hunger always gnawing, gnawing? to have to get up and make a bow when Mr. Bumble the beadle entered the common room? to have to listen to Miss Prim, who came to give me her ideas of the next world? If I were eighty, I own I should not like to have to sleep with another gentleman of my own age, gouty, a bad sleeper, kicking in his old dreams, and snoring; to march down my vale of years at word of command, accommodating my tottering old steps to those of the other prisoners in my dingy, hopeless old gang; to hold out a trembling hand for a sickly pittance of gruel, and say, "Thank you, mam!" to Miss Prim, when she has done reading her sermon. John! when Goody Twoshoes comes next Friday, I desire she may not be disturbed by theological controversies. You have a very fair voice, and I heard you and the maids singing a hymn very sweetly the other night, and was thankful that our humble household should be in such harmony. Poor old Twoshoes is so old and toothless and quaky, that she can't sing a bit; but don't be giving yourself airs over her, because she can't sing and you can. Make her comfortable at our kitchen hearth. Set that old kettle to sing by our hob. Warm her old stomache with nut-brown ale and a toast laid in the fire. Be kind to the poor old school-girl of ninety, who has had leave to come out for a day of Christmas holiday. Shall there be many more Christmases for thee? Think of the ninety she has seen already; the four score and ten cold, cheerless, nipping New Years!

If you were in her place, would you like to have a remembrance of better early days, when you were young, and happy, and loving, perhaps; or would you prefer to have no past on which your mind could rest? About the year 1788, Goody, were your cheeks rosy, and your eyes bright, and did some young fellow in powder and a pig-tail look in them? We may grow old, but to us some stories never are old. On a sudden they rise up, not dead, but living, — not forgotten, but freshly remembered. The eyes gleam on us as they used to do. The dear voice thrills in our hearts. The rapture of the meeting, the terrible, terrible parting, again and again the tragedy is acted over. Yesterday, in the street, I saw a pair of eyes so like two which used to brighten at my coming once, that the whole past came back as I walked lonely, in the rush of the Strand, and I was young again in the midst of joys and sorrows, alike sweet and sad, alike sacred, and fondly remembered.

If I tell a tale out of school, will any harm come to my old school-girl? Once, a lady gave her a half-sovereign, which was a source of great pain and anxiety to Goody Twoshoes. She sewed it away in her old stays somewhere, thinking here at least was a safe investment — (*vestis* — a vest — an investment, — pardon me, thou poor old thing, but I cannot help the pleasantry). And what do you think? Another pensionnaire of the establishment cut the coin out of Goody's stays, — *an old woman who went upon two crutches!* Faugh, the old witch! What? Violence amongst these toothless, tottering, trembling, feeble ones? Robbery amongst the penniless? Dogs coming and snatching Lazarus's crumbs out of his lap? Ah, how indignant Goody was as she told the story! To that pond at Potsdam where the carps live for hundreds of hundreds of years, with hunches of blue mould on their back, I dare say the little Prince and Princess of Preussen-Britannien come sometimes with crumbs and cakes to feed the mouldy ones. Those eyes may have goggled from beneath the weeds at Napoleon's jack-boots: they have seen Frederick's lean shanks reflected in their pool; and perhaps Monsieur de Voltaire has fed them, — and now, for a crumb of biscuit they will fight, push, hustle, rob, squabble, gobble, relapsing into their tranquillity when the ignoble struggle is over. Sans souci, indeed! It is mighty well writing "Sans souci" over the gate; but where is the gate through which Care has not slipped? She perches on the shoulders of the sentry in the sentry-box: she whispers the porter sleeping in his arm-chair: she glides up the staircase, and lies down between the king and queen in their bed-royal: this very night I dare say she will perch upon poor old Goody Twoshoes's meagre bolster, and whisper, "Will the gentleman and those ladies ask me again? No, no; they will forget poor old Twoshoes." Goody! For shame of yourself! Do not be cynical. Do not mistrust your fellow-creatures. What? Has the Christmas morning dawned upon thee ninety times? For four-score and ten years has it been thy lot to totter on this earth, hungry and obscure? Peace and goodwill to thee, let us say at this Christmas season. Come, drink, eat, rest awhile at our hearth, thou poor old pilgrim! And of the bread which God's bounty gives us, I pray, brother reader, we may not forget to set aside a part for those noble and silent poor, from whose innocent hands war has torn the means of labor. Enough! As I hope for beef at Christmas, I vow a note shall be sent to Saint Lazarus Union House, in which Mr. Roundabout requests the honor of Mrs. Twoshoes's company on Friday, 26th December.

DESSEIN'S.

ARRIVED by the night-mail packet from Dover. The passage had been rough, and the usual consequences had ensued. I was disinclined to travel farther that night on my road to Paris, and knew the Calais hotel of old as one of the cleanest, one of the dearest, one of the most comfortable hotels on the continent of Europe. There is no town more French than Calais. That charming old Hôtel Dessein, with its court, its gardens, its lordly kitchen, its princely waiter, — a gentleman of the old school, who has welcomed the finest company in Europe, — have long been known to me. I have read complaints in The Times, more than once, I think, that the Dessein bills are dear. A bottle of soda-water certainly costs — well, never mind how much. I remember as a boy, at the Ship at Dover (imperante Carolo Decimo), when, my place to London being paid, I had but 12*s.* left after a certain little Paris excursion (about which my benighted parents never knew anything), ordering for dinner a whiting, a beefsteak, and a glass of negus, and the bill was, dinner 7*s.*, glass of negus 2*s.*, waiter 6*d.*, and only half-a-crown left, as I was a sinner, for the guard and coachman on the way to London! And I *was* a sinner. I had gone without leave. What a long, dreary, guilty, forty hours'

journey it was from Paris to Calais, I remember! How did I come to think of this escapade, which occurred in the Easter vacation of the year 1830? I always think of it when I am crossing to Calais. Guilt, sir, guilt remains stamped on the memory, and I feel easier in my mind now that it is liberated of this old peccadillo. I met my college tutor only yesterday. We were travelling, and stopped at the same hotel. He had the very next room to mine. After he had gone into his apartment, having shaken me quite kindly by the hand, I felt inclined to knock at his door, and say, "Doctor Bentley, I beg your pardon, but do you remember, when I was going down at the Easter vacation in 1830, you asked me where I was going to spend my vacation? And I said, with my friend Slingsby, in Huntingdonshire. Well, sir, I grieve to have to confess that I told you a fib. I had got £20 and was going for a lark to Paris, where my friend Edwards was staying." There, it is out. The Doctor will read it, for I did not wake him up after all to make my confession, but protest he shall have a copy of this Roundabout sent to him when he returns to his lodge.

They gave me a bedroom there; a very neat room on the first floor, looking into the pretty garden. The hotel must look pretty much as it did a hundred years ago when he visited it. I wonder whether he paid his bill? Yes: his journey was just begun. He had borrowed or got the money somehow. Such a man would spend it liberally enough when he had it, give generously, — nay, drop a tear over the fate of the poor fellow whom he relieved. I don't believe a word he says, but I never accused him of stinginess about money. That is a fault of much more virtuous people than he. Mr. Laurence is ready enough with his purse when there are anybody's guineas in it. Still, when I went to bed in the room, in *his* room, — when I think how I admire, dislike, and have abused him, — a certain dim feeling of apprehension filled my mind at the midnight hour. What if I should see his lean figure in the black satin breeches, his sinister smile, his long thin finger pointing to me in the moonlight (for I am in bed, and have popped my candle out), and he should say, "You mistrust me, you hate me, do you? And you, don't you know how Jack, Tom, and Harry, your brother authors, hate *you?*" I grin and laugh in the moonlight, in the midnight, in the silence. "O you ghost in black satin breeches and a wig! I like to be hated by some men," I say. "I know men whose lives are a scheme, whose laughter is a conspiracy, whose smile means something else, whose hatred is a cloak, and I had rather these men should hate me than not."

"My good sir," says he, with a ghastly grin on his lean face, "you have your wish."

"*Après?*" I say. "Please let me go to sleep. I sha'n't sleep any the worse because —"

"Because there are insects in the bed, and they sting you?" (This is only by way of illustration, my good sir; the animals don't bite me now. All the house at present seems to me excellently clean.) "'T is absurd to affect this indifference. If you are thin-skinned, and the reptiles bite, they keep you from sleep."

"There are some men who cry out at a flea-bite as loud as if they were torn by a vulture," I growl.

"Men of the *genus irritable*, my worthy good gentleman! — and you are one."

"Yes, sir, I am of the profession, as you say; and I dare say make a great shouting and crying at a small hurt."

"You are ashamed of that quality by which you earn your subsistence, and such reputation as you have? Your sensibility is your livelihood, my worthy friend. You feel a pang of pleasure or pain? It is noted in your memory, and some day or other makes its appearance in your manuscript. Why, in your last Roundabout rubbish you mention reading your first novel on the day when King George IV. was crowned. I remember him in his cradle at St. James's, a lovely little babe; a gilt Chinese railing was before him, and I dropped the tear of sensibility as I gazed on the sleeping cherub."

"A tear, — a fiddlestick, Mr. STERNE," I growled out, for of course I knew my friend in the wig and satin breeches to be no other than the notorious, nay, celebrated Mr. Laurence Sterne.

"Does not the sight of a beautiful infant charm and melt you, *mon ami?* If not, I pity you. Yes, he was beautiful. I was in London the year he was born. I used to breakfast at the Mount Coffee-house. I did not become the fashion until two years later, when my "Tristram" made his appearance, who has held his own for a hundred years. By the way, *mon bon monsieur*, how many authors of your present time will last till the next century? Do you think Brown will?"

I laughed with scorn as I lay in my bed (and so did the ghost give a ghastly snigger).

"Brown!" I roared. "One of the most over-rated men that ever put pen to paper."

"What do you think of Jones?"

I grew indignant with this old cynic. "As a reasonable ghost, come out of the other world, you don't mean," I said, "to ask me a serious opinion of Mr. Jones? His books may be very good reading for maid-servants and school-boys, but you don't ask *me* to read them? As a scholar yourself you must know that —"

"Well, then, Robinson?"

"Robinson, I am told, has merit. I dare say; I never have been able to read his books, and can't, therefore, form any opinion about Mr. Robinson. At least you will allow that I am not speaking in a prejudiced manner about *him*."

"Ah! I see you men of letters have your cabals and jealousies, as we had in my time. There was an Irish fellow by the name of Gouldsmith, who used to abuse me; but he went into no genteel company, — and faith! it mattered little, his praise or abuse. I never was more surprised than when I heard that Mr. Irving, an American gentleman of parts and elegance, had wrote the fellow's life. To make a hero of that man, my dear sir, 't was ridiculous! You followed in the fashion, I hear, and chose to lay a wreath before this queer little idol. Preposterous! A pretty writer, who has turned some neat couplets. Bah! I have no patience with Master Posterity, that has chosen to take up this fellow, and make a hero of him! And there was another gentleman of my time, Mr. Thiefcatcher Fielding, forsooth! a fellow with the strength, and the tastes, and the manners of a porter! What madness has possessed you all to bow before that Calvert Butt of a man? — a creature without elegance or sensibility! The dog had spirits, certainly. I remember my Lord Bathurst praising them: but as for reading his books — *ma foi*, I would as lief go and dive for tripe in a cellar. The man's vulgarity stifles me. He wafts me whiffs of gin. Tobacco and onions are in his great coarse laugh, which choke me, *pardi;* and I don't think much better of the other fellow, — the Scots' gallipot purveyor, — Peregrine Clinker, Humphrey Random, — how did the fellow call his rubbish? Neither of these men had the *bel air*, the *bon ton*, the *je ne sçais quoy*. Pah! If I meet them in my walks by our Stygian river, I give them a wide berth, as that hybrid apothecary fellow would say. An ounce of civet, good apothecary; horrible, horrible! The mere thought of the coarseness of those men gives me the *chair de poule.* Mr. Fielding, especially, has no more sensibility than a butcher in Fleet Market. He takes his heroes out of alehouse kitchens, or worse places still. And this is the person whom Posterity has chosen to honor along with me, — *me!* Faith, Monsieur Posterity, you have put me in pretty company, and I see you are no wiser than we were in our time. Mr. Fielding, forsooth! Mr. Tripe and Onions! Mr. Cowheel and Gin! Thank you for nothing, Monsieur Posterity!"

"And so," thought I, "even among these Stygians this envy and quarrelsomeness (if you will permit me the word) survive. What a pitiful meanness! To be sure, I can understand this feeling to a certain extent; a sense of justice will prompt it. In my own case, I often feel myself forced to protest against the absurd praises lavished on contemporaries. Yesterday, for instance, Lady Jones was good enough to praise one of my works. *Très bien.* But in the very next minute she began, with quite as great enthusiasm, to praise Miss Hobson's last romance. My good creature, what is that woman's praise worth who absolutely admires the writings of Miss Hobson? I offer a friend a bottle of '44 claret, fit for a pontifical supper. "This is capital wine," says he; "and now we have finished the bottle, will you give me a bottle of that ordinaire we drank the other day?" Very well, my good man. You are a good judge, — of ordinaire, I dare say. Nothing so provokes my anger, and rouses my sense of justice, as to hear other men undeservedly praised. In a word, if you wish to remain friends with me, don't praise anybody. You tell me that the Venus de' Medici is beautiful, or Jacob Omnium is tall. *Que diable!* Can't I judge for myself? Have n't I eyes and a foot-rule? I don't think the Venus *is* so handsome, since you press me. She is pretty, but she has no expression. And as for Mr. Omnium, I can see much taller men in a fair for twopence."

"And so," I said, turning round to Mr. Sterne, "you are actually jealous of Mr. Fielding? O you men of letters, you men of letters! Is not the world (your world, I mean) big enough for all of you?"

I often travel in my sleep. I often of a night find myself walking in my night-gown about the gray streets. It is awkward at first, but somehow nobody makes any remark. I glide along over the ground with my naked feet. The mud does not wet them. The passers-by do not tread on them. I am wafted over the ground, down the stairs, through the doors. This sort of travelling, dear friends, I am sure you have all of you indulged.

Well, on the night in question (and, if you wish to know the precise date, it was the 31st of September last), after having some little conversation with Mr. Sterne in our bedroom, I must have got up, though I protest I don't know how, and come down stairs with him into the coffee-room of the Hôtel Dessein, where the moon was shining, and a cold supper was laid out. I forget what we had — "vol au vent d'œufs de Phénix — agneau aux pistaches à la Barmécide," — what matters what we had? As regards supper this is certain, the less you have of it the better.

That is what one of the guests remarked, — a shabby old man in a wig, and such a dirty, ragged, disreputable dressing-gown that I should have been quite surprised at him, only one never *is* surprised in dr— under certain circumstances.

"I can't eat 'em now," said the greasy man (with his false old teeth, I wonder he could eat anything). "I remember Alvanley eating three suppers once at Carlton House, — one night *de petite comité*."

"*Petit comité*, sir," said Mr. Sterne.

"Dammy, sir, let me tell my own story my own way. I say, one night at Carlton House, playing at blind hookey with York, Wales, Tom Raikes, Prince Boothby, and Dutch Sam the boxer, Alvanley ate three suppers, and won three and twenty hundred pounds in ponies. Never saw a fellow with such an appetite except Wales in his *good* time. But he destroyed the finest digestion a man ever had with maraschino, by Jove, — always at it."

"Try mine," said Mr. Sterne.

"What a doosid queer box," says Mr. Brummell.

"I had it from a Capuchin friar in this town. The box is but a horn one; but to the nose of sensibility Araby's perfume is not more delicate."

"I call it doosid stale old rappee," says Mr. Brummell — (as for me I declare I could not smell anything at all in either of the boxes). "Old boy in smock-frock, take a pinch?"

The old boy in the smock-frock, as Mr. Brummell called him, was a very old man, with long white beard, wearing, not a smock-frock, but a shirt; and he had actually nothing else save a rope round his neck, which hung behind his chair in the queerest way.

"Fair sir," he said, turning to Mr. Brummell, "when

the Prince of Wales and his father laid siege to our town — "

"What nonsense are you talking, old cock?" says Mr. Brummell; "Wales was never here. His late Majesty George IV. passed through on his way to Hanover. My good man, you don't seem to know what's up at all. What is he talkin' about the siege of Calais? I lived here fifteen years! Ought to know. What's his old name?"

"I am Master Eustace, of Saint Peter," said the old gentleman in the shirt. "When my Lord King Edward laid siege to this city — "

"Laid siege to Jericho!" cries Mr. Brummell. "The old man is cracked, — cracked, sir!"

"— Laid siege to this city," continued the old man, "I and five more promised Messire Gautier de Mauny that we would give ourselves up as ransom for the place. And we came before our Lord King Edward, attired as you see, and the fair queen begged our lives out of her gramercy."

"Queen, nonsense! you mean the Princess of Wales, — pretty woman, *petit nez retroussé*, grew monstrous stout?" suggested Mr. Brummell, whose reading was evidently not extensive. "Sir Sydney Smith was a fine fellow, great talker, hook-nose, so has Lord Cochrane, so has Lord Wellington. She was very sweet on Sir Sydney."

"Your acquaintance with the history of Calais does not seem to be considerable," said Mr. Sterne to Mr. Brummell, with a shrug.

"Don't it, bishop? — for I conclude you are a bishop by your wig. I know Calais as well as any man. I lived here for years before I took that confounded consulate at Caen. Lived in this hotel, then at Leleux's. People used to stop here. Good fellows used to ask for poor George Brummell; Hertford did, so did the Duchess of Devonshire. Not know Calais indeed! That is a good joke. Had many a good dinner here: sorry I ever left it."

"My Lord King Edward," chirped the queer old gentleman in the shirt, "colonized the place with his English, after we had yielded it up to him. I have heard tell they kept it for nigh three hundred years, till my Lord de Guise took it from a fair Queen, Mary of blessed memory, a holy woman. Eh, but Sire Gautier of Mauny was a good knight, a valiant captain, gentle and courteous withal! Do you remember his ransoming the — "

"What is the old fellow twaddlin' about?" cries Brummell. He is talking about some knight? — I never spoke to a knight, and very seldom to a baronet. Firkins, my butterman, was a knight, — a knight and alderman. Wales knighted him once on going into the city."

"I am not surprised that the gentleman should not understand Messire Eustace of St. Peter's," said the ghostly individual addressed as Mr. Sterne. "Your reading doubtless has not been very extensive?"

"Dammy, sir, speak for yourself!" cries Mr. Brummell, testily. "I never professed to be a reading man, but I was as good as my neighbors. Wales was n't a reading man; York was n't a reading man; Clarence was n't a reading man; Sussex was, but he was n't a man in society. I remember reading your "Sentimental Journey," old boy: read it to the duchess at Beauvoir, I recollect, and she cried over it. Doosid clever, amusing book, and does you great credit. Birron wrote doosid clever books, too; so did Monk Lewis. George Spencer was an elegant poet, and my dear Duchess of Devonshire, if she had not been a grande dame, would have beat 'em all, by George. Wales could n't write: he could sing, but he could n't spell."

"Ah, you know the great world? so did I in my time, Mr. Brummell. I have had the visiting tickets of half the nobility at my lodgings in Bond Street. But they left me there no more cared for than last year's calendar," sighed Mr. Sterne. "I wonder who is the mode in London now? One of our late arrivals, my Lord Macaulay, has prodigious merit and learning, and, faith, his histories are more amusing than any novels, my own included."

"Don't know, I'm sure; not in my line. Pick this bone of chicken," says Mr. Brummell, trifling with a skeleton bird before him.

"I remember in this city of Calais worse fare than yon bird," said old Mr. Eustace, of Saint Peter. "Marry, sirs, when my Lord King Edward laid siege to us, lucky was he who could get a slice of horse for his breakfast, and a rat was sold at the price of a hare."

"Hare is coarse food, never tasted rat," remarked the Beau. *Table-d'hôte* poor fare enough for a man like me, who has been accustomed to the best of cookery. But rat — stifle me! I could n't swallow that: never could bear hardship at all."

"We had to bear enough when my Lord of England pressed us. 'T was pitiful to see the faces of our women as the siege went on, and hear the little ones asking for dinner."

"Always a bore, children. At dessert, they are bad enough, but at dinner they 're the deuce and all," remarked Mr. Brummell.

Messire Eustace, of St. Peter, did not seem to pay

much attention to the Beau's remarks, but continued his own train of thought as old men will do.

"I hear," said he, "that there has actually been no war between us of France and you men of England for wellnigh fifty year. Ours has ever been a nation of warriors. And besides her regular found men-at-arms, 't is said the English of the present time have more than a hundred thousand of archers with weapons that will carry for half a mile. And a multitude have come amongst us of late from a great Western country, never so much as heard of in my time, — valiant men and great drawers of the long-bow, and they say they have ships in armor that no shot can penetrate. Is it so? Wonderful; wonderful! The best armor, gossips, is a stout heart."

"And if ever manly heart beat under shirt-frill, thine is that heart, Sir Eustace!" cried Mr. Sterne, enthusiastically.

"We, of France, were never accused of lack of courage, sir, in so far as I know," said Messire Eustace. "We have shown as much in a thousand wars with you English by sea and land; and sometimes we conquered, and sometimes, as is the fortune of war, we were discomfited. And notably in a great sea-fight which befell off Ushant on the first of June —— Our amiral, Messire Villaret Joyeuse, on board his galleon named the *Vengeur*, being sore pressed by an English bombard, rather than yield the crew of his ship to mercy, determined to go down with all on board of her: and, to the cry of Vive la Répub—— or, I would say, of Notre Dame à la Rescousse, he and his crew all sank to an immortal grave —"

"Sir," said I, looking with amazement at the old gentleman, "surely, surely, there is some mistake in your statement. Permit me to observe that the action of the first of June took place five hundred years after your time, and —"

"Perhaps I am confusing my dates," said the old gentleman, with a faint blush. "You say I am mixing up the transactions of my time on earth with the story of my successors? It may be so. We take no count of a few centuries more or less in our dwelling by the darkling Stygian river. Of late, there came amongst us a good knight, Messire de Cambronne, who fought against you English in the country of Flanders, being captain of the guard of my Lord the King of France, in a famous battle where you English would have been utterly routed but for the succor of the Prussian heathen. This Méssire de Cambronne, when bidden to yield by you of England, answered this, 'The guard dies but never surrenders'; and fought a long time afterwards, as became a good knight. In our wars with you of England it may have pleased the Fates to give you the greater success, but on our side, also, there has been no lack of brave deeds performed by brave men."

"King Edward may have been the victor, sir, as being the strongest, but you are the hero of the siege of Calais!" cried Mr. Sterne. "Your story is sacred, and your name has been blessed for five hundred years. Wherever men speak of patriotism and sacrifice, Eustace, of Saint Pierre, shall be beloved and remembered. I prostrate myself before the bare feet which stood before King Edward. What collar of chivalry is to be compared to that glorious order which you wear? Think, sir, how, out of the myriad millions of our race, you, and some few more, stand forth as exemplars of duty and honor. *Fortunati nimium!*"

"Sir," said the old gentleman, "I did but my duty at a painful moment; and 't is matter of wonder to me that men talk still, and glorify such a trifling matter. By our Lady's grace, in the fair kingdom of France, there are scores of thousands of men, gentle and simple, who would do as I did. Does not every sentinel at his post, does not every archer in the front of battle, brave it, and die where his captain bids him? Who am I that I should be chosen out of all France to be an example of fortitude? I braved no tortures, though these I trust I would have endured with a good heart. I was subject to threats only. Who was the Roman knight of whom the Latin clerk Horatius tells?"

"A Latin clerk? Faith, I forget my Latin," says Mr. Brummell. "Ask the parson here."

"Messire Regulus, I remember, was his name. Taken prisoner by the Saracens, he gave his knightly word, and was permitted to go seek a ransom among his own people. Being unable to raise the sum that was a fitting ransom for such a knight, he returned to Afric, and cheerfully submitted to the tortures which the Paynims inflicted. And 't is said he took leave of his friends as gayly as though he were going to a village kermes, or riding to his garden house in the suburb of the city."

"Great, good, glorious man!" cried Mr. Sterne, very much moved. "Let me embrace that gallant hand, and bedew it with my tears! As long as honor lasts thy name shall be remembered. See this dew-drop twinkling on my cheek! 'T is the sparkling tribute that Sensibility pays to Valor. Though in my life and practice I may turn from Virtue, believe me, I never have ceased to honor her! Ah, Virtue! Ah, Sensibility! O —"

Here Mr. Sterne was interrupted by a monk of the

Order of St. Francis who stepped into the room, and begged us all to take a pinch of his famous old rappee. I suppose the snuff was very pungent, for, with a great start, I woke up; and now perceived that I must have been dreaming altogether. Dessein's of now-a-days is not the Dessein's which Mr. Sterne, and Mr. Brummell, and I, recollect in the good old times. The town of Calais has bought the old hotel, and Dessein has gone over to Quillacq's. And I was there yesterday. And I remember old diligences, and old postilions in pig-tails and jack-boots, who were once as alive as I am, and whose cracking whips I have heard in the midnight many and many a time. Now, where are they? Behold, they have been ferried over Styx, and have passed away into limbo.

I wonder what time does my boat go? Ah! Here comes the waiter bringing me my little bill.

ON A PEAR-TREE.

 GRACIOUS reader no doubt has remarked that these humble sermons have for subjects some little event which happens at the preacher's own gate, or which falls under his peculiar cognizance. Once, you may remember, we discoursed about a chalk-mark on the door. This morning Betsy, the housemaid, comes with a frightened look, and says, "Law, mum! there 's three bricks taken out of the garden-wall, and the branches broke, and all the pears taken off the pear-tree!" Poor peaceful suburban pear-tree! Jail-birds have hopped about thy branches, and robbed them of their smoky fruit. But those bricks removed; that ladder evidently prepared, by which unknown marauders may enter and depart from my little Englishman's castle; is not this a subject of thrilling interest, and may it not *be continued in a future number?* — that is the terrible question. Suppose, having escaladed the outer wall, the miscreants take a fancy to storm the castle? Well — well! we are armed; we are numerous; we are men of tremendous courage, who will defend our spoons with our lives; and there are barracks close by (thank goodness!) whence, at the noise of our shouts and firing at least a thousand bayonets will bristle to our rescue.

What sound is yonder? A church bell. I might go myself, but how listen to the sermon? I am thinking of those thieves who have made a ladder of my wall, and a prey of my pear-tree. They may be walking to church at this moment, neatly shaved, in clean linen, with every outward appearance of virtue. If I went, I know I should be watching the congregation, and thinking, "Is that one of the fellows who came over my wall?" If, after the reading of the eighth Commandment, a man sang out with particular energy, "Incline our hearts to keep this law," I should think, "Aha, Master Basso, did you have pears for breakfast this morning?" Crime is walking round me, that is clear. Who is the perpetrator? . . . . What a changed aspect the world has, since these last few lines were written! I have been walking round about my premises, and in consultation with a gentleman in a single-breasted blue coat, with pewter buttons, and a tape ornament on the collar. He has looked at the holes in the wall, and the amputated tree. We have formed our plan of defence, —*perhaps of attack.* Perhaps some day you may read in the papers: "DARING ATTEMPT AT BURGLARY, — HEROIC VICTORY OVER THE VILLAINS," &c., &c. Rascals as yet unknown! perhaps you, too, may read these words, and may be induced to pause in your fatal intention. Take the advice of a sincere friend, and keep off. To find a man writhing in my man-trap, another mayhap impaled in my ditch, to pick off another from my tree (scoundrel! as though he were a pear), will give me no pleasure; but such things may happen. Be warned in time, villains! Or, if you *must* pursue your calling as cracksmen, have the goodness to try some other shutters. Enough! subside into your darkness, children of night!

Thieves! we seek not to have *you* hanged, — you are but as pegs whereon to hang others.

I may have said before, that if I were going to be hanged myself, I think I should take an accurate note of my sensations, request to stop at some public-house on the road to Tyburn, and be provided with a private room and writing materials, and give an account of my state of mind. Then, gee up, carter! I beg your reverence to continue your apposite, though not novel, remarks on my situation; — and so we drive up to Tyburn turnpike, where an expectant crowd, the obliging sheriffs, and the dexterous and rapid Mr. Ketch are already in waiting.

A number of laboring people are sauntering about our streets, and taking their rest on this holiday, — fellows who have no more stolen my pears than they have robbed the crown jewels out of the Tower, — and I say I cannot help thinking in my own mind, "Are you the rascal who got over my wall last night?" Is the suspicion haunting my mind written on my countenance? I trust not. What if one man after another were to come up to me and say, "How dare you, sir, suspect me in your mind of stealing your fruit? Go be hanged, you and your jargonels!" You rascal thief! it is not merely three halfp'orth of sooty fruit you rob me of, it is my peace of mind, — my artless innocence and trust in my fellow-creatures, my childlike belief that everything they say is true. How can I hold out the hand of friendship in this condition, when my first impression is, "My good sir, I strongly suspect that you were up my pear-tree last night?" It is a dreadful state of mind. The core is black; the death-stricken fruit drops on the bough, and a great worm is within, — fattening and feasting and wriggling! Who stole the pears? I say. Is it you, brother? Is it you, madam? Come! are you ready to answer, — *respondere parati et cantare pares?* (O shame! shame!)

Will the villains ever be discovered and punished who stole my fruit? Some unlucky rascals who rob orchards are caught up the tree at once. Some rob through life with impunity. If I, for my part, were to try and get up the smallest tree, on the darkest night, in the most remote orchard, I wager any money I should be found out, — be caught by the leg in a man-trap, or have Towler fastening on me. I always am found out; have been; shall be. It's my luck. Other men will carry off bushels of fruit, and get away undetected, unsuspected; whereas I know woe and punishment would fall upon me were I to lay my hand on the smallest pippin. So be it. A man who has this precious self-knowledge will surely keep his hands from picking and stealing, and his feet upon the paths of virtue.

I will assume, my benevolent friend and present reader, that you yourself are virtuous, not from a fear of punishment, but from a sheer love of good: but as you and I walk through life, consider what hundreds of thousands of rascals we must have met, who have not been found out at all. In high places and low, in Clubs and on 'Change, at church, or the balls and routs of the nobility and gentry, how dreadful it is for benevolent beings like you and me to have to think these undiscovered though not unsuspected scoundrels are swarming! What is the difference between you and a galley-slave? Is yonder poor wretch at the hulks not a man and a brother too? Have you ever forged, my dear sir? Have you ever cheated your neighbor? Have you ever ridden to Hounslow Heath and robbed the mail? Have you ever entered a first-class railway carriage, where an old gentleman sat alone in a sweet sleep, daintily murdered him, taken his pocket-book, and got out at the next station? You know that this circumstance occurred in France a few months since. If we have travelled in France this autumn we may have met the ingenious gentleman who perpetrated this daring and successful *coup*. We may have found him a well-informed and agreeable man. I have been acquainted with two or three gentlemen who have been discovered after — after the performance of illegal actions. What? That agreeable, rattling fellow we met was the celebrated Mr. John Sheppard? Was that amiable, quiet gentleman in spectacles the well-known Mr. Fauntleroy? In Hazlitt's admirable paper, "Going to a Fight," he describes a dashing sporting fellow who was in the coach, and who was no less a man than the eminent destroyer of Mr. William Weare. Don't tell me that you would not like to have met (out of business) Captain Sheppard, the Reverend Doctor Dodd, or others rendered famous by their actions and misfortunes, by their lives and their deaths. They are the subjects of ballads, the heroes of romance. A friend of mine had the house in May Fair, out of which poor Doctor Dodd was taken handcuffed. There was the paved hall over which he stepped. That little room at the side was, no doubt, the study where he composed his elegant sermons. Two years since I had the good fortune to partake of some admirable dinners in Tyburnia, — magnificent dinners indeed; but rendered doubly interesting from the fact that the house was that occupied by the late Mr. Sadleir. One night the late Mr. Sadleir took tea in that dining-room, and, to the surprise of his butler, went out, having put into his pocket his own cream-jug. The next morning, you know, he was found dead on Hampstead Heath, with the cream-jug lying by him, into which he had poured the poison by which he died. The idea of the ghost of the late gentleman flitting about the room gave a strange interest to the banquet. Can you fancy him taking his tea alone in the dining-room? He empties that cream-jug and puts it in his pocket; and then he opens yonder door, through which he is never to pass again. Now he crosses the hall: and hark! the hall-door shuts upon him, and his steps die away. They are gone into the night. They traverse the sleeping city. They lead him into the fields, where the gray morning is beginning to glimmer. He pours something from a bottle into a little silver jug. It touches his lips, the lying lips. Do they quiver a prayer ere that awful draught is swallowed? When the sun rises they are dumb.

I neither knew this unhappy man, nor his countryman — Laërtes let us call him — who is at present in exile, having been compelled to fly from remorseless creditors. Laërtes fled to America, where he earned his bread by his pen. I own to having a kindly feeling towards this scapegrace, because, though an exile, he did not abuse the country whence he fled. I have heard that he went away taking no spoil with him, — penniless almost; and on his voyage he made acquaintance with a certain Jew; and when he fell sick, at New York, this Jew befriended him, and gave him help and money out of his own store, which was but small. Now, after they had been awhile in the strange city, it happened that the poor Jew spent all his little money, and he too fell ill, and was in great penury. And now it was Laërtes who befriended that Ebrew Jew. He fee'd doctors; he fed and tended the sick and hungry. Go to, Laërtes! I know thee not. It may be thou art justly *exul patriæ*. But the Jew shall intercede for thee, thou not, let us trust, hopeless Christian sinner.

Another exile to the same shore I knew: who did not? Julius Cæsar hardly owed more money than Cucedicus: and, gracious powers! Cucedicus, how did you manage to spend and owe so much? All day he was at work for his clients; at night he was occupied in the Public Council. He neither had wife nor children. The rewards which he received from his orations were enough to maintain twenty rhetoricians. Night after night I have seen him eating his frugal meal, consisting but of a fish, a small portion of mutton, and a small measure of Iberian or Trinacrian wine, largely diluted with the sparkling waters of Rhenish Gaul. And this was all he had; and this man earned and paid away talents upon talents; and fled, owing who knows how many more! Does a man earn fifteen thousand pounds a year, toiling by day, talking by night, having horrible unrest in his bed, ghastly terrors at waking, seeing an officer lurking at every corner, a sword of justice forever hanging over his head, — and have for his sole diversion a newspaper, a lonely mutton-chop, and a little sherry and seltzer-water? In the German stories we read how men sell themselves to — a certain Personage, and that Personage cheats them. He gives them wealth; yes, but the gold pieces turn into worthless leaves. He sets them before splendid banquets; yes, but what an awful grin that black footman has who lifts up the dish-cover; and don't you smell a peculiar sulphurous odor in the dish? Faugh! take it away; I can't eat. He promises them splendors and triumphs. The conqueror's car rolls glittering through the city, the multitudes shout and huzzah. Drive on, coachman. Yes, but who is that hanging on behind the carriage? Is this the reward of eloquence, talents, industry? Is this the end of a life's labor? Don't you remember how, when the dragon was infesting the neighborhood of Babylon, the citizens used to walk dismally out of evenings, and look at the valleys round about strewed with the bones of the victims whom the monster had devoured? O insatiate brute, and most disgusting, brazen, and scaly reptile! Let us be thankful, children, that it has not gobbled us up too. Quick. Let us turn away, and pray that we may be kept out of the reach of his horrible maw, jaw, claw!

When I first came up to London, — as innocent as Monsieur Gil Blas, — I also fell in with some pretty acquaintances, found my way into several caverns, and delivered my purse to more than one gallant gentleman of the road. One I remember especially, — one who never eased me personally of a single maravedi, — one than whom I never met a bandit more gallant, courteous, and amiable. Rob me? Rolando feasted me; treated me to his dinner and his wine; kept a generous table for his friends, and I know was most liberal to many of them. How well I remember one of his speculations! It was a great plan for smuggling tobacco. Revenue officers were to be bought off; silent ships were to ply on the Thames; cunning depôts were to be established, and hundreds of thousands of pounds to be made by the *coup*. How his eyes kindled as he propounded the scheme to me! How easy and certain it seemed! It might have succeeded: I can't say; but the bold and merry, the hearty and kindly Rolando came to grief, — a little matter of imitated signatures occasioned a Bank persecution of Rolando the Brave. He walked about armed, and vowed he would never be taken alive: but taken he was; tried, condemned, sentenced to perpetual banishment; and I heard that for some time he was universally popular in the colony which had the honor to possess him. What a song he could sing! 'T was when the cup was sparkling before us, and heaven gave a portion of its blue, boys, blue, that I remember the song of Roland at the old Piazza Coffee-house. And now where is the old Piazza Coffee-house? Where is Thebes? where is Troy? where is the Colossus of Rhodes? Ah, Rolando, Rolando! thou wert a gallant captain, a cheery, a handsome, a merry. At *me* thou never presentedst pistol. Thou badest the bumper of Burgundy fill, fill for me, giving those who preferred it champagne. *Cœlum non animum*, &c. Do you think he has reformed now that he has crossed the sea, and changed the air? I have my own opinion. Howbeit, Rolando, thou wert a most kindly and hospitable bandit. And I love not to think of thee with a chain at thy shin.

Do you know how all these memories of unfortunate men have come upon me? When they came to frighten me this morning by speaking of my robbed pears, my perforated garden wall, I was reading an article in the "Saturday Review" about Rupilius. I have sat near that young man at a public dinner, and beheld him in a gilded uniform. But yesterday he lived in splendor, had long hair, a flowing beard, a jewel at his neck, and a smart surtout. So attired, he stood but yesterday in court; and to-day he sits over a bowl of prison cocoa, with a shaved head, and in a felon's jerkin.

That beard and head shaved, that gaudy deputy-lieutenant's coat exchanged for felon uniform, and your daily bottle of champagne for prison cocoa, my poor Rupilius, what a comfort it must be to have the business brought to an end! Champagne was the honorable gentleman's drink in the House of Commons dining-room, as I am informed. What uncommonly dry champagne that must have been! When we saw him outwardly happy, how miserable he must have been! when we thought him prosperous, how dismally poor! When the great Mr. Harker, at the public dinners, called out: "Gentlemen, charge your glasses, and please silence for the honorable Member for Lambeth!" how that honorable Member must have writhed inwardly! One day, when there was a talk of a gentleman's honor being questioned, Rupilius said, "If any man doubted mine, I would knock him down." But that speech was in the way of business. The Spartan boy, who stole the fox, smiled while the beast was gnawing him under his cloak: I promise you Rupilius had some sharp fangs gnashing under his. We have sat at the same feast, I say; we have paid our contribution to the same charity. Ah! when I ask this day for my daily bread, I pray not to be led into temptation, and to be delivered from evil.

ON A MEDAL OF GEORGE THE FOURTH.

BEFORE me lies a coin bearing the image and superscription of King George IV., and of the nominal value of two-and-sixpence. But an official friend at a neighboring turnpike says the piece is hopelessly bad; and a chemist tested it, returning a like unfavorable opinion. A cabman, who had brought me from a club, left it with the club porter, appealing to the gent who gave it a pore cabby, at ever so much o'clock of a rainy night, which he hoped he would give him another. I have taken that cabman at his word. He has been provided with a sound coin. The bad piece is on the table before me, and shall have a hole drilled through it, as soon as this essay is written, by a loyal subject who does not desire to deface the Sovereign's fair image, but to protest against the rascal who has taken her name in vain. *Fid. Def.*, indeed! Is that what you call defending the faith? You dare to forge your Sovereign's name, and pass your scoundrel pewter as her silver? I wonder who you are, wretch and most consummate trickster? This forgery is so complete that even now I am deceived by it, — I can't see the difference between the base and sterling metal. Perhaps this piece is a little lighter; — I don't know. A little softer; — is it? I have not bitten it, not being a connoisseur in the tasting of pewter or silver. I take the word of three honest men, though it goes against me: and though I have given two-and-sixpence worth of honest consideration for the counter, I shall not attempt to implicate anybody else in my misfortune, or transfer my ill-luck to a deluded neighbor.

I say the imitation is so curiously successful, the stamping, milling of the edges, lettering, and so forth, are so neat, that even now, when my eyes are open, I cannot see the cheat. How did those experts, the cabman, and pikeman, and tradesman, come to find it out? How do they happen to be more familiar with pewter and silver than I am? You see, I put out of the question another point which I might argue without fear of defeat, namely, the cabman's statement that I gave him this bad piece of money. Suppose every cabman who took me a shilling fare were to drive away and return presently with a bad coin and an assertion that I had given it to him? This would be absurd and mischievous; an encouragement of vice amongst men who already are subject to temptations. Being *homo,* I think if I were a cabman myself, I might sometimes stretch a furlong or two in my calculations of distance. But don't come *twice,* my man, and tell me I have given you a bad half-crown. No, no! I have paid once like a gentleman, and once is enough. For instance, during the Exhibition time I was stopped by an old country-woman in black, with a huge umbrella, who, bursting into tears, said to me, "Master, be this the way to Harlow, in Essex?" "This the way to Harlow? This is the way to Exeter, my good lady, and you will arrive there if you walk about 170 miles in your present direction," I answered courteously, replying to the old creature. Then she fell a-sobbing as though her old heart would break. She had a daughter a-dying at Harlow.

She had walked already "vifty dree mile" that day. Tears stopped the rest of her discourse, so artless, genuine, and abundant, that — I own the truth — I gave her, in I believe genuine silver, a piece of the exact size of that coin which forms the subject of this essay. Well. About a month since, near to the very spot where I had met my old woman, I was accosted by a person in black, a person in a large draggled cap, a person with a huge umbrella, who was beginning, "I say, master, can you tell me if this be the way to Har——" but here she stopped. Her eyes goggled wildly. She started from me, as Macbeth turned from Macduff. She would not engage with me. It was my old friend of Harlow, in Essex. I dare say she has informed many other people of her daughter's illness, and her anxiety to be put upon the right way to Harlow. Not long since a very gentlemanlike man, Major Delamere let us call him (I like the title of Major very much), requested to see me, named a dead gentleman who he said had been our mutual friend, and on the strength of this mutual acquaintance, begged me to cash his check for five pounds!

It is these things, my dear sir, which serve to make a man cynical. I do conscientiously believe that, had I cashed the Major's check, there would have been a difficulty about payment on the part of the respected bankers on whom he drew. On your honor and conscience, do you think that old widow who was walking from Tunbridge Wells to Harlow had a daughter ill, and was an honest woman at all? The daughter could n't always, you see, be being ill, and her mother on her way to her dear child through Hyde Park. In the same way some habitual sneerers may be inclined to hint that the cabman's story was an invention, — or at any rate, choose to ride off (so to speak) on the doubt. No. My opinion, I own, is unfavorable as regards the widow from Tunbridge Wells, and Major Delamere; but, believing the cabman was honest, I am glad to think he was not injured by the reader's most humble servant.

What a queer, exciting life this rogue's march must be: this attempt of the bad half-crowns to get into circulation! Had my distinguished friend the Major knocked at many doors that morning, before operating on mine? The sport must be something akin to the pleasure of tiger or elephant hunting. What ingenuity the sportsman must have in tracing his prey, — what daring and caution in coming upon him! What coolness in facing the angry animal (for, after all, a man on whom you draw a check *à bout portant* will be angry)! What a delicious thrill of triumph, if you can bring him down! If I have money at the banker's and draw for a portion of it over the counter, that is mere prose, — any dolt can do that. But, having no balance, say, I drive up in a cab, present a check at Coutts's, and, receiving the amount, drive off? What a glorious morning's sport that has been! How superior in excitement to the common transactions of every-day life! . . . . I must tell a story; it is against myself, I know, but it *will* out, and perhaps my mind will be the easier.

More than twenty years ago, in an island remarkable for its verdure, I met, four or five times, one of the most agreeable companions with whom I have passed a night. I heard that evil times had come upon this gentleman; and, overtaking him in a road near my own house one evening, I asked him to come home to dinner. In two days he was at my door again. At breakfast-time was this second appearance. He was in a cab (of course he was in a cab, they always are, these unfortunate, these courageous men). To deny myself was absurd. My friend could see me over the parlor blinds, surrounded by my family, and cheerfully partaking the morning meal. Might he have a word with me? and can you imagine its purport? By the most provoking delay, — his uncle the admiral not being able to come to town till Friday, — would I cash him a check? I need not say it would be paid on Saturday without fail. I tell you that man went away with money in his pocket, and I regret to add that his gallant relative has not *come to town yet!*

Laying down the pen, and sinking back in my chair, here, perhaps, I fall into a five minutes' reverie, and think of one, two, three, half a dozen cases in which I have been content to accept that sham promissory coin in return for sterling money advanced. Not a reader, whatever his age, but could tell a like story. I vow and believe there are men of fifty, who will dine well to-day, who have not paid their school debts yet, and who have not taken up their long-protested promises to pay. Tom, Dick, Harry, my boys, I owe you no grudge, and rather relish that wince with which you will read these meek lines and say, "He means me." Poor Jack in Hades! Do you remember a certain pecuniary transaction, and a little sum of money you borrowed "until the meeting of Parliament"? Parliament met often in your lifetime: Parliament has met since: but I think I should scarce be more surprised if your ghost glided into the room now, and laid down the amount of our little account, than I should have been if you had paid me in your lifetime with the actual acceptances of the Bank of England. You asked to borrow, but you never intended to pay. I would as soon have believed that a promissory note of

Sir John Falstaff (accepted by Messrs. Bardolph and Nym, and payable in Aldgate,) would be as sure to find payment, as that note of the departed — nay, lamented — Jack Thriftless.

He who borrows, meaning to pay, is quite a different person from the individual here described. Many — most, I hope — took Jack's promise for what it was worth, — and quite well knew that when he said, "Lend me," he meant "Give me" twenty pounds. "Give me change for this half-crown," said Jack; I know it's a pewter piece, and you gave him the change in honest silver, and pocketed the counterfeit gravely.

What a queer consciousness that must be which accompanies such a man in his sleeping, in his waking, in his walk through life, by his fireside with his children round him! "For what we are going to receive," &c., — he says grace before his dinner. "My dears! Shall I help you to some mutton? I robbed the butcher of the meat. I don't intend to pay him. Johnson, my boy, a glass of champagne? Very good, is n't it? Not too sweet. Forty-six. I get it from So-and-so, whom I intend to cheat." As eagles go forth and bring home to their eaglets the lamb or the pavid kid, I say there are men who live and victual their nests by plunder. We all know highway robbers in white neckcloths, domestic bandits, marauders, passers of bad coin. What was yonder check which Major Delamere proposed I should cash but a piece of bad money? What was Jack Thriftless's promise to pay? Having got his booty, I fancy Jack or the Major returning home, and wife and children gathering round about him. Poor wife and children! They respect papa very likely. They don't know he is false coin. Maybe the wife has a dreadful inkling of the truth, and, sickening, tries to hide it from the daughters and sons. Maybe she is an accomplice: herself a brazen forgery. If Turpin and Jack Sheppard were married, very likely Mesdames Sheppard and Turpin did not know, at first, what their husbands' real profession was, and fancied, when the men left home in the morning, they only went away to follow some regular and honorable business. Then a suspicion of the truth may have come; then a dreadful revelation; and presently we have the guilty pair robbing together, or passing forged money each on his own account. You know Doctor Dodd? I wonder whether his wife knows that he is a forger, and scoundrel? Has she had any of the plunder, think you, and were the darling children's new dresses bought with it? The Doctor's sermon last Sunday was certainly charming, and we all cried. Ah, my poor Dodd! Whilst he is preaching most beautifully, pocket-handkerchief in hand, he is peering over the pulpit cushions, looking out piteously for Messrs. Peachum and Lockit from the police-office. By Doctor Dodd you understand I would typify the rogue of respectable exterior, not committed to jail yet, but not undiscovered. We all know one or two such. This very sermon, perhaps, will be read by some, or more likely, — for, depend upon it, your solemn hypocritic scoundrels don't care much for light literature, — more likely, I say, this discourse will be read by some of their wives, who think, "Ah mercy! does that horrible cynical wretch know how my poor husband blacked my eye, or abstracted mamma's silver teapot, or forced me to write So-and-so's name on that piece of stamped paper, or what not?" My good creature, I am not angry with *you*. If your husband has broken your nose, you will vow that he had authority over your person, and a right to demolish any part of it; if he has conveyed away your mamma's teapot, you will say that she gave it to him at your marriage, and it was very ugly, and what not: if he takes your aunt's watch, and you love him, you will carry it erelong to the pawnbroker's, and perjure yourself, — O, how you will perjure yourself, — in the witness-box! I know this is a degrading view of woman's noble nature, her exalted mission, and so forth, and so forth. I know you will say this is bad morality. Is it? Do you, or do you not, expect your womankind to stick by you for better or for worse? Say I have committed a forgery, and the officers come in search of me, is my wife, Mrs. Dodd, to show them into the dining-room, and say, "Pray step in, gentlemen! My husband has just come home from church. That bill with my Lord Chesterfield's acceptance, I am bound to own, was never written by his lordship, and the signature is in the doctor's handwriting"? I say, would any man of sense, or honor, or fine feeling, praise his wife for telling the truth under such circumstances? Suppose she made a fine grimace, and said, "Most painful as my position is, most deeply as I feel for my William, yet truth must prevail, and I deeply lament to state that the beloved partner of my life *did* commit the flagitious act with which he is charged, and is at this present moment located in the two-pair back, up the chimney, whither it is my duty to lead you." Why, even Dodd himself, who was one of the greatest humbugs who ever lived, would not have had the face to say that he approved of his wife telling the truth in such a case. Would you have had Flora Macdonald beckon the officers, saying, "This way, gentlemen! You will find the young chevalier asleep in that cavern." Or don't you prefer her to be *splendide mendax*, and ready at all risks to save him? If ever I lead a rebellion, and my women betray me, may I be hanged but I will not forgive them; and if ever I steal a teapot, and *my* women don't stand up for me, pass the articles under their shawls, whisk down the street with it, outbluster the policeman, and utter any amount of fibs before Mr. Beak; those beings are not what I take them to be, and — for a fortune — I won't give them so much as a bad half-crown.

Is conscious guilt a source of unmixed pain to the bosom which harbors it? Has not your criminal, on the contrary, an excitement, an enjoyment within quite unknown to you and me who never did anything wrong in our lives? The housebreaker must snatch a fearful joy as he walks unchallenged by the policeman with his sack full of spoons and tankards. Do not cracksmen, when assembled together, entertain themselves with stories of glorious old burglaries which they or by-gone heroes have committed? But that my age is mature and my habits formed I should really just like to try a little criminality. Fancy passing a forged bill to your banker; calling on a friend and sweeping his sideboard of plate, his hall of umbrellas and coats; and then going home to dress for dinner, say, — and to meet a bishop, a judge, and a police magistrate or so, and talk more morally than any man at table! How I should chuckle (as my host's spoons clinked softly in my pocket) whilst I was uttering some noble speech about virtue, duty, charity! I wonder do we meet garroters in society? In an average tea-party, now, how many returned convicts are there? Does John Footman, when he asks permission to go and spend the evening with some friends, pass his time in thuggee; waylay and strangle an old gentleman or two; let himself into your house, with the house-key, of course, and appear as usual with the shaving-water when you ring your bell in the morning? The very possibility of such a suspicion invests John with a new and romantic interest in my mind. Behind the grave politeness of his countenance I try and read the lurking treason. Full of this pleasing subject, I have been talking thief-stories with a neighbor. The neighbor tells me how some friends of her's used to keep a jewel-box under a bed in their room; and, going into the room, they thought they heard a noise under the bed. They had the courage to look. The cook was under the bed, — under the bed with the jewel-box. Of course she said she had come for purposes connected with her business; but this was absurd. A cook under a bed is not there for professional purposes. A relation of mine had a box containing diamonds under her bed, which diamonds she told me were to be mine. Mine! One day, at dinner-time, between the entrées and the roast, a cab drove away from my relative's house containing the box wherein lay the diamonds. John laid the dessert, brought the coffee, waited all the evening, — and O, how frightened he was when he came to learn that his mistress's box had been conveyed out of her own room, and it contained diamonds, — "Law bless us, did it now?" I wonder whether John's subsequent career has been prosperous? Perhaps the gentlemen from Bow Street were all in the wrong when they agreed in suspecting John as the author of the robbery. His noble nature was hurt at the suspicion. You conceive he would not like to remain in a family where they were mean enough to suspect him of stealing a jewel-box out of a bedroom, — and the injured man and my relatives soon parted. But, inclining (with my usual cynicism) to think that he did steal the valuables, think of his life for the month or two whilst he still remains in the service! He shows the officers over the house, agrees with them that the *coup* must have been made by persons familiar with it; gives them every assistance; pities his master and mistress with a manly compassion; points out what a cruel misfortune it is to himself as an honest man, with his living to get and his family to provide for, that this suspicion should fall on him. Finally, he takes leave of his place, with a deep though natural melancholy that ever he had accepted it. What 's a thousand pounds to gentlefolks? A loss, certainly; but they will live as well without the diamonds as with them. But to John his Hhhohor was worth more than diamonds, his Hhonor was. Whohever is to give him back his character? Who is to prevent hany one from saying, "Ho yes. This is the butler which was in the family where the diamonds was stole?" &c.

I wonder has John prospered in life subsequently? If he is innocent, he does not interest me in the least. The interest of the case lies in John's behavior supposing him to be guilty. Imagine the smiling face, the daily service, the orderly performance of duty, whilst within John is suffering pangs lest discovery should overtake him. Every bell of the door which he is obliged to open may bring a police officer. The accomplices may peach. What an exciting life John's must have been for a while. And now, years and years after, when pursuit has long ceased, and detection is impossible, does he ever revert to the little transaction? Is it possible those diamonds cost a thousand pounds? What a rogue the fence must have been who only gave him so and so! And I pleasingly picture to myself an old ex-butler and an ancient receiver of stolen goods meeting and talking over this matter, which dates from times so early that the Queen's fair image could only just have begun to be coined or forged.

I choose to take John at the time when his little peccadillo is suspected, perhaps, but when there is no specific charge of robbery against him. He is not yet convicted: he is not even on his trial; how then can we venture to say he is guilty? Now think what scores of men and women walk the world in a like predicament; and what false coin passes current! Pinchbeck strives to pass off his history as sound coin. He knows it is only base metal, washed over with a thin varnish of learning. Poluphloisbos puts his sermons in circulation: sounding brass, lackered over with white metal, and marked with the stamp and image of piety. What say you to Drawcansir's reputation as a military commander? to Tibbs's pretensions to be a fine gentleman? to Sapphira's claims as a poetess, or Rodoessa's as a beauty? His bravery, his piety, high birth, genius, beauty, — each of these deceivers would palm his falsehood on us, and have us accept his forgeries as sterling coin. And we talk here, please to observe, of weaknesses rather than crimes. Some of us have more serious things to hide than a yellow cheek behind a raddle of rouge, or a white poll under a wig of jetty curls. You know, neighbor, there are not only false teeth in this world, but false tongues: and some make up a bust and an appearance of strength with padding, cotton, and what not; while another kind of artist tries to take you in by wearing under his waistcoat, and perpetually thumping, an immense sham heart. Dear sir, may yours and mine be found, at the right time, of the proper size and in the right place.

And what has this to do with half-crowns, good or bad? Ah, friend! may our coin, battered, and clipped, and defaced though it be, be proved to be Sterling Silver on the day of the Great Assay!

ON ALEXANDRINES.

A LETTER TO SOME COUNTRY COUSINS.

EAR COUSINS, — Be pleased to receive herewith a packet of Mayall's photographs, and copies of "Illustrated News," "Illustrated Times," "London Review," "Queen," and "Observer," each containing an account of the notable festivities of the past week. If besides these remembrances of home you have a mind to read a letter from an old friend, behold here it is. When I was at school, having left my parents in India, a good-natured captain or colonel would come sometimes and see us Indian boys, and talk to us about papa and mamma, and give us coins of the realm, and write to our parents, and say, "I drove over yesterday and saw Tommy at Dr. Birch's. I took him to the George, and gave him a dinner. His appetite is fine. He states that he is reading Cornelius Nepos, with which he is much interested. His masters report," &c. And though Dr. Birch wrote by the same mail a longer, fuller, and official statement, I have no doubt the distant parents preferred the friend's letter, with its artless, possibly ungrammatical, account of their little darling.

I have seen the young heir of Britain. These eyes have beheld him and his bride, — on Saturday in Pall Mall (when they stopped for a while before the house of

Smith, Elder, and Co., and all within admired a lovely cloak of purple velvet and sable worn by a lady of whose appearance the photographers will enable you to judge), and on Tuesday, in the nave of St. George's Chapel at Windsor, when the young Princess Alexandra of Denmark passed by with her blooming procession of bridesmaids; and half an hour later, when the Princess of Wales came forth from the chapel, her husband by her side robed in the purple mantle of the famous Order which his forefather established here five hundred years ago. We were to see her yet once again, when her open carriage passed out of the Castle gate to the station of the near railway which was to convey her to Southampton.

Since womankind existed, has any woman ever had such a greeting? At ten hours' distance, there is a city far more magnificent than ours. With every respect for Kensington turnpike, I own that the Arc de l'Etoile at Paris is a much finer entrance to an imperial capital. In our black, orderless, zigzag streets, we can show nothing to compare with the magnificent array of the Rue de Rivoli, that enormous regiment of stone stretching for five miles and presenting arms before the Tuileries. Think of the late Fleet Prison and Waithman's Obelisk, and of the Place de la Concorde and the Luxor Stone! "The finest site in Europe," as Trafalgar Square has been called by some obstinate British optimist, is disfigured by trophies, fountains, columns, and statues so puerile, disorderly, and hideous, that a lover of the arts must hang the head of shame as he passes to see our dear old queen city arraying herself so absurdly; but when all is said and done, we can show one or two of the greatest sights in the world. I doubt if any Roman festival was as vast or striking as the Derby day, or if any Imperial triumph could show such a prodigious muster of faithful people as our young Princess saw on Saturday, when the nation turned out to greet her. The calculators are squabbling about the numbers of hundreds of thousands, of millions, who came forth to see her and bid her welcome. Imagine beacons flaming, rockets blazing, yards manned, ships and forts saluting with their thunder, every steamer and vessel, every town and village from Ramsgate to Gravesend, swarming with happy gratulation; young girls with flowers, scattering roses before her; staid citizens and aldermen pushing and squeezing and panting to make the speech, and bow the knee, and bid her welcome! Who is this who is honored with such a prodigious triumph, and received with a welcome so astonishing? A year ago we had never heard of her. I think about her pedigree and family not a few of us are in the dark still, and I own, for my part, to be much puzzled by the allusions of newspaper genealogists and bards and skalds to "Vikings," Berserkers, and so forth. But it would be interesting to know how many hundreds of thousands of photographs of the fair bright face have by this time made it beloved and familiar in British homes. Think of all the quiet country nooks from Land's End to Caithness, where kind eyes have glanced at it. The farmer brings it home from market; the curate from his visit to the Cathedral town; the rustic folk peer at it in the little village shop window; the squire's children gaze on it round the drawing-room table: every eye that beholds it looks tenderly on its bright beauty and sweet, artless grace, and young and old pray God bless her. We have an elderly friend (a certain Goody Twoshoes, who has been mentioned before in the pages of this Magazine), and who inhabits, with many other old ladies, the Union-house of the parish of St. Lazarus in Soho. One of your cousins from this house went to see her, and found Goody and her companion crones all in a flutter of excitement about the marriage. The whitewashed walls of their bleak dormitory were ornamented with prints out of the illustrated journals, and hung with festoons and true-lover's knots of tape and colored paper; and the old bodies had had a good dinner, and the old tongues were chirping and clacking away, all eager, interested, sympathizing; and one very elderly and rheumatic Goody, who is obliged to keep her bed (and has, I trust, an exaggerated idea of the cares attending on royalty), said, " Pore thing, pore thing! I pity her." Yes, even in that dim place there was a little brightness and a quavering huzza, a contribution of a mite subscribed by those dozen poor old widows to the treasure of loyalty with which the nation endows the Prince's bride.

Three hundred years ago, when our dread Sovereign Lady Elizabeth came to take possession of her realm and capital city, Holingshed, if you please (whose pleasing history of course you carry about with you), relates in his fourth volume folio, that, — " At hir entring the citie, she was of the people receiued maruellous intierlie, as appeared by the assemblies, praiers, welcommings, cries, and all other signes which argued a woonderfull earnest loue": and at various halting-places on the royal progress children habited like angels appeared out of allegoric edifices and spoke verses to her: —

Welcome, O Queen, as much as heart can think,
  Welcome again, as much as tongue can tell,
Welcome to joyous tongues and hearts that will not shrink.
  God thee preserve, we pray, and wish thee ever well!

Our new Princess, you may be sure, has also had her

Alexandrines, and many minstrels have gone before her singing her praises. Mr. Tupper, who begins in very great force and strength, and who proposes to give her no less than eight hundred thousand welcomes in the first twenty lines of his ode, is not satisfied with this most liberal amount of acclamation, but proposes at the end of his poem a still more magnificent subscription. Thus we begin, " A hundred thousand welcomes, a hundred thousand welcomes." (In my copy the figures are in the well-known Arabic numerals, but let us have the numbers literally accurate) : —

A hundred thousand welcomes!
A hundred thousand welcomes!
  And a hundred thousand more!
O happy heart of England,
Shout aloud and sing, land,
As no land sang before ;
And let the pæans soar
And ring from shore to shore,
A hundred thousand welcomes,
And a hundred thousand more;
  And let the cannons roar,
  The joy-stunned city o'er.
And let the steeples chime it
A hundred thousand welcomes,
And a hundred thousand more;
  And let the people rhyme it
  From neighbor's door to door,
  From every man's heart's core,
A hundred thousand welcomes
And a hundred thousand more.

This contribution, in twenty not long lines, of 900,000 (say nine hundred thousand) welcomes is handsome indeed ; and shows that when our bard is inclined to be liberal, he does not look to the cost. But what is a sum of 900,000 to his further proposal ? —

O let all these declare it,
Let miles of shouting swear it,
  In all the years of yore,
  Unparalleled before!
And thou, most welcome Wand'rer
  Across the Northern Water,
Our England's ALEXANDRA,
  Our dear adopted daughter,—

Lay to thine heart, conned o'er and o'er,
  In future years remembered well,
  The magic fervor of this spell
That shakes the land from shore to shore,
And makes all hearts and eyes brim o'er;
  Our hundred thousand welcomes,
  Our fifty million welcomes,
And a hundred million more!

Here we have, besides the most liberal previous subscription, a further call on the public for no less than one hundred and fifty million one hundred thousand welcomes for her Royal Highness. How much is this per head for all of us in the three kingdoms? Not above five welcomes apiece, and I am sure many of us have given more than five hurrahs to the fair young Princess.

Each man sings according to his voice, and gives in proportion to his means. The guns at Sheerness, "from their adamantine lips" (which had spoken in quarrelsome old times a very different language), roared a hundred thundering welcomes to the fair Dane. The maidens of England strewed roses before her feet at Gravesend when she landed. Mr. Tupper, with the million and odd welcomes, may be compared to the thundering fleet; Mr. Chorley's song to the flowerets scattered on her Royal Highness's happy and carpeted path:—

Blessings on that fair face!
  Safe on the shore
Of her home-dwelling place,
  Stranger no more.

Love, from her household shrine
  Keep sorrow far!
May, for her hawthorn twine,
June, bring sweet eglantine,
Autumn, the golden vine,
  Dear Northern Star!

Hawthorn for May, eglantine for June, and in autumn a little tass of the golden vine for our Northern Star. I am sure no one will grudge the Princess these simple enjoyments, and of the produce of the last-named pleasing plant, I wonder how many bumpers were drunk to her health on the happy day of her bridal? As for the Laureate's verses, I would respectfully liken his Highness to a giant showing a beacon-torch on "a windy headland." His flaring torch is a pine-tree, to be sure, which nobody can wield but himself. He waves it: and four times in the midnight he shouts mightily, "Alexandra!" and the Pontic pine is whirled into the ocean and Enceladus goes home.

Whose muse, whose cornemuse, sounds with such plaintive sweetness from Arthur's Seat, while Edinburgh and Musselburgh lie rapt in delight, and the mermaids come flapping up to Leith shore to hear the exquisite music? Sweeter piper Edina knows not than Aytoun, the Bard of the Cavaliers, who has given in his frank adhesion to the reigning dynasty. When a most beautiful, celebrated, and unfortunate princess, whose memory the Professor loves,— when Mary, wife of Francis the Second, King of France, and by her own right proclaimed Queen of Scotland and England (poor soul!), entered Paris with her young bridegroom, good Peter Ronsard wrote of her,—

Toi qui as veu l'excellence de celle
Qui rend le ciel de l'Escosse envieux,

Dy hardiment, contentez vous mes yeux,
Vous ne verrez jamais chose plus belle.*

Vous ne verrez jamais chose plus belle. Here is an Alexandrine written three hundred years ago, as simple as *bon jour.* Professor Aytoun is more ornate. After elegantly complimenting the spring, and a description of her Royal Highness's well-known ancestors, "the Berserkers," he bursts forth, —

The Rose of Denmark comes, the Royal Bride!
O loveliest Rose! our paragon and pride, —
Choice of the Prince whom England holds so dear, —
What homage shall we pay
To one who has no peer?
What can the bard or wildered minstrel say
More than the peasant, who, on bended knee,
Breathes from his heart an earnest prayer for thee?
Words are not fair, if that they would express
Is fairer still; so lovers in dismay
Stand all abashed before that loveliness
They worship most, but find no words to pray.
Too sweet for incense! (bravo!) Take our loves instead, —
Most freely, truly, and devoutly given;
Our prayer for blessings on that gentle head,
For earthly happiness and rest in heaven!
May never sorrow dim those dove-like eyes,
But peace as pure as reigned in Paradise,
Calm and untainted on creation's eve,
Attend thee still! May holy angels, &c.

This is all very well, my dear country cousins. But will you say "Amen" to this prayer? I won't. Assuredly our fair Princess will shed many tears out of the "dovelike eyes," or the heart will be little worth. Is she to know no parting, no care, no anxious longing, no tender watches by the sick, to deplore no friends and kindred, and feel no grief? Heaven forbid! When a bard or wildered minstrel writes so, best accept his own con-

* Quoted in "Mignet's Life of Mary."

fession, that he is losing his head. On the day of her entrance into London who looked more bright and happy than the Princess? On the day of the marriage, the fair face wore its marks of care already, and looked out quite grave, and frightened almost, under the wreaths and lace and orange-flowers. Would you have had her feel no tremor? A maiden on the bridegroom's threshold, a Princess led up to the steps of a throne? I think her pallor and doubt became her as well as her smiles. That, I can tell you, was *our* vote who sat in X compartment, let us say, in the nave of St. George's Chapel at Windsor, and saw a part of one of the brightest ceremonies ever performed there.

My dear cousin Mary, you have an account of the dresses; and I promise you there were princesses besides the bride whom it did the eyes good to behold. Around the bride sailed a bevy of young creatures so fair, white, and graceful that I thought of those fairy-tale beauties who are sometimes princesses, and sometimes white swans. The Royal Princesses and the Royal Knights of the Garter swept by in prodigious robes and trains of purple velvet, thirty shillings a yard, my dear, not of course including the lining, which, I have no doubt, was of the richest satin, or that costly "miniver" which we used to read about in poor Jerrold's writings. The young princes were habited in kilts; and by the side of the Princess Royal trotted such a little wee solemn Highlander! He is the young heir and chief of the famous clan of Brandenburg. His eyrie is amongst the Eagles, and I pray no harm may befall the dear little chieftain.

The heralds in their tabards were marvellous to behold, and a nod from Rouge Croix gave me the keenest gratification. I tried to catch Garter's eye, but either I could n't or he would n't. In his robes, he is like one of the Three Kings in old missal illuminations. Gold Stick in waiting is even more splendid. With his gold rod and robes and trappings of many colors, he looks like a royal enchanter, and as if he had raised up all this scene of glamour by a wave of his glittering wand. The silver trumpeters wear such quaint caps, as those I have humbly tried to depict on the playful heads of children. Behind the trumpeters came a drum-bearer, on whose back a gold-laced drummer drubbed his march.

When the silver clarions had blown, and, under a clear chorus of white-robed children chanting round the organ, the noble procession passed into the chapel, and was hidden from our sight for a while, there was silence, or from the inner chapel ever so faint a hum. Then hymns arose, and in the lull we knew that prayers were being said, and the sacred rite performed which joined Albert Edward to Alexandra his wife. I am sure hearty prayers were offered outside the gate as well as within for that princely young pair, and for their Mother and Queen. The peace, the freedom, the happiness, the order which her rule guarantees, are part of my birthright as an Englishman, and I bless God for my share. Where else shall I find such liberty of action, thought, speech, or laws which protect me so well? Her part of her compact with her people, what sovereign ever better performed? If ours sits apart from the festivities of the day, it is because she suffers from a grief so recent that the loyal heart cannot master it as yet, and remains *treu und fest* to a beloved memory. A part of the music which celebrates the day's service was composed by the husband who is gone to the place where the just and pure of life meet the reward promised by the Father of all of us to good and faithful servants who have well done here below. As this one gives in his account, surely we may remember how the Prince was the friend of all peaceful arts and learning; how he was true and fast always to duty, home, honor; how, through a life of complicated trials, he was sagacious, righteous, active, and self-denying. And as we trace in the young faces of his many children the father's features and likeness, what Englishman will not pray that they may have inherited also some of the great qualities which won for the Prince Consort the love and respect of our country?

The papers tell us how, on the night of the marriage of the Prince of Wales, all over England and Scotland illuminations were made, the poor and children were feasted, and in village and city thousands of kindly schemes were devised to mark the national happiness and sympathy. "The bonfire on Coptpoint at Folkestone was seen in France," the *Telegraph* says, "more clearly than even the French marine lights could be seen at Folkestone." Long may the fire continue to burn! There are European coasts (and inland places) where the liberty light has been extinguished, or is so low that you can't see to read by it, — there are great Atlantic shores where it flickers and smokes very gloomily. Let us be thankful to the honest guardians of ours, and for the kind sky under which it burns bright and steady.

THE NOTCH ON THE AXE.

A STORY À LA MODE.

PART I.

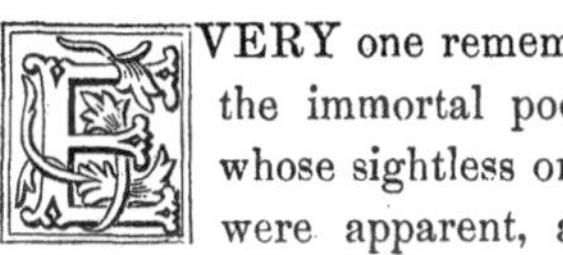

EVERY one remembers in the Fourth Book of the immortal poem of your Blind Bard (to whose sightless orbs no doubt Glorious Shapes were apparent, and Visions Celestial), how Adam discourses to Eve of the Bright Visitors who hovered round their Eden, —

"Millions of spiritual creatures walk the earth,
Unseen both when we wake and when we sleep."

"'How often,' says Father Adam, 'from the steep of echoing hill or thicket, have we heard celestial voices to the midnight air, sole, or responsive to each other's notes, singing!' After the Act of Disobedience, when the erring pair from Eden took their solitary way, and went forth to toil and trouble on common earth, — though the Glorious Ones no longer were visible, you cannot say they were gone? It was not that the Bright Ones were absent, but that the dim eyes of rebel man no longer could see them. In your chamber hangs a picture of one whom you never knew, but whom you have long held in tenderest regard, and who was painted for you by a friend of mine, the Knight of Plympton. She communes with you. She smiles on you. When your spirits are low, her bright eyes shine on you and cheer you. Her innocent sweet smile is a caress to you. She never fails to soothe you with her speechless prattle. You love her. She is alive with you. As you extinguish your candle and turn to sleep, though your eyes see her not, is she not there still smiling? As you lie in the night awake, and thinking of your duties, and the morrow's inevitable toil oppressing the busy, weary, wakeful brain as with a remorse, the crackling fire flashes up for a moment in the grate, and she is there, your little Beauteous Maiden, smiling with her sweet eyes! When moon is down, when fire is out, when curtains are drawn, when lids are closed, is she not there, the little Beautiful One, though invisible, present and smiling still? Friend, the Unseen Ones are round about us. Does it not seem as if the time were drawing near when it shall be given to men to behold them?"

The print of which my friend spoke, and which, indeed, hangs in my room, though he has never been there, is that charming little winter piece of Sir Joshua, representing the little Lady Caroline Montagu, afterwards Duchess of Buccleuch. She is represented as standing in the midst of a winter landscape, wrapped in muff and cloak: and she looks out of her picture with a smile so exquisite that a Herod could not see her without being charmed.

"I beg your pardon, Mr. Pinto," I said to the person with whom I was conversing. (I wonder, by the way, that I was not surprised at his knowing how fond I am of this print.) "You spoke of the Knight of Plympton. Sir Joshua died, 1792: and you say he was your dear friend?"

As I spoke I chanced to look at Mr. Pinto; and then it suddenly struck me: Gracious powers! Perhaps you *are* a hundred years old, now I think of it. You look more than a hundred. Yes, you may be a thousand years old for what I know. Your teeth are false. One eye is evidently false. Can I say that the other is not? If a man's age may be calculated by the rings round his eyes, this man may be as old as Methuselah. He has no beard. He wears a large curly glossy brown wig, and his eyebrows are painted a deep olive-green. It was odd to hear this man, this walking mummy, talking sentiment, in these queer old chambers in Shepherd's Inn.

Pinto passed a yellow bandanna handkerchief over his awful white teeth, and kept his glass eye steadily fixed on me. "Sir Joshua's friend?" said he (you perceive, eluding my direct question). "Is not every one that knows his pictures Reynolds's friend? Suppose I tell you that I have been in his painting room scores of times, and that his sister Thé has made me tea, and his sister Toffy has made coffee for me? You will only say I am an old ombog." (Mr. Pinto, I remarked, spoke all languages with an accent equally foreign.) "Suppose I tell you that I knew Mr. Sam Johnson, and did not like him? that I was at that very ball at Madame Cornelis's, which you have mentioned in one of your little — what do you call them? — bah! my memory begins to fail me, — in one of your little Whirligig Papers? Suppose I tell you that Sir Joshua has been here, in this very room?"

Have you, then, had these apartments for — more — than — seventy years?" I asked.

"They look as if they had not been swept for that time, — don't they? Hey? I did not say that I had them for seventy years, but that Sir Joshua has visited me here."

"When?" I asked, eying the man sternly, for I began to think he was an impostor.

He answered me with a glance still more stern: "Sir Joshua Reynolds was here this very morning, with Angelica Kaufmann, and Mr. Oliver Goldschmidt. He is still very much attached to Angelica, who still does not care for him. Because he is dead (and I was in the fourth mourning coach at his funeral) is that any reason why he should not come back to earth again? My good sir, you are laughing at me. He has sat many a time on that very chair which you are occupying. There are several spirits in the room now, whom you cannot see. Excuse me." Here he turned round as if he was addressing somebody, and began rapidly speaking a language unknown to me. "It is Arabic," he said; "a bad *patois*, I own. I learned it in Barbary, when I was a prisoner amongst the Moors. In anno 1609, bin ick aldus ghekledt gheghaen. Ha! you doubt me: look at me well. At least I am like — "

Perhaps some of my readers remember a paper of which the figure of a man carrying a barrel formed the initial letter, and which I copied from an old spoon now in my possession. As I looked at Mr. Pinto, I do declare he looked so like the figure on that old piece of plate that I started and felt very uneasy. "Ha!" said he, laughing through his false teeth (I declare they were false, — I could see utterly toothless gums working up and down behind the pink coral), "you see I wore a beard den; I am shafed now; perhaps you tink I am *a spoon.* Ha, ha!" And as he laughed he gave a cough which I thought would have coughed his teeth out, his glass eye out, his wig off, his very head off; but he stopped this convulsion by stumping across the room and seizing a little bottle of bright pink medicine, which, being opened, spread a singular acrid aromatic odor through the apartment; and I thought I saw — but of this I cannot take an affirmation — a light green and violet flame flickering round the neck of the phial as he opened it. By the way, from the peculiar stumping noise which he made in crossing the bare-boarded apartment, I knew at once that my strange entertainer had a wooden leg. Over the dust which lay quite thick on the boards, you could see the mark of one foot very neat and pretty, and then a round O, which was naturally the impression made by the wooden stump. I own I had a queer thrill as I saw that mark, and felt a secret comfort that it was not *cloven*.

In this desolate apartment in which Mr. Pinto had invited me to see him, there were three chairs, one bottomless, a little table on which you might put a breakfast-tray, and not a single other article of furniture. In the next room, the door of which was open, I could see a magnificent gilt dressing-case, with some splendid diamond and ruby shirt-studs lying by it, and a chest of drawers, and a cupboard apparently full of clothes.

Remembering him in Baden Baden in great magnificence, I wondered at his present denuded state. "You have a house elsewhere, Mr. Pinto?" I said.

"Many," says he. "I have apartments in many cities. I lock dem up, and do not cary mosh logish."

I then remembered that his apartment at Baden, where I first met him, was bare, and had no bed in it.

"There is, then, a sleeping-room beyond?"

"This is the sleeping-room." (He pronounces it *dis.*) Can this, by the way, give any clew to the nationality of this singular man?

"If you sleep on these two old chairs you have a rickety couch; if on the floor, a dusty one."

"Suppose I sleep up dere?" said this strange man, and

he actually pointed up to the ceiling. I thought him mad, or what he himself called an ombog. "I know. You do not believe me; for why should I deceive you? I came but to propose a matter of business to you. I told you I could give you the clew to the mystery of the Two Children in Black, whom we met at Baden, and you came to see me. If I told you, you would not believe me. What for try and convinz you? Ha hey?" And he shook his hand once, twice, thrice, at me, and glared at me out of his eye in a peculiar way.

Of what happened now I protest I cannot give an accurate account. It seemed to me that there shot a flame from his eye into my brain, whilst behind his *glass* eye there was a green illumination as if a candle had been lit in it. It seemed to me that from his long fingers two quivering flames issued, sputtering, as it were, which penetrated me, and forced me back into one of the chairs, — the broken one, — out of which I had much difficulty in scrambling, when the strange glamour was ended. It seemed to me that, when I was so fixed, so transfixed in the broken chair, the man floated up to the ceiling, crossed his legs, folded his arms as if he was lying on a sofa, and grinned down at me. When I came to myself he was down from the ceiling, and, taking me out of the broken cane-bottomed chair, kindly enough, — "Bah!" said he, "it is the smell of my medicine. It often gives the vertigo. I thought you would have had a little fit. Come into the open air." And we went down the steps, and into Shepherd's Inn, where the setting sun was just shining on the statue of Shepherd; the laundresses were trapesing about; the porters were leaning against the railings; and the clerks were playing at marbles, to my inexpressible consolation.

"You said you were going to dine at the Gray's-inn Coffee-house," he said. I was. I often dine there. There is excellent wine at the Gray's-inn Coffee-house; but I declare I NEVER SAID SO. I was not astonished at his remark; no more astonished than if I was in a dream. Perhaps I *was* in a dream. Is life a dream? Are dreams facts? Is sleeping being really awake? I don't know. I tell you I am puzzled. I have read "The Woman in White," "The Strange Story," — not to mention that story stranger than fiction in the "Cornhill Magazine," — that story for which THREE credible witnesses are ready to vouch. I have read that Article in "The Times" about Mr. Foster. I have had messages from the dead; and not only from the dead, but from people who never existed at all. I own I am in a state of much bewilderment; but, if you please, will proceed with my simple, my artless story.

Well, then. We passed from Shepherd's Inn into Holborn, and looked for a while at Woodgate's bric-à-brac shop, which I never can pass without delaying at the windows, — indeed, if I were going to be hung, I would beg the cart to stop, and let me have one look more at that delightful *omnium gatherum.* And passing Woodgate's, we come to Gale's little shop, No. 47, which is also a favorite haunt of mine.

Mr. Gale happened to be at his door, and as we exchanged salutations, "Mr. Pinto," I said, "will you like to see a real curiosity in this curiosity shop? Step into Mr. Gale's little back room."

In that little back parlor there are Chinese gongs; there are old Saxe and Sèvres plates; there is Fürstenberg, Carl. Theodor, Worcester, Amstel, Nankin and other jimcrockery. And in the corner what do you think there is? There is an actual GUILLOTINE. If you doubt me, go and see, — Gale, High Holborn, No. 47. It is a slim instrument, much slighter than those which they make now; — some nine feet high, narrow, a pretty piece of upholstery enough. There is the hook over which the rope used to play which unloosened the dreadful axe above; and look! dropped into the orifice where the head used to go, — there is THE AXE itself, all rusty with A GREAT NOTCH IN THE BLADE.

As Pinto looked at it, — Mr. Gale was not in the room, I recollect, — happening to have been just called out by a customer who offered him three pound fourteen and sixpence for a blue Shepherd in *pâte tendre*, — Mr. Pinto gave a little start, and seemed *crispé* for a moment. Then he looked steadily towards one of those great porcelain stools which you see in gardens, — and, — it seemed to me, — I tell you I won't take my affidavit, — I may have been maddened by the six glasses I took of that pink elixir, — I may have been sleep-walking, perhaps am as I write now, — I may have been under the influence of that astounding MEDIUM into whose hands I had fallen, — but I vow I heard Pinto say, with rather a ghastly grin at the porcelain stool,

"Nay, nefer shague your gory locks at me,
Dou canst not say I did it."

(He pronounced it, by the way, I *dit* it, by which I *know* that Pinto was a German.)

I heard Pinto say those very words, and sitting on the porcelain stool I saw, dimly at first, then with an awful distinctness, — a ghost, — an *eidolon*, — a form, — A HEADLESS MAN seated, with his head in his lap, which wore an expression of piteous surprise.

At this minute, Mr. Gale entered from the front shop

to show a customer some delf plates; and he did not see — but *we did* — the figure rise up from the porcelain stool, shake its head, which it held in its hand, and which kept its eyes fixed sadly on us, and disappear behind the guillotine.

"Come to the Gray's-inn Coffee-house," Pinto said, "and I will tell you how *the notch came to the axe.*" And we walked down Holborn at about thirty-seven minutes past six o'clock.

If there is anything in the above statement which astonishes the reader, I promise him that in the next chapter of this little story he will be astonished still more.

PART II.

"YOU will excuse me," I said to my companion, "for remarking, that when you addressed the — the individual sitting on the porcelain stool, with his head in his lap, your ordinarily benevolent features" — (this I confess was a bouncer, for between ourselves a more sinister and ill-looking rascal than Mons. P. I have seldom set eyes on) — "your ordinarily handsome face wore an expression that was by no means pleasing. You grinned at the individual just as you did at me when you went up to the cei——, pardon me, as I *thought* you did, when I fell down in a fit in your chambers"; and I qualified my words in a great flutter and tremble; I did not care to offend the man, — I did not *dare* to offend the man. I thought once or twice of jumping into a cab and flying; of taking refuge in Day and Martin's Blacking Warehouse; of speaking to a policeman, but not one would come. I was this man's slave. I followed him like his dog. I *could* not get away from him. So, you see, I went on meanly conversing with him, and affecting a simpering confidence. I remember when I was a little boy at school, going up fawning and smiling in this way to some great hulking bully of a sixth-form boy. So I said in a word, "Your ordinarily handsome face wore a disagreeable expression," &c.

"It is ordinarily *very* handsome," said he, with such a leer at a couple of passers-by, that one of them cried, "O, crikey, here 's a precious guy!" and a child, in its nurse's arms, screamed itself into convulsions. "*O, oui, che suis très-choli garçon, bien peau, cerdainement,*" continued Mr. Pinto; "but you were right. That — that person was not very well pleased, when he saw me. There was no love lost between us, as you say; and the world never knew a more worthless miscreant. I hate him, *voyez-vouz?* I hated him alife; I hate him dead. I hate him man; I hate him ghost: and he know it, and tremble before me. If I see him twenty tausend years hence — and why not? — I shall hate him still. You remarked how he was dressed?"

"In black satin breeches and striped stockings; a white piqué waistcoat, a gray coat, with large metal buttons, and his hair in powder. He must have worn a pigtail — only — "

"Only it was *cut off!* Ha, ha, ha!" Mr. Pinto cried, yelling a laugh, which, I observed, made the policemen stare very much. "Yes. It was cut off by the same blow which took off the scoundrel's head, — ho, ho, ho!" And he made a circle with his hook-nailed finger round his own yellow neck, and grinned with a horrible triumph. "I promise you that fellow was surprised when he found his head in the pannier. Ha, ha! Do you ever cease to hate those whom you hate?" — fire flashed terrifically from his glass eye, as he spoke — "or to love dose whom you once loved. O, never, never!" And here his natural eye was bedewed with tears. "But here we are at the Gray's-inn Coffee-house. James, what is the joint?"

That very respectful and efficient waiter brought in the bill of fare, and I, for my part, chose boiled leg of pork and pease-pudding, which my acquaintance said would do as well as anything else; though I remarked he only trifled with the pease-pudding, and left all the pork on the plate. In fact, he scarcely ate anything. But he drank a prodigious quantity of wine; and I must say that my friend Mr. Hart's port wine is so good that I myself took — well, I should think I took three glasses. Yes, three, certainly. *He,* — I mean Mr. P., — the old rogue, was insatiable: for we had to call for a second bottle in no time. When that was gone, my companion wanted another. A little red mounted up to his yellow cheeks as he drank the wine, and he winked at it in a strange manner. "I remember," said he, musing, "when port wine was scarcely drunk in this country, — though the Queen liked it, and so did Harley; but Bolingbroke did n't, — he drank Florence and champagne. Dr. Swift put water to his wine. 'Jonathan,' I once said to him — but bah! *autres temps, autres mœurs.* Another magnum, James."

This was all very well. "My good sir," I said, "it may suit *you* to order bottles of '20 port, at a guinea a bottle; but that kind of price does not suit me. I only happen to have thirty-four and sixpence in my pocket, of which I want a shilling for the waiter, and eighteen-pence for my cab. You rich foreigners and *swells* may spend what you like" (I had him there: for my friend's dress was as shabby as an old-clothes-man's); "but a man with a family, Mr. What-d'you-call'im, cannot afford to spend seven or eight hundred a year on his dinner alone."

"Bah!" he said. "Nunkey pays for all, as you say. I will what you call stant the dinner, if you are *so poor!*" and again he gave that disagreeable grin, and placed an odious crooked-nailed, and by no means clean finger to his nose. But I was not so afraid of him now, for we were in a public place; and the two half-glasses of port wine had, you see, given me courage.

"What a pretty snuff-box!" he remarked, as I handed him mine, which I am still old-fashioned enough to carry. It is a pretty old gold box enough, but valuable to me especially as a relic of an old, old relative, whom I can just remember as a child, when she was very kind to me. "Yes; a pretty box. I can remember when many ladies, — most ladies, carried a box, — nay, two boxes, — *tabatière* and *bonbonnière*. What lady carries snuff-box now, hey? Suppose your astonishment if a lady in an assembly were to offer you a *prise?* I can remember a lady with such a box as this, with a *tour*, as we used to call it then; with *paniers*, with a tortoise-shell cane, with the prettiest little high-heeled velvet shoes in the world! — ah! that was a time, that was a time! Ah, Eliza, Eliza, I have thee now in my mind's eye! At Bungay on the Waveney, did I not walk with thee, Eliza? Aha, did I not love thee? Did I not walk with thee then? Do I not see thee still?"

This was passing strange. My ancestress — but there is no need to publish her revered name — did indeed live at Bungay Saint Mary's, where she lies buried. She used to walk with a tortoise-shell cane. She used to wear little black velvet shoes, with the prettiest high heels in the world.

"Did you — did you — know, then, my great gr-ndm-ther?" I said.

He pulled up his coat-sleeve, — "Is that her name?" he said.

"Eliza ——"

There, I declare, was the very name of the kind old creature written in red on his arm.

"*You* knew her old," he said, divining my thoughts (with his strange knack); "*I* knew her young and lovely. I danced with her at the Bury ball. Did I not, dear, dear Miss ——?"

As I live, he here mentioned dear gr-nny's *maiden* name. Her maiden name was —— Her honored married name was ——

"She married your great gr-ndf-th-r the year Poseidon won the Newmarket Plate," Mr. Pinto dryly remarked.

Merciful powers! I remember, over the old shagreen knife and spoon case on the sideboard in my gr-nny's parlor, a print by Stubbs of that very horse. My grandsire, in a red coat and his fair hair flowing over his shoulders, was over the mantel-piece, and Poseidon won the Newmarket Cup in the year 1783!

"Yes; you are right. I danced a minuet with her at Bury that very night, before I lost my poor leg. And I quarrelled with your grandf—, ha!"

As he said "Ha!" there came three quiet little taps on the table, — it is the middle table in the Gray's-inn Coffee-house, under the bust of the late Duke of W-ll-ngt-n.

"I fired in the air," he continued; "did I not?" (Tap, tap, tap.) "Your grandfather hit me in the leg. He married three months afterwards. 'Captain Brown,'

I said, 'who could see Miss Sm-th without loving her?' She is there! She is there!" (Tap, tap, tap.) "Yes, my first love —"

But here there came tap, tap, which everybody knows means "No."

"I forgot," he said, with a faint blush stealing over his wan features, "she was not my first love. In Germ—— in my own country — there *was* a young woman — "

Tap, tap, tap. There was here quite a lively little treble knock; and when the old man said, "But I loved thee better than all the world, Eliza," the affirmative signal was briskly repeated.

And this I declare UPON MY HONOR. There was, I have said, a bottle of port wine before us, — I should say a decanter. That decanter was LIFTED UP, and out of it into our respective glasses two bumpers of wine were poured. I appeal to Mr. Hart, the landlord, — I appeal to James, the respectful and intelligent waiter, if this statement is not true? And when we had finished that magnum, and I said, — for I did not now in the least doubt of her presence, — "Dear gr-nny, may we have another magnum?" the table *distinctly* rapped "No."

"Now, my good sir," Mr. Pinto said, who really began to be affected by the wine, "you understand the interest I have taken in you. I loved Eliza ——" (of course I don't mention family names). "I knew you had that box which belonged to her, — I will give you what you like for that box. Name your price at once, and I pay you on the spot."

"Why, when we came out, you said you had not sixpence in your pocket."

"Bah! give you anything you like, — fifty, — a hundred, — a tausend pound."

"Come, come," said I, "the gold of the box may be worth nine guineas, and the *façon* we will put at six more."

"One tausend guineas!" he screeched. "One tausand and fifty pound, dere!" and he sank back in his chair, — no, by the way, on his bench, for he was sitting with his back to one of the partitions of the boxes, as I dare say James remembers.

"*Don't* go on in this way," I continued, rather weakly, for I did not know whether I was in a dream. "If you offer me a thousand guineas for this box I *must* take it. Must n't I, dear gr-nny?"

The table most distinctly said, "Yes"; and putting out his claws to seize the box, Mr. Pinto plunged his hooked nose into it, and eagerly inhaled some of my 47 with a dash of Hardman.

"But stay, you old harpy!" I exclaimed, being now in a sort of rage, and quite familiar with him. "Where is the money? Where is the check?"

"James, a piece of note-paper and a receipt stamp!"

"This is all mighty well, sir," I said, but I don't know you; I never saw you before. I will trouble you to hand me that box back again, or give me a check with some known signature."

"Whose? Ha, HA, HA!"

The room happened to be very dark. Indeed, all the waiters were gone to supper, and there were only two gentlemen snoring in their respective boxes. I saw a hand come quivering down from the ceiling, — a very pretty hand, on which was a ring with a coronet, with a lion rampant gules for a crest. *I saw that hand take a dip of ink and write across the paper.* Mr. Pinto then, taking a gray receipt stamp out of his blue leather pocket-book, fastened it on to the paper by the usual process; and the hand then wrote across the receipt stamp, went across the table and shook hands with Pinto, and then, as if waving him an adieu, vanished in the direction of the ceiling.

There was the paper before me, wet with the ink. There was the pen which THE HAND had used. Does anybody doubt me? *I have that pen now.* A cedar stick of a not uncommon sort, and holding one of Gillott's pens. It is in my inkstand now, I tell you. Anybody may see it. The handwriting on the check, for such the document was, was the writing of a female. It ran thus: "London, midnight, March 31, 1862. Pay the bearer one thousand and fifty pounds. Rachel Sidonia. To Messrs. Sidonia, Pozzosanto, & Co., London."

"Noblest and best of women!" said Pinto, kissing the sheet of paper with much reverence; "my good Mr. Roundabout, I suppose you do not question *that* signature?"

Indeed, the house of Sidonia, Pozzosanto, & Co. is known to be one of the richest in Europe, and as for the Countess Rachel, she was known to be the chief manager of that enormously wealthy establishment. There was only one little difficulty, *the Countess Rachel died last October.*

I pointed out this circumstance, and tossed over the paper to Pinto with a sneer.

"*C'est à brendre ou à laisser,*" he said with some heat. "You literary men are all imbrudent; but I did not tink you such a fool *wie* dis. Your box is not worth twenty pound, and I offer you a tausend because I know you want money to pay dat rascal Tom's college bills." (This strange man actually knew that my scapegrace

Tom has been a source of great expense and annoyance to me.) "You see money costs me nothing, and you refuse to take it! Once, twice; will you take this check in exchange for your trumpery snuff-box?"

What could I do? My poor granny's legacy was valuable and dear to me, but after all a thousand guineas are not to be had every day. "Be it a bargain," said I. "Shall we have a glass of wine on it?" says Pinto; and to this proposal I also unwillingly acceded, reminding him, by the way, that he had not yet told me the story of the headless man.

"Your poor gr-ndm-ther was right, just now, when she said she was not my first love. 'T was one of those *banales* expressions" (here Mr. P. blushed once more) "which we use to women. We tell each she is our first passion. They reply with a similar illusory formula. No man is any woman's first love; no woman any man's. We are in love in our nurse's arms, and women coquette with their eyes before their tongue can form a word. How could your lovely relative love me? I was far, far too old for her. I am older than I look. I am so old that you would not believe my age were I to tell you. I have loved many and many a woman before your relative. It has not always been fortunate for them to love me. Ah, Sophronia! Round the dreadful circus where you fell, and whence I was dragged corpse-like by the heels, there sat multitudes more savage than the lions which mangled your sweet form! Ah, *tenez!* when we marched to the terrible stake together at Valladolid, — the Protestant and the J——. But away with memory! Boy! It was happy for thy grandam that she loved me not.

"During that strange period," he went on, "when the

teeming Time was great with the revolution that was speedily to be born, I was on a mission in Paris with my excellent, my maligned friend, Cagliostro. Mesmer was one of our band. I seemed to occupy but an obscure rank in it; though, as you know, in secret societies the humble man may be a chief and director, — the ostensible leader but a puppet moved by unseen hands. Never mind who was chief, or who was second. Never mind my age. It boots not to tell it: why shall I expose myself to your scornful incredulity, — or reply to your questions in words that are familiar to you, but which yet you cannot understand? Words are symbols of things which you know, or of things which you don't know. If you don't know them, to speak is idle." (Here I confess Mr. P. spoke for exactly thirty-eight minutes, about physics, metaphysics, language, the origin and destiny of man, during which time I was rather bored, and, to relieve my *ennui*, drank a half-glass or so of wine.) "Love, friend, is the fountain of youth! It may not happen to me once, — once in an age: but when I love, then I am young. I loved when I was in Paris. Bathilde, Bathilde, I loved thee, — ah, how fondly! Wine, I say, more wine! Love is ever young. I was a boy at the little feet of Bathilde de Béchamel, — the fair, the fond, the fickle, ah, the false!" The strange old man's agony was here really terrific, and he showed himself much more agitated than he had been when speaking about my gr-ndm-th-r.

"I thought Blanche might love me. I could speak to her in the language of all countries, and tell her the lore of all ages. I could trace the nursery legends which she loved up to their Sanscrit source, and whisper to her the darkling mysteries of Egyptian Magi. I could chant for her the wild chorus that rang in the dishevelled Eleusinian revel: I could tell her, and I would, the watchword never known but to one woman, the Saban queen, which Hiram breathed in the abysmal ear of Solomon. — You don't attend. Psha! you have drunk too much wine!" Perhaps I may as well own that I was *not* attending, for he had been carrying on for about fifty-seven minutes; and I don't like a man to have *all* the talk to himself.

"Blanche de Béchamel was wild, then, about this secret of Masonry. In early, early days I loved, I married a girl fair as Blanche, who, too, was tormented by curiosity, who, too, would peep into my closet, — into the only secret I guarded from her. A dreadful fate befell poor Fatima. An *accident* shortened her life. Poor thing! she had a foolish sister who urged her on. I always told her to beware of Ann. She died. They said her brothers killed her. A gross falsehood. *Am* I dead? If I were, could I pledge you in this wine?"

"Was your name," I asked, quite bewildered, "was your name, pray, then, ever Blueb——"

"Hush! the waiter will overhear you. Methought we were speaking of Blanche de Béchamel. I loved her, young man. My pearls, and diamonds, and treasure, my wit, my wisdom, my passion, I flung them all into the child's lap. I was a fool! Was strong Samson not as weak as I? Was Solomon the Wise much better when Balkis wheedled him? I said to the king — But enough of that, I spake of Blanche de Béchamel.

"Curiosity was the poor child's foible. I could see, as I talked to her, that her thoughts were elsewhere (as yours, my friend, have been absent once or twice to-night). To know the secret of Masonry was the wretched child's mad desire. With a thousand wiles, smiles, caresses, she strove to coax it from me, — from *me*, — ha! ha!

"I had an apprentice, — the son of a dear friend, who died by my side at Rossbach, when Soubise, with whose army I happened to be, suffered a dreadful defeat for neglecting my advice. The young Chevalier Goby de Mouchy was glad enough to serve as my clerk, and help in some chemical experiments in which I was engaged with my friend Dr. Mesmer. Bathilde saw this young man. Since women were, has it not been their business to smile and deceive, to fondle and lure? Away! From the very first it has been so!" And as my companion spoke, he looked as wicked as the serpent that coiled round the tree, and hissed a poisoned counsel to the first woman.

"One evening I went, as was my wont, to see Blanche. She was radiant; she was wild with spirits; a saucy triumph blazed in her blue eyes. She talked, she rattled in her childish way. She uttered, in the course of her rhapsody, a hint — an intimation — so terrible that the truth flashed across me in a moment. Did I ask her? She would lie to me. But I know how to make falsehood impossible. And I *ordered her to go to sleep*."

At this moment the clock (after its previous convulsions) sounded TWELVE. And as the new Editor of the Cornhill Magazine — and *he*, I promise you, won't stand any nonsense — will only allow seven pages, I am obliged to leave off at THE VERY MOST INTERESTING POINT OF THE STORY.

PART III.

ARE you of our fraternity? I see you are not. The secret which Mademoiselle de Béchamel confided to me in her mad triumph and wild hoyden spirits, — she was but a child, poor thing, poor thing, scarce fifteen : — but I love them young, — a folly not unusual with the old!" (Here Mr. Pinto thrust his knuckles into his hollow eyes; and, I am sorry to say, so little regardful was he of personal cleanliness, that his tears made streaks of white over his gnarled dark hands.) "Ah, at fifteen, poor child, thy fate was terrible! Go to! It is not good to love me, friend. They prosper not who do. I divine you. You need not say what you are thinking — "

In truth, I was thinking, if girls fall in love with this sallow, hooked-nosed, glass-eyed, wooden-legged, dirty, hideous old man, with the sham teeth, they have a queer taste. *That* is what I was thinking.

"Jack Wilks said the handsomest man in London had but half an hour's start of him. And, without vanity, I am scarcely uglier than Jack Wilks. We were members of the same club at Medenham Abbey, Jack and I, and had many a merry night together. Well, sir, I — Mary of Scotland knew me but as a little hunchbacked music-master; and yet, and yet, I think, *she* was not indifferent to her David Riz—— and *she* came to misfortune. They all do, — they all do!"

"Sir, you are wandering from your point!" I said, with some severity. For, really, for this old humbug to hint that he had been the baboon who frightened the club at Medenham, that he had been in the Inquisition at Valladolid, — that, under the name of D. Riz, as he called it, he had known the lovely Queen of Scots, — was a *little* too much. "Sir," then I said, "you were speaking about a Miss de Béchamel. I really have not time to hear all your biography."

"Faith, the good wine gets into my head." (I should think so, the old toper! Four bottles all but two glasses.) "To return to poor Blanche. As I sat laughing, joking with her, she let slip a word, a little word, which filled me with dismay. Some one had told her a part of the Secret, — the secret which has been divulged scarce thrice in three thousand years, — the Secret of the Freemasons. Do you know what happens to those uninitiate who learn that secret? to those wretched men the initiate who reveal it?"

As Pinto spoke to me, he looked through and through me with his horrible piercing glance, so that I sat quite uneasily on my bench. He continued: "Did I question her awake? I knew she would lie to me. Poor child! I loved her no less because I did not believe a word she said. I loved her blue eye, her golden hair, her delicious voice, that was true in song, though when she spoke, false as Eblis! You are aware that I possess in rather a remarkable degree what we have agreed to call the mesmeric power. I set the unhappy girl to sleep. *Then* she was obliged to tell me all. It was as I had surmised. Goby de Mouchy, my wretched, besotted, miserable secretary, in his visits to the château of the old Marquis de Béchamel, who was one of our society, had seen Blanche. I suppose it was because she had been warned that he was worthless, and poor, artful, and a coward, she loved him. She wormed out of the besotted wretch the secrets of our Order. 'Did he tell you the NUMBER ONE?' I asked.

"She said, 'Yes.'

"'Did he,' I further inquired, 'tell you the —'

"'O, don't ask me, don't ask me!' she said, writhing on the sofa, where she lay in the presence of the Marquis de Béchamel, her most unhappy father. Poor Béchamel, poor Béchamel! How pale he looked as I spoke! 'Did he tell you,' I repeated with a dreadful calm, 'the NUMBER TWO?' She said, 'Yes.'

"The poor old marquis rose up, and clasping his hands, fell on his knees before Count Cagl—— Bah! I went by a different name then. Vat's in a name? Dat vich ve call a Rosicrucian by any other name vil smell as sveet. 'Monsieur,' he said, 'I am old, — I am rich. I have five hundred thousand livres of rentes in Picardy. I have half as much in Artois. I have two hundred and eighty thousand on the Grand Livre. I am promised by my sovereign a dukedom and his orders, with a reversion to my heir. I am a Grandee of Spain of the First Class, and Duke of Volovento. Take my titles, my ready money, my life, my honor, everything I have in the world, but don't ask the THIRD QUESTION.'

"'Godefroid de Bouillon, Comte de Béchamel, Grandee of Spain and Prince of Volovento, in our Assembly what was the oath you swore?'". The old man writhed as he remembered its terrific purport.

"Though my heart was racked with agony, and I would have died, ay, cheerfully" (died, indeed, as if *that* were a penalty!) "to spare yonder lovely child a pang, I said to her calmly, 'Blanche de Béchamel, did Goby de Mouchy tell you secret NUMBER THREE?'

"She whispered a *oui* that was quite faint, faint and small. But her poor father fell in convulsions at her feet.

"She died suddenly that night. Did I not tell you

these I love come to no good? When General Bonaparte crossed the Saint Bernard, he saw in the convent an old monk with a white beard, wandering about the corridors, cheerful and rather stout, but mad, — mad as a March hare. 'General,' I said to him, 'did you ever see that face before?' He had not. He had not mingled much with the higher classes of our society before the Revolution. *I* knew the poor old man well enough; he was the last of a noble race, and I loved his child."

"And did she die by — ?"

"Man! did I say so? Do I whisper the secrets of the Vehmgericht? I say she died that night; and he, — he, the heartless, the villain, the betrayer, — you saw him seated in yonder curiosity-shop, by yonder guillotine, with his scoundrelly head in his lap.

"You saw how slight that instrument was? It was one of the first which Guillotin made, and which he showed to private friends in a *hangar* in the Rue Picpus, where he lived. The invention created some little conversation amongst scientific men at the time, though I remember a machine in Edinburgh of a very similar construction, two hundred — well, many, many years ago, — and at a breakfast which Guillotin gave he showed us the instrument, and much talk arose amongst us as to whether people suffered under it.

"And now I must tell you what befell the traitor who had caused all this suffering. Did he know that the poor child's death was A SENTENCE? He felt a cowardly satisfaction that with her was gone the secret of his treason. Then he began to doubt. I had MEANS to penetrate all his thoughts, as well as to know his acts. Then he became a slave to a horrible fear. He fled in abject terror to a convent. They still existed in Paris; and behind the walls of Jacobins the wretch thought himself secure. Poor fool! I had but to set one of my somnambulists to sleep. Her spirit went forth and spied the shuddering wretch in his cell. She described the street, the gate, the convent, the very dress which he wore, and which you saw to-day.

"And now *this* is what happened. In his chamber in the Rue St. Honoré, at Paris, sat a man *alone*, — a man who has been maligned, a man who has been called a knave and charlatan, a man who has been persecuted even to the death, it is said, in Roman Inquisitions, forsooth, and elsewhere. Ha! ha! A man who has a mighty will.

"And looking towards the Jacobin Convent (of which, from his chamber, he could see the spires and trees), this man WILLED. And it was not yet dawn. And he willed; and one who was lying in his cell in the Convent of Jacobins, awake and shuddering with terror for a crime which he had committed, fell asleep.

"But though he was asleep his eyes were open.

"And after tossing and writhing, and clinging to the pallet, and saying, 'No, I will not go,' he rose up and donned his clothes, — a gray coat, a vest of white piqué, black satin small-clothes, ribbed silk stockings, and a white stock with a steel buckle; and he arranged his hair, and he tied his queue, all the while being in that strange somnolence which walks, which moves, which FLIES sometimes, which sees, which is indifferent to pain, which OBEYS. And he put on his hat, and he went forth from his cell; and though the dawn was not yet, he trod the corridors as seeing them. And he passed into the cloister, and then into the garden where lie the ancient dead. And he came to the wicket, which Brother Jerome was opening just at the dawning. And the crowd was already waiting with their cans and bowls to receive the alms of the good brethren.

"And he passed through the crowd and went on his way through, and the few people then abroad who marked him, said, 'Tiens! How very odd he looks! He looks like a man walking in his sleep!' This was said by various persons: —

"By milk-women, with their cans and carts, coming into the town.

"By roysterers, who had been drinking at the taverns of the Barrier, for it was Mid-Lent.

"By the sergeants of the watch, who eyed him sternly as he passed near their halberds.

"But he passed on unmoved by the halberds,

"Unmoved by the cries of the roysterers,

"By the market-women coming with their milk and eggs.

"He walked through the Rue St. Honoré, I say: —

"By the Rue Rambuteau,

"By the Rue St. Antoine,

"By the King's Château of the Bastille,

"By the Faubourg St. Antoine.

"And he came to No. 29 in the Rue Picpus, — a house which then stood between a court and garden, —

"That is, there was a building of one story, with a great coach-door.

"Then there was a court, around which were stables, coach-houses, offices.

"Then there was a house, — a two-storied house, with a *perron* in front.

"Behind the house was a garden, — a garden of two hundred and fifty French feet in length.

"And as one hundred feet of France equal one hundred and six feet of England, this garden, my friends, equalled exactly two hundred and sixty-five feet of British measure.

"In the centre of the garden was a fountain and a statue, — or, to speak more correctly, two statues. One was recumbent, — a man. Over him, sabre in hand, stood a woman.

"The man was Olofernes. The woman was Judith. From the head, from the trunk, the water gushed. It was the taste of the doctor; — was it not a droll of taste?

"At the end of the garden was the doctor's cabinet of study. My faith, a singular cabinet, and singular pictures! —

"Decapitation of Charles Premier at Vitehall.

"Decapitation of Montrose at Edimbourg.

"Decapitation of Cinq Mars. When I tell you that he was a man of a taste charming!

"Through this garden, by these statues, up these stairs, went the pale figure of him who, the porter said, knew the way of the house. He did. Turning neither right nor left, he seemed to walk *through* the statues, the obstacles, the flower-beds, the stairs, the door, the tables, the chairs.

"In the corner of the room was THAT INSTRUMENT which Guillotin had just invented and perfected. One day he was to lay his own head under his own axe. Peace be to his name! With him I deal not!

"In a frame of mahogany, neatly worked, was a board with a half-circle in it, over which another board fitted. Above was a heavy axe, which fell — you know how. It was held up by a rope, and when this rope was untied, or cut, the steel fell.

"To the story which I now have to relate you may give credence, or not, as you will. The sleeping man went up to that instrument.

"He laid his head in it, asleep.

"Asleep!

"He then took a little penknife out of the pocket of his white dimity waistcoat.

"He cut the rope, asleep!

"The axe descended on the head of the traitor and villain. The notch in it was made by the steel buckle of his stock, which was cut through.

"A strange legend has got abroad that after the deed was done, the figure rose, took the head from the basket, walked forth through the garden, and by the screaming porters at the gate, and went and laid itself down at the Morgue. But for this I will not vouch. Only of this be sure. 'There are more things in heaven and earth, Horatio, than are dreamed of in your philosophy.' More and more the light peeps through the chinks. Soon, amidst music ravishing, the curtain will rise, and the glorious scene be displayed. Adieu! Remember me. Ha! 't is dawn," Pinto said. And he was gone.

I am ashamed to say that my first movement was to clutch the check which he had left with me, and which I was determined to present the very moment the bank opened. I know the importance of these things, and that men *change their mind* sometimes. I sprang through the streets to the great banking-house of Manasseh, in Duke Street. It seemed to me as if I actually flew as I walked. As the clock struck ten I was at the counter and laid down my check.

The gentleman who received it, who was one of the Hebrew persuasion, as were the other two hundred clerks of the establishment, having looked at the draft with terror in his countenance, then looked at me, then called to himself two of his fellow clerks, and queer it was to see all their aquiline beaks over the paper.

"Come, come!" said I, "don't keep me here all day. Hand me over the money, short, if you please!" for I was, you see, a little alarmed, and so determined to assume some extra bluster.

"Will you have the kindness to step into the parlor to the partners?" the clerk said, and I followed him.

"What, *again?*" shrieked a bald-headed, red-whiskered gentleman, whom I knew to be Mr. Manasseh. "Mr. Salathiel, this is too bad! Leave me with this gentleman, S." And the clerk disappeared.

"Sir," he said, "I know how you came by this; the Count de Pinto gave it you. It is too bad! I honor my parents; I honor *their* parents; I honor their bills! But this one of grandma's is too bad, — it is, upon my word, now! She 've been dead these five-and-thirty years. And this last four months she has left her burial-place and took to drawing on our 'ouse! It 's too bad, grandma; it is too bad!" and he appealed to me, and tears actually trickled down his nose.

"Is it the Countess Sidonia's check or not?" I asked, haughtily.

"But, I tell you, she 's dead! It 's a shame! — it 's a shame! — it is, grandmamma!" and he cried, and wiped his great nose in his yellow pocket-handkerchief. "Look year, — will you take pounds instead of guineas? She 's dead, I tell you! It 's no go! Take the pounds, — one tausand pound! — ten nice, neat, crisp hundred-pound notes, and go away vid you, do?"

"I will have my bond, sir, or nothing," I said; and I

put on an attitude of resolution which I confess surprised even myself.

"Wery vell," he shrieked, with many oaths, "then you shall have noting, — ha, ha, ha! — noting but a policeman! Mr. Abednego, call a policeman! Take that, you humbug and impostor!" and here, with an abundance of frightful language which I dare not repeat, the wealthy banker abused and defied me.

Au bout du compte, what was I to do, if a banker did not choose to honor a check drawn by his dead grandmother? I began to wish I had my snuff-box back. I began to think I was a fool for changing that little old-fashioned gold for this slip of strange paper.

Meanwhile the banker had passed from his fit of anger to a paroxysm of despair. He seemed to be addressing some person invisible, but in the room: "Look here, ma'am, you 've really been coming it too strong. A hundred thousand in six months, and now a thousand more! The 'ouse can't stand it; it *won't* stand it, I say! What? Oh! mercy, mercy!"

As he uttered these words, A HAND fluttered over the table in the air! It was a female hand, — that which I had seen the night before. That female hand took a pen from the green-baize table, dipped it in a silver inkstand, and wrote on a quarter of a sheet of foolscap on the blotting-book, "How about the diamond robbery? If you do not pay, I will tell him where they are."

What diamonds? what robbery? what was this mystery? That will never be ascertained, for the wretched man's demeanor instantly changed. "Certainly, sir; — O, certainly," he said, forcing a grin. "How will you have the money, sir? All right, Mr. Abednego. This way out."

"I hope I shall often see you again," I said; on which I own poor Manasseh gave a dreadful grin, and shot back into his parlor.

I ran home, clutching the ten delicious, crisp hundred pounds, and the dear little fifty which made up the account. I flew through the streets again. I got to my chambers. I bolted the outer doors. I sank back in my great chair, and slept. . . . .

My first thing on waking was to feel for my money. Perdition! Where was I? Ha! — on the table before me was my grandmother's snuff-box, and by its side one of those awful — those admirable — sensation novels, which I had been reading, and which are full of delicious wonder.

But that the guillotine is still to be seen at Mr. Gale's, No. 47, High Holborn, I give you MY HONOR. I suppose I was dreaming about it. I don't know. What is dreaming? What is life? Why should n't I sleep on the ceiling? — and am I sitting on it now, or on the floor? I am puzzled. But enough. If the fashion for sensation novels goes on, I tell you I will write one in fifty volumes. For the present, DIXI. But between ourselves, this Pinto, who fought at the Colosseum, who was nearly being roasted by the Inquisition, and sang duets at Holyrood, I am rather sorry to lose him after three little bits of Roundabout Papers. *Et vous?*

JUNE, 1862.

DE FINIBUS.

HEN Swift was in love with Stella, and despatching her a letter from London thrice a month by the Irish packet, you may remember how he would begin letter No. XXIII., we will say, on the very day when XXII. had been sent away, stealing out of the coffee-house or the assembly so as to be able to prattle with his dear; "never letting go her kind hand, as it were," as some commentator or other has said in speaking of the Dean and his amour. When Mr. Johnson, walking to Dodsley's, and touching the posts in Pall Mall as he walked, forgot to pat the head of one of them, he went back and imposed his hands on it, — impelled I know not by what superstition. I have this I hope not dangerous mania too. As soon as a piece of work is out of hand, and before going to sleep, I like to begin another: it may be to write only half a dozen lines: but that is something towards Number the Next. The printer's boy has not yet reached Green Arbor Court with the copy. Those people who were alive half an hour since, Pendennis, Clive Newcome, and (what do you call him? what was the name of the last hero? I remember now!) Philip Firmin, have hardly drunk their glass of wine, and the mammas have only this minute got the children's cloaks on, and have been bowed out of my

premises, — and here I come back to the study again: *tamen usque recurro.* How lonely it looks now all these people are gone! My dear, good friends, some folks are utterly tired of you, and say, "What a poverty of friends the man has! He is always asking us to meet those Pendennises, Newcomes, and so forth. Why does he not introduce us to some new characters? Why is he not thrilling like Twostars, learned and profound like Threestars, exquisitely humorous and human like Fourstars? Why, finally, is he not somebody else?" My good people, it is not only impossible to please you all, but it is absurd to try. The dish which one man devours, another dislikes. Is the dinner of to-day not to your taste? Let us hope to-morrow's entertainment will be more agreeable. . . . . I resume my original subject. What an odd, pleasant, humorous, melancholy feeling it is to sit in the study, alone and quiet, now all these people are gone who have been boarding and lodging with me for twenty months! They have interrupted my rest: they have plagued me at all sorts of minutes: they have thrust themselves upon me when I was ill, or wished to be idle, and I have growled out a "Be hanged to you, can't you leave me alone now?" Once or twice they have prevented my going out to dinner. Many and many a time they have prevented my coming home, because I knew they were there waiting in the study, and a plague take them! and I have left home and family, and gone to dine at the Club, and told nobody where I went. They have bored me, those people. They have plagued me at all sorts of uncomfortable hours. They have made such a disturbance in my mind and house, that sometimes I have hardly known what was going on in my family, and scarcely have heard what my neighbor said to me. They are gone at last; and you would expect me to be at ease? Far from it. I should almost be glad if Woolcomb would walk in and talk to me; or Twysden reappear, take his place in that chair opposite me, and begin one of his tremendous stories.

Madmen, you know, see visions, hold conversations with, even draw the likeness of people invisible to you and me. Is this making of people out of fancy madness? and are novel-writers at all entitled to strait-waistcoats? I often forget people's names in life; and in my own stories contritely own that I make dreadful blunders regarding them; but I declare, my dear sir, with respect to the personages introduced into your humble servant's fables, I know the people utterly, — I know the sound of their voices. A gentleman came in to see me the other day, who was so like the picture of Philip Firmin in Mr. Walker's charming drawings in the Cornhill Magazine, that he was quite a curiosity to me. The same eyes, beard, shoulders, just as you have seen them from month to month. Well, he is not like the Philip Firmin in my mind. Asleep, asleep in the grave, lies the bold, the generous, the reckless, the tender-hearted creature whom I have made to pass through those adventures which have just been brought to an end. It is years since I heard the laughter ringing, or saw the bright blue eyes. When I knew him both were young. I become young as I think of him. And this morning he was alive again in this room, ready to laugh, to fight, to weep. As I write, do you know, it is the gray of evening; the house is quiet; everybody is out; the room is getting a little dark, and I look rather wistfully up from the paper with perhaps ever so little fancy that HE MAY COME IN. ——— No? No movement. No gray shade, growing more palpable, out of which at last look the well-known eyes. No, the printer came and took him away with the last page of the proofs. And with the printer's boy did the whole *cortège* of ghosts flit away, invisible? Ha! stay! what is this? Angels and ministers of grace! The door opens, and a dark form — enters, bearing a black, — a black suit of clothes. It is John. He says it is time to dress for dinner.

* * * * *

Every man who has had his German tutor, and has been coached through the famous Faust of Goethe (thou wert my instructor, good old Weissenborn, and these eyes beheld the great master himself in dear little Weimar town!) has read those charming verses which are prefixed to the drama, in which the poet reverts to the time when his work was first composed, and recalls the friends, now departed, who once listened to his song. The dear shadows rise up around him, he says; he lives in the past again. It is to-day which appears vague and visionary. We humbler writers cannot create Fausts, or raise up monumental works that shall endure for all ages; but our books are diaries, in which our own feelings must of necessity be set down. As we look to the page written last month, or ten years ago, we remember the day and its events; the child ill, mayhap, in the adjoining room, and the doubts and fears which racked the brain as it still pursued its work; the dear old friend who read the commencement of the tale, and whose gentle hand shall be laid in ours no more. I own for my part that, in reading pages which this hand penned formerly, I often lose sight of the text under my eyes. It is not the words I see; but that past day; that by-gone page of life's history; that tragedy, comedy it may be, which our little home company was enacting; that merry-making which we shared; that funeral which we followed; that bitter, bitter grief which we buried.

And such being the state of my mind, I pray gentle readers to deal kindly with their humble servant's manifold short-comings, blunders, and slips of memory. As sure as I read a page of my own composition, I find a fault or two, half a dozen. Jones is called Brown. Brown, who is dead, is brought to life. Aghast, and months after the number was printed, I saw that I had called Philip Firmin, Clive Newcome. Now Clive Newcome is the hero of another story by the reader's most obedient writer. The two men are as different, in my mind's eye, as — as Lord Palmerston and Mr. Disraeli, let us say. But there is that blunder at page 990, line 76, volume 84 of the Cornhill Magazine, and it is past mending; and I wish in my life I had made no worse blunders or errors than that which is hereby acknowledged.

Another Finis written. Another milestone passed on this journey from birth to the next world! Sure it is a subject for solemn cogitation. Shall we continue this story-telling business and be voluble to the end of our age? Will it not be presently time, O prattler, to hold your tongue, and let younger people speak? I have a friend, a painter, who, like other persons who shall be nameless, is growing old. He has never painted with such laborious finish as his works now show. This master is still the most humble and diligent of scholars. Of Art, his mistress, he is always an eager, reverent pupil. In his calling, in yours, in mine, industry and humility will help and comfort us. A word with you. In a pretty large experience I have not found the men who write books superior in wit or learning to those who don't write at all. In regard of mere information, non-writers must often be superior to writers. You don't expect a lawyer in full practice to be conversant with all kinds of literature; he is too busy with his law; and so a writer is commonly too busy with his own books to be able to bestow attention on the works of other people. After a day's work (in which I have been depicting, let us say, the agonies of Louisa on parting with the Captain, or the atrocious behavior of the wicked Marquis to Lady Emily) I march to the Club, proposing to improve my mind and keep myself "posted up," as the Americans phrase it, with the literature of the day. And what happens? Given, a walk after luncheon, a pleasing book, and a most comfortable arm-chair by the fire, and you know the rest. A doze ensues. Pleasing book drops suddenly, is picked up once with an air of some confusion, is laid presently softly in lap; head falls on comfortable arm-chair cushion; eyes close; soft nasal music is heard. Am I telling Club secrets? Of afternoons, after lunch, I say, scores of sensible fogies have a doze. Perhaps I have fallen asleep over that very book to which "Finis" has just been written. And if the writer sleeps, what happens to the readers? says Jones, coming down upon me with his lightning wit. What? You *did* sleep over it? And a very good thing too. These eyes have more than once seen a friend dozing over pages which this hand has written. There is a vignette somewhere in one of my books of a friend so caught napping with "Pendennis," or the "Newcomes," in his lap; and if a writer can give you a sweet, soothing, harmless sleep, has he not done you a kindness? So is the author who excites and interests you worthy of your thanks and benedictions. I am troubled with fever and ague, that seizes me at odd intervals and prostrates me for a day. There is cold fit, for which, I am thankful to say, hot brandy-and-water is prescribed, and this induces hot fit, and so on. In one or two of these fits I have read novels with the most fearful contentment of mind. Once, on the Mississippi, it was my dearly beloved "Jacob Faithful"; once at Frankfort, O. M., the delightful *Vingt Ans Après* of Monsieur Dumas; once at Tonbridge Wells, the thrilling "Woman in White"; and these books gave me amusement from morning till sunset. I remember those ague fits with a great deal of pleasure and gratitude. Think of a whole day in bed, and a good novel for a companion! No cares; no remorse about idleness; no visitors; and the Woman in White or the Chevalier d'Artagnan to tell me stories from dawn to night! "Please, ma'am, my master's compliments, and can he have the third volume?" (This message was sent to an astonished friend and neighbor who lent me, volume by volume, the "W. in W.") How do you like your novels? I like mine strong, "hot with," and no mistake; no love-making; no observations about society; little dialogue, except where the characters are bullying each other; plenty of fighting; and a villain in the cupboard, who is to suffer tortures just before Finis. I don't like your melancholy Finis. I never read the history of a consumptive heroine twice. If I might give a short hint to an impartial writer (as the Examiner used to say in old days), it would be to act, *not* à la mode le pays de Pole (I think that was the phraseology), but *always* to give quarter. In the story of Philip, just come to an end, I have the permission of the author to state that he was going to drown the two villains of the piece — a certain Doctor F—— and a certain Mr. T. H—— on board the *President*, or some other tragic ship, — but you see I relented. I pictured to myself

Firmin's ghastly face amid the crowd of shuddering people on that reeling deck in the lonely ocean, and thought, "Thou ghastly lying wretch, thou shalt not be drowned: thou shalt have a fever only; a knowledge of thy danger; and a chance — ever so small a chance — of repentance." I wonder whether he *did* repent when he found himself in the yellow-fever, in Virginia? The probability is, he fancied that his son had injured him very much, and forgave him on his deathbed. Do you imagine there is a great deal of genuine right-down remorse in the world? Don't people rather find excuses which make their minds easy; endeavor to prove to themselves that they have been lamentably belied and misunderstood; and try and forgive the persecutors who *will* present that bill when it is due; and not bear malice against the cruel ruffian who takes them to the police-office for stealing the spoons? Years ago I had a quarrel with a certain well-known person (I believed a statement regarding him which his friends imparted to me, and which turned out to be quite incorrect). To his dying day that quarrel was never quite made up. I said to his brother, "Why is your brother's soul still dark against me? It is I who ought to be angry and unforgiving; for I was in the wrong." In the region which they now inhabit (for Finis has been set to the volumes of the lives of both here below), if they take any cognizance of our squabbles, and tittle-tattles, and gossips on earth here, I hope they admit that my little error was not of a nature unpardonable. If you have never committed a worse, my good sir, surely the score against you will not be heavy. Ha, *dilectissimi fratres!* It is in regard of sins *not* found out that we may say or sing (in an undertone, in a most penitent and lugubrious minor key), *Miserere nobis miseris peccatoribus.*

Among the sins of commission which novel-writers not seldom perpetrate, is the sin of grandiloquence, or tall-talking, against which, for my part, I will offer up a special *libera me.* This is the sin of schoolmasters, governesses, critics, sermoners, and instructors of young or old people. Nay (for I am making a clean breast, and liberating my soul), perhaps of all the novel-spinners now extant, the present speaker is the most addicted to preaching. Does he not stop perpetually in his story and begin to preach to you? When he ought to be engaged with business, is he not forever taking the Muse by the sleeve, and plaguing her with some of his cynical sermons? I cry *peccavi* loudly and heartily. I tell you I would like to be able to write a story which should show no egotism whatever, — in which there should be no reflections, no cynicism, no vulgarity (and so forth), but an incident in every other page, a villain, a battle, a mystery in every chapter. I should like to be able to feed a reader so spicily as to leave him hungering and thirsting for more at the end of every monthly meal.

Alexandre Dumas describes himself, when inventing the plan of a work, as lying silent on his back for two whole days on the deck of a yacht in a Mediterranean port. At the end of the two days he arose, and called for dinner. In those two days he had built his plot. He had moulded a mighty clay, to be cast presently in perennial brass. The chapters, the characters, the incidents, the combinations were all arranged in the artist's brain ere he set a pen to paper. My Pegasus won't fly, so as to let me survey the field below me. He has no wings, he is blind of one eye certainly, he is restive, stubborn, slow; crops a hedge when he ought to be galloping, or gallops when he ought to be quiet. He never will show off when I want him. Sometimes he goes at a pace which surprises me. Sometimes, when I most wish him to make the running, the brute turns restive, and I am obliged to let him take his own time. I wonder do other novel-writers experience this fatalism? They *must* go a certain way, in spite of themselves. I have been surprised at the observations made by some of my characters. It seems as if an occult Power was moving the pen. The personage does or says something, and I ask, how the Dickens did he come to think of that? Every man has remarked in dreams, the vast dramatic power which is sometimes evinced,—I won't say the surprising power, for nothing does surprise you in dreams. But those strange characters you meet make instant observations of which you never can have thought previously. In like manner, the imagination foretells things. We spake anon of the inflated style of some writers. What also if there is an *afflated* style,—when a writer is like a Pythoness on her oracle tripod, and mighty words, words which he cannot help, come blowing, and bellowing, and whistling, and moaning through the speaking pipes of his bodily organ? I have told you it was a very queer shock to me the other day when, with a letter of introduction in his hand, the artist's (not my) Philip Firmin walked into this room, and sat down in the chair opposite. In the novel of "Pendennis," written ten years ago, there is an account of a certain Costigan, whom I had invented (as I suppose authors invent their personages out of scraps, heel-taps, odds and ends of characters). I was smoking in a tavern parlor one night, and this Costigan came into the room alive,—the very man,—the most remarkable resemblance of the printed sketches of the man, of the rude drawings in which I had depicted him. He had the same little coat, the same battered hat, cocked on one eye, the same twinkle in that eye. "Sir," said I, knowing him to be an old friend whom I had met in unknown regions, "sir," I said, "may I offer you a glass of brandy and water?" — "*Bedad, ye may,*" says he, "*and I'll sing ye a song tu.*" Of course he spoke with an Irish brogue. Of course he had been in the army. In ten minutes he pulled out an army agent's account, whereon his name was written. A few months after we read of him in a police court. How had I come to know him, to divine him? Nothing shall convince me that I have not seen that man in the world of spirits. In the world of spirits and water I know I did; but that is a mere quibble of words. I was not surprised when he spoke in an Irish brogue. I had had cognizance of him before somehow. Who has not felt that little shock which arises when a person, a place, some words in a book (there is always a collocation) present themselves to you, and you know that you have before met the same person, words, scene, and so forth?

They used to call the good Sir Walter the "Wizard of the North." What if some writer should appear who can write so *enchantingly* that he shall be able to call into actual life the people whom he invents? What if Mignon, and Margaret, and Goetz von Berlichingen are alive now (though I don't say they are visible), and Dugald Dalgetty and Ivanhoe were to step in at that open window by the little garden yonder? Suppose Uncas and our noble old Leather-Stocking were to glide silent in? Suppose Athos, Porthos, and Aramis should enter with a noiseless swagger, curling their mustachios? And dearest Amelia Booth, on Uncle Toby's arm; and Tittlebat Titmouse, with his hair dyed green; and all the Crummles company of comedians, with the Gil Blas troop; and Sir Roger de Coverley; and the greatest of all crazy gentlemen, the Knight of La Mancha, with his blessed squire? I say to you, I look rather wistfully towards the window, musing upon these people. Were any of them to enter, I think I should not be very much frightened. Dear old friends, what pleasant hours I have had with them! We do not see each other very often, but when we do, we are ever happy to meet. I had a capital half hour with Jacob Faithful last night; when the last sheet was corrected, when "Finis" had been written, and the printer's boy, with the copy, was safe in Green Arbour Court.

So you are gone, little printer's boy, with the last scratches and corrections on the proof, and a fine flourish by way of Finis at the story's end. The last corrections? I say those last corrections seem never to be finished. A plague upon the weeds! Every day, when I walk in my own little literary garden-plot, I spy some, and should like to have a spud, and root them out. Those idle words, neighbor, are past remedy. That turning back to the old pages produces anything but elation of mind. Would you not pay a pretty fine to be able to cancel some of them? O, the sad old pages, the dull old pages! O, the cares, the *ennui*, the squabbles, the repetitions, the old conversations over and over again! But now and again a kind thought is recalled, and now and again a dear memory. Yet a few chapters more, and then the last: after which, behold Finis itself come to an end, and the Infinite begun.

Cambridge: Printed by Welch, Bigelow, & Co.

www.ingramcontent.com/pod-product-compliance
Lightning Source LLC
LaVergne TN
LVHW011157110826
845150LV00006B/1239

* 9 7 8 1 4 2 5 5 4 5 8 4 0 *